TOP CAREERS
FOR
ART
GRADUATES

Also available
Top Careers for Business Graduates
Top Careers for Communications Graduates
Top Careers for Economics Graduates
Top Careers for History Graduates
Top Careers for Liberal Arts Graduates

Art
Graduates

☑®
Checkmark Books®
An imprint of Facts On File, Inc.

Checkmark Books
An imprint of Facts On File, Inc.
132 West 31st Street
New York NY 10001

Library of Congress Cataloging-in-Publication Data

Top Careers for Art Graduates.
    p. cm.
Summary: Describes a wide variety of careers which involve art.
Includes bibliographical references and index.
    ISBN 0-8160-5565-3 (pb : alk. paper)
    1. Art—Vocational guidance. [1. Art—Vocational guidance.
    2. Vocational guidance.] I. Title.
N8350.T66 2004
702′.3′73—dc22   2003019377

Checkmark Books are available at special discounts when purchased in bulk quantities for businesses, associations, institutions, or sales promotions. Please call our Special Sales Department in New York at (212) 967-8800 or (800) 322-8755.

You can find Facts On File on the World Wide Web at http://www.factsonfile.com

Text design by David Strelecky

Cover design by Cathy Rincon

Printed in the United States of America

MP Hermitage 10 9 8 7 6 5 4 3 2 1

This book is printed on acid-free paper.

CONTENTS

SECTION I

WHY DO YOU NEED A COLLEGE DEGREE?

More people are receiving college degrees than ever before. In 2000, more than 1 million students earned their bachelor's degrees. By 2001, 58 percent of all individuals between the ages of 25 and 29 had completed some portion of their college education. The National Center for Education Statistics reports that 29 percent of this same age group held at least a bachelor's degree.

Given the large number of college graduates entering the workforce, many employers now require a college degree for jobs that previously had lower educational requirements. This "educational upgrading" has occurred primarily in occupations that are considered desirable and that pay well.

Employers want workers with good communication, teamwork, and problem-solving skills. They want workers who are able to learn quickly, can adapt and adjust to workplace challenges, and who have the desire to excel and achieve. Above all, they want college graduates.

This book does more than stress the importance of a college degree. Also included is information on how to define and evaluate your skills and interests, determining if an art major is the right choice for you, making the most of your college experience, and translating your college degree and experience into a satisfying and rewarding career.

The following is a brief description of the contents.

SECTION I

Introduction: Meet the Art Major provides an overview of college majors most often associated with an art education. It also provides basic information on colleges and universities, suggested courses, skills, potential employers, starting salaries, and further avenues of exploration.

Chapter 1: Your High School Years will help you select a major and prepare for college study while you are still in high school. Here you will read about suggested courses, self-assessment tests, methods of exploring your major of interest, and how to choose a college.

Chapter 2: Making the Most of Your Experience as an Art Major will help you make the best use of your college years—even if you are unsure of a major. Topics include typical art curricula, the benefits of a minor, methods of exploring careers, and preparing for the workforce.

Chapter 3: Taking Your Art Degree to Work offers tips on finding direction after graduation, job searching, improving your resume, applying for jobs online, tips for successful interviewing, and the benefits of a graduate degree.

Section I also includes informative interviews with college professors and workers in the field who will provide further insight on the art major and its career options. You will also find helpful and interesting sidebars with information about the art field, tips on finding a scholarship, lists of top graduate programs, recommended books for further reading, and a glossary of terms most often associated with the art industry.

SECTION II

The second half of the book profiles 34 careers in the field of art. Each article discusses the occupation in detail.

The **Quick Facts** section provides a brief summary of the career including recommended school subjects, personal skills, work environment, minimum educational requirements, salary ranges, certification or licensing requirements, and employment outlook. This section also provides acronyms and identification numbers for the following government classification indexes: the *Dictionary of Occupational Titles* (DOT), the Guide to Occupational Exploration (GOE), the National Occupational Classification (NOC) Index, and the Occupational Information Network (O*NET)-Standard Occupational Classification System (SOC) index. The DOT, GOE, and O*NET-SOC indexes have been created by the U.S. government; the NOC index is Canada's career classification system. Readers can use the identification numbers listed in the Quick Facts section to access further information on a career. Print editions of the DOT (*Dictionary of Occupational Titles*. Indianapolis, Ind.: JIST Works, 1991) and GOE (*The Complete Guide for Occupational Exploration*. Indianapolis, Ind.: JIST Works, 1993) are available from libraries, and electronic versions of the NOC (http://www23.hrdc-drhc.gc.ca/2001/e/generic/welcome.shtml) and O*NET-SOC (http://online.onetcenter.org) are available on the World Wide Web. When no DOT, GOE, NOC, or O*NET-SOC numbers are listed, this means that the U.S. Department of Labor or the Human Resources Development Canada have not created a numerical designation for this career. In this instance, you will see the acronym "N/A," or not available.

The **Overview** section is a brief introductory description of the duties and responsibilities involved in this career. A career may have a variety of job titles. When this is the case, alternative career titles are presented.

The **History** section describes the history of the particular job as it relates to the overall development of its industry or field.

The Job describes in detail the primary and secondary duties of the job.

Requirements discusses high school and postsecondary education and training requirements, certification or licensing, if necessary, and any other personal requirements for success in the job. The majority of the careers in *Top Careers for Art Graduates* require a minimum of a bachelor's degree, but we have also included a few careers that may have a minimum educational requirement of a graduate degree. For example, the careers of archivist and college art professor require a master's or doctorate degree, but individuals with a bachelor's degree may be able to find work at a community college. Conversely, the book includes a few careers that require less than a college degree; however, some college-level business courses are highly recommended for these positions. Examples include the job of antique and art dealer, costume designer, furniture designer, and illustrator.

Exploring offers suggestions on how to gain some experience in or knowledge of the particular job before making a firm educational and financial commitment. While in high school or the early years of college, you can learn about clubs and other activities, for example, which will give you a better understanding of the job.

The **Employers** section gives an overview of typical places of employment for the job and may also include specific employment numbers from the U.S. Department of Labor.

Starting Out discusses the best ways to land that first job, be it through a college placement office, newspaper ads, or personal contacts.

The **Advancement** section describes what kind of career path to expect from the job and how to get there.

Earnings lists salary ranges and describes the typical fringe benefits.

The **Work Environment** section describes the typical surroundings and conditions of employment—whether indoors or outdoors, noisy or quiet, social or independent, and so on. Also discussed are typical hours worked, any seasonal fluctuations, and the stresses and strains of the job.

The **Outlook** section summarizes the job in terms of the general economy and industry projections. For the most part, Outlook information is obtained from the Bureau of Labor Statistics and is supplemented by information taken from professional associations. Job growth terms follow those used in the *Occupational Outlook Handbook.*

- Growth described as "much faster than the average" means an increase of 36 percent or more.
- Growth described as "faster than the average" means an increase of 21–35 percent.
- Growth described as "about as fast as the average" means an increase of 10–20 percent.
- Growth described as "more slowly than the average" means an increase of 3–9 percent.
- Growth described as having "little or no change" means an increase of 0–2 percent.
- "Decline" means a decrease of 1 percent or more.

Each career article concludes with **For More Information,** which lists organizations that can provide career information on training, education, internships, scholarships, and job placement.

Whether you are a high school student just beginning to think about a college major, a college student interested in learning more about career options, or a graduate thinking about changing careers, this book will help you learn more about the art major and the career options available to those with this background.

MEET THE ART MAJOR

WHAT IS ART?
Art comprises many creative forms, from the traditional visual art forms of illustration and sculpture to the industrial art forms of graphic design and blueprint sketches. Though artists' work can differ dramatically, those who produce art must have one common quality: creativity. Artists choose a medium, such as oil paints, charcoal, metal, or computers, to express their ideas. Their efforts result in works that elicit various responses and emotions in viewers.

However, not all artists—and art majors—create works of art. Some decide to study the work of others, teach art history to other students, or specialize in restoring artistic works. These professionals must have a profound appreciation for artistic works and their creators and be well educated in the origin and history of art from around the world, how different pieces are created, and how to promote and preserve art for future generations.

According to the U.S. Department of Education, approximately 58,791 students graduated with an undergraduate degree in art in 2000. Another 10,918 graduated with a master's degree, and 1,127 graduated with a doctorate.

WHAT COURSES WILL I TAKE?
Art education varies tremendously depending on the art career that you choose. Museum curators will have a much different curriculum than jewelry designers. However, most art majors will take classes in art history, basic drawing and illustration, sculpture, design methods, and computer imaging.

WHAT WILL I LEARN?
Students will learn about the history and evolution of art, from paintings to sculpture to architecture. They also learn about the techniques and methods of their particular medium and how to develop their skills and personal style as an artist. Because art has been influ-

enced by the technological revolution just as much as other industries, students will learn computer skills. They work with software programs that aid in design, illustration, printmaking, sketching, or other forms of art. Even if an artist creates work without computer assistance, he or she should become familiar with the technology that is available and that may be used by his or her peers.

WHERE WILL I WORK AND HOW MUCH WILL I EARN?

Art majors work all over the world in a variety of industries as visual artists, as corporate employees in advertising, architecture, or design firms, as elementary, high school, or college educators, as museum directors—the list is endless. As a result, earnings vary depending on the career. A "starving artist" just starting his or her career may earn nothing until he or she sells a work. However, an art director with a large advertising firm can earn more than $100,000 a year.

The majority of art majors don't choose the field for monetary reasons; most choose the major because of a passion for or talent in art.

You can learn more about art careers and training from books, periodicals, and online resources. Here are a few good websites to start your exploration.

Ask Joan of Art! (from the Smithsonian American Art Museum)
http://nmaa-ryder.si.edu/study/nav-joan.html

Princeton Review: Career Resources
http://www.princetonreview.com/cte

Career Guide for Art History Majors
http://www.utexas.edu/cofa/career/documents/arthistguide.pdf

CHAPTER 1

YOUR HIGH SCHOOL YEARS

It's never too early to think about your future. Even if you are in high school, college is just around the corner, and soon enough you'll be throwing your graduation cap in the air, ready to enter the workforce. The earlier you begin to think about your interests and how they might relate to a career, the more confident you will be about your career choices in the coming years.

SUGGESTED COURSES

If you are interested in being an art major, while in high school take various art classes, including basic drawing and illustration, shop, blueprint sketching, photography, and ceramics. To build a broad educational base, take classes in mathematics, English, history, and science. These classes will not only prepare you for more advanced college classes, but they will enhance your understanding of art history and artistic works. History and sociology classes will help you understand art movements in their cultural contexts. Mathematics classes will help you with technical aspects of your career, such as visualizing a blueprint sketch as a full-scale building or being able to mix and measure art materials, such as paints or photography chemicals. Computer classes are also useful. Many artists use computers in their daily work, whether it's to design a company's logo, illustrate a children's book, or digitally manipulate pieces of art.

Ask your adviser or college counselor to suggest other classes that will prepare you for an art major.

INTERVIEW: Kelsey Sauber Olds

Kelsey Sauber Olds owns and operates his own furniture design shop, KSO Furniture (http://www.ksofurniture.com) in Madison, Wisconsin.

He was kind enough to discuss his work and educational background with the editors of Top Careers for Art Graduates.

Q. What is your work schedule?

A. I work a regular 9:00 A.M.–5:00 P.M. schedule during weekdays and work an additional six to eight hours on weekends.

Q. Where do you work? Do you travel for your job?

A. I have a storefront showroom where I display my furniture and work on pieces in a workshop behind the store. I travel occasionally to meet with out-of-town clients and to deliver pieces.

Q. How did you train for this job? What was your college major?

A. I was a studio art major at Kenyon College (Ohio) where I focused on sculpture. This taught me a familiarity with the materials and some of the equipment I use today and gave me a strong sense of design and invaluable problem-solving skills. In the field of furniture making specifically, I am self-taught.

Q. Did you participate in any internships or apprenticeships?

A. I had an apprenticeship at a fine art gallery in Minneapolis and worked with a banjo maker, but I did not have any formal training in furniture making.

Q. How/where did you get your first job in this field? What did you do?

A. When I decided to design and make furniture full time, I started my own company, KSO Furniture, in Madison.

Q. What kinds of sources are available to someone looking to get into this field?

A. There are many helpful books, magazines, and websites, but the most valuable sources are other furniture makers themselves. I advise those starting out in the field to acquaint themselves with as many furniture makers as possible and not be shy about asking questions.

Q. What are the most important personal and professional qualities for people in your career?

A. Among the many personal qualities this field requires are flexibility and self-discipline. Individuals need to be able to weather the ups and downs by staying focused and be comfortable wearing many hats. Good presentation and communication skills are also a must.

While this is a field that relies heavily on aesthetics and technical skill, the most important professional qualities to have are business skills. My livelihood depends on my ability to run my business well.

Q. What are some of the pros and cons of your job?

A. The best thing about my job is that it is entirely mine. I am doing exactly what I want to be doing and have complete control of my days. I am making a living doing something that I am passionate about and do it on my own terms. This is a rare and wonderful position to be in.

   The dramatically outweighed cons are that there is no steady paycheck, no health care benefits, and no paid vacation time and sick days. There is uncertainty, whether I am booked up for a month or for a year, in never knowing when or from where that next job is going to come.

Q. What advice would you offer students as they prepare to pursue an arts-related career?

A. Go out on a limb. That's where the fruit is.

ASSESSMENT TESTS

Self-assessment tests can help you decide if an art major is right for you. Taking these tests while you're in high school is a good idea, as they can help you decide what to look for in a college and plan your courses accordingly. Depending on the test, questions help you evaluate your college and career options by focusing on your values, interests, academic strength, and personality. The following are some of the more popular tests available (Note that some of these tests require a fee. Talk to your high school guidance counselor or adviser for more details.):

- Career Key: Developed by Lawrence K. Jones, a college professor specializing in career counseling and development, this website hosts a quick and easy assessment to help you explore jobs that fit your career type, such as artistic or enterprising. After answering questions about your interests and skills, the Career Key develops a list of appropriate jobs that fit your responses. Visit http://www.careerkey.org to take your own assessment test.

- Kuder Career Planning System: The Kuder test can help you evaluate your interests, skills, and values. Suggested college majors and careers are ranked based on survey responses. For sample tests and more information, visit http://www.kuder.com.

- Myers-Briggs Type Indicator: This assessment test will help you identify your personality type using four general, but opposite, dispositions: extraversion/introversion, sensate/intuitive, thinking/feeling, and judging/perceiving. Based on your test responses, you may be categorized as one of 16 personality types. Although most organizations charge a fee for this test, you can visit http://www.humanmetrics.com/cgi-win/JTypes1.htm for a free test based on the Myers-Briggs Type Indicator. Also visit http://www.cpp-db.com.

- Princeton Review Career Quiz: This quick and easy multiple-choice survey will help you determine your worker "type" (such as careful/orderly or quick/random) and your main work interests (such as artistic/creative or mechanical/technical). To try it out, visit http://www.princetonreview.com/cte/quiz.

OTHER WAYS TO EXPLORE

Although self-assessment tests are useful, there are many other ways to explore your potential interest and skill in art.

- If your high school has an art club, be sure to join it and stay active. Some clubs sponsor field trips to museums, plays, galleries, or other sites to expand your exposure to different forms of art. Other clubs invite guest artists to come to the school, show off their work, and lead a group discussion.

- If your school doesn't offer an art club, check out the National 4-H Council website (http://www.fourhcouncil.edu). This organization offers an annual photography contest and other opportunities for involvement.

- Because many artists go into business for themselves, you may want to consider joining a club for young entrepreneurs. Meetings may cover developing skills in leadership, money management, working with people, and much more. Junior Achievement (JA) is a national organization that works to instill business skills in young adults and empower them to be

the leaders of the future. Check out JA's website (http://www.
ja.org) to see if a chapter is located near you.

- Take part in other events in the arts community, such as participating in school and local plays, musicals, arts and crafts fairs, or art contests.
- If you are interested in a design career, work on your school paper or yearbook, or help design programs for school plays or other productions.
- Keep up on the latest developments in the art industry. Depending on which area of art you hope to pursue, helpful publications include *American Artist* (http://www.myamericanartist.com), *ARTnews* (http://www.artnewsonline.com), *Archaeology* (http://www.archaeology.org), and *Architectural Digest* (http://www.archdigest.com).
- Explore the Internet and play games that develop your artistic skills. The Albright-Knox Art Gallery in Buffalo, New York, has developed a fun site for younger students called ArtGames (http://www.albrightknox.org/artgames). Here you can learn about famous paintings and sculpture through interactive games. Another fun site, The Art Room (http://www.arts.ufl.edu/art/rt_room), developed by the Department of Art Education at the University of Florida, offers ideas for art projects and a gallery of works done by young adults around the world.

There is also a wealth of information on the art industry available on the Internet. Listed below are a few good sites to explore:

About: Art History
http://arthistory.about.com

About: Drawing/Sketching
http://drawsketch.about.com

High School Hub: Art and Music
http://highschoolhub.org/hub/art.cfm

Kid's Catalog Web: Explore Arts & Crafts
http://kcweb.denver.lib.co.us/kcweb/servlet/kcExplore

CHOOSING A COLLEGE
Deciding on a college can be as daunting as choosing a major or career. You have a lot to consider before making a decision, such as

size, location, cost, and curriculum, among other factors. Students who have decided on an art career may choose to attend an art school that has a good reputation. However, not all students have a clear-cut idea of their future career path. For this reason, they may choose a college with a broad spectrum of options. There are many resources you can use that will help you narrow your choices.

Guidance Counselors

Your high school's guidance counselor should be one of the first people you consult when weighing your college options. He or she will have information on programs, application deadlines, campus environments, and financial aid opportunities. Some guidance counselors keep track of recent high school graduates and may be able to give you names and contact information of students at schools in which you have interest.

Before you meet with your counselor, make a list of the things you are looking for in a school. Do you want a small or large campus? Do you want to be in rural or urban surroundings? What is your tuition range? Keep this list and all other college information organized in a folder or binder so that you can find the appropriate information when you need it.

College Recruiters

Most high schools host several different recruiters from colleges and universities across the country, possibly including those from art schools. Acting as school representatives, these recruiters talk with groups of students about their schools' educational programs, faculty, campus life, tuition and other expenses, and scholarship and loan opportunities. In addition to making presentations, recruiters field questions from students.

Because recruiters are there for your benefit, take full advantage of the opportunity to meet with them, learn more about their school, and ask your own questions. If there is a college that you are interested in that will not be represented at your high school, ask your guidance counselor for assistance in scheduling a meeting with a representative.

College Fairs

College fairs are also good places to meet college recruiters. These gatherings of college and university admissions representatives take place throughout the United States. At these fairs, you can gather brochures about schools and talk to representatives one on one.

They can answer your questions about educational programs, courses offered, admissions and financial aid requirements, campus activities, and any other information that will help you narrow your college options. Some fairs even specialize in an academic area, such as the study of art.

Just like you did before visiting your guidance counselor, make a list of the things you are looking for in a school (size, programs, locations, etc.), and focus your attention on schools that seem to fit these preliminary guidelines. Be sure to bring a pen, some paper, and a large folder or binder to hold your college information and notes. Visit http://www.nacac.com/fairs.html for more helpful tips and a list of college fairs, organized by date. This website also features a listing of college fairs aimed specifically at students interested in studying the visual and performing arts.

Contact Colleges Yourself

To learn more about colleges, you can also take matters into your own hands. Contact the schools' admissions offices directly to obtain their catalogs. You can also view catalogs and other information on colleges at their websites. Visit CollegeSource Online (http://www.collegesource.org) to view over 25,000 college catalogs in complete, original page format.

To learn more about art schools on the Internet, check out the following websites:

ArtSchools.com
http://www.artschools.com

Art Schools & Colleges
http://www.art-schools-colleges.com

Explore Art Schools
http://www.glencoe.com/sec/art/student/studio/activities/
   expl.htm

INTERVIEW: John Michalczyk

John Michalczyk is the chair of the Fine Arts Department and co-director of the Film Studies Program at Boston College. He spoke to the editors of Top Careers for Art Graduates *about his program and share advice with students considering this course of study.*

Q. What areas of art do you specialize in and teach?

A. I teach film history and documentary film history/production. My courses cover Latin American cinema, European film, propaganda film, documentary film, the Holocaust, and the arts, among others.

Q. How long have you been teaching?

A. I have taught at Boston College since 1974.

Q. Beyond the obvious, for what types of jobs does a film studies major prepare students?

A. In film, our first priority is to develop solid visual and critical thinking within the student by situating the program in a liberal arts environment. For students who want to specialize in film, we work closely with them on developing technical skills such as shooting and editing. We try to prepare students for the "reel world" by encouraging them to work in internships or assist the faculty with their own productions.

The types of jobs that recent students have worked in or are presently working in are endless. Some of our graduates have gone on to become feature directors and producers, famous actors (Chris O'Donnell, for one), film editors, scriptwriters, television producers, and photographers. Immediately after graduation, many film majors go on to graduate school in film or work as interns for PBS, local documentary film companies, or local commercial production houses. One recent graduate is teaching film and the media to underprivileged students.

Q. What are the most important personal and professional qualities for art/film majors?

A. Personal qualities: You should be open to all different kinds of film experiences to be able to find the niche that fulfills you.

Professional qualities: You should adapt to various film jobs so that you can build up experience and contacts. Also, put an emphasis on creative thinking when working in film—you need to be able to think outside of the proverbial box. Develop a strong liberal arts background as a basis for understanding society. Ideas often come from reading and exposure to new educational areas.

Q. When the typical student enters your program, what are his or her expectations?

A. Often the student who enters the program feels that he/she could become another Steven Spielberg or another major director. By the end of the program, the student sees that there are many niches in the film business, such as writing, law, advertising, finance, editing, cinematography, etc.

Q. What advice would you offer art majors as they graduate and look for jobs?

A. Be open to new ventures, but don't stray too far from your ideal. Use your first job as a stepping stone to another, but one from which you can learn fresh things. If the new job is lethal, don't self-destruct over it. Try another area of film and re-invent yourself.

Q. Are there any misconceptions about this major that you'd like to clear up, or warnings that you'd like to give students about careers in this field?

A. The film world is a very challenging and frustrating one, especially in the New York or California film scenes. It is difficult to break into and demands patience. The work is not glamorous; an 18-hour day might be very common at times.

Q. Are there any changes in this job market that students should expect? Have certain areas of this field been especially promising in recent years?

A. The job opportunities are slimmer these past two years, given the current economy. Fewer companies are able to hire the staff they need because of financial restraints. This may be a temporary phase of the market. Television employers, such as HBO, the History Channel, and PBS are still interested in the kinds of background we provide in our film program.

Q. What is the future of the Film Studies Program at Boston College?

A. Our film studies program formally began in 1983, but film has been a part of the larger liberal arts program since the 1960s. In 1998, the film major was introduced with eight majors and 40 minors. Currently, there are approximately 50 majors and 50 minors. Students from other disciplines take our courses for electives and core liberal arts classes. The program continues to grow; however, we are often unable to accommodate all of the students who are interested in the curriculum.

CAMPUS VISITS:
GIVING SCHOOLS A TEST DRIVE

You can talk to counselors, students, and recruiters until you're blue in the face (not recommended), but the best way to gauge your interest in a college is through a campus visit. Campus visits allow you to go beyond a school's neatly crafted brochure and walk the streets, meet the students and faculty, sample a few classes, and even taste the dining hall "delicacies."

However, just showing up on campus is not recommended; schedule your visit with an admissions counselor to make the most of your visit. Most likely, an admissions representative will match you with a student of similar interests who will show you around campus.

Before you leave home, make a list of the facilities and school features that you'd like to see. For example, if you're visiting an art school and have an interest in photography, you should be sure to see the school's photography lab and studio. Share this list with your student guide or college representative so you'll be sure to check out all these sites and experiences during your stay. Campus visits can be fun: you can see (and even spend the night in) a dorm, sample the fine cuisine from the campus cafeteria, and most importantly, attend a class or two.

Setting up a formal campus tour also lets the admissions department know that you are interested in the school. If time allows, you might even be asked for a short interview with an admissions counselor during your visit. Again, be prepared with a list of questions to ask the counselor.

If you are unable to visit colleges, check out the website CampusTours (http://www.campustours.com), which offers virtual campus tours of over 850 colleges and universities.

LAST, BUT NOT LEAST

Your family, friends, college counselors, and teachers are great sources of help and guidance when picking out a school. But in the end, make sure you choose a school that is right for *you*.

For more information on choosing the right college for you, visit

Adventures in Education
http://www.adventuresineducation.org

College Board
http://www.collegeboard.com

College Is Possible
http://www.collegeispossible.org

CollegeNet
http://www.collegenet.com

Colleges.com
http://www.colleges.com

Princeton Review
http://www.princetonreview.com

CHAPTER 2

MAKING THE MOST OF YOUR EXPERIENCE AS AN ART MAJOR

So you've made it to college. Your bags are unpacked, the pictures of your family and friends are on display, and the Yaffa blocks are set up and holding every piece of clothing you own. You have your shower shoes, your blacklight, and your minifridge. You seem to be in good shape. But what about your academic goals? If you haven't already, how are you going to decide on a major, let alone your life's direction, in just a year?

If you are uncertain about your major, don't worry—you'll be in good company. Most college freshmen (and some unfortunate seniors) don't yet know their major or career goals. Most schools have general educational requirements that must be fulfilled by all students, no matter what their chosen major. Freshman year is a great time not only to complete these required classes, but to learn the basics of a lot of different subject areas. These introductory-level classes (biology, psychology, English 101, and, yes, introduction to illustration) should help you identify the fields you excel in and enjoy, which is a good indicator of a potential college major.

If you are reading this book, you are probably considering a major in art. Congratulations: You are joining a group that annually welcomes 60,000 talented individuals who will become tomorrow's artists, designers, architects, and other art professionals. Your college courses will prepare you for the challenges that lie ahead in the working world: finding a job or being able to sell your work on your own, earning enough money to support your craft, forming good working relationships with managers, clients, and buyers, and advancing in your career. Your college background will help you conquer these challenges if you plan carefully and make wise choices. Some of the more important choices you will make will involve choosing your classes.

SUGGESTED COURSES

All colleges offer different curricula. Your required courses will depend on your art specialty, such as ceramics, photography, printmaking, costume design, interior design, architecture, or film, just to name a few. Examples of "core" art classes include color theory, basic sketching, black-and-white photography, woodworking, pottery, and art history.

Many artists also study elements of computer science as part of their major. Many students may overlook the importance of computers and their use in artists' work. Computers are used to create, manipulate, store, and edit images, to communicate with co-workers, managers, and clients, and to conduct research and evaluations of other works of art. Some jobs are inseparable from computers, such as those of architects, desktop publishing specialists, editors, and graphic designers. Most jobs in today's workplace involve some computer use. At the very least, you should be comfortable using word processing programs, such as Microsoft Word or Corel WordPerfect. Most artists will also need to be able to use more specialized computer programs, such as QuarkXpress or Adobe Photoshop to design and layout a books, or Adobe Illustrator to create pictures for a textbook. Another useful skill for any field is the ability to write or alter a website. Knowledge of a basic programming language such as HTML will be extremely useful, especially if you plan to create art for online use.

DON'T FORGET A MINOR

If you know exactly what you'd like to do after you graduate, consider choosing a specific minor to complement your art degree. For example, if you want to be a high school art teacher, a minor in secondary education would be wise (although it may already be a requirement for your major). When deciding on a minor, two good things to consider are how the courses will fit into and complement the workload for your major, and how the knowledge and skill you acquire from the minor might affect your career.

INTERVIEW: Pamela Berger

Pamela Berger is a professor at Boston College, specializing in medieval art and art history research for historical feature films. Berger was kind enough to speak to the editors of Top Careers for Art Graduates *about her program and the field of art in general.*

Q. Beyond preparing students to work as a professional artist, what other types of jobs can art majors pursue?

A. Visual education prepares one for a variety of different kinds of work. Art majors can go on to work at art galleries or historical societies. They could become architects, go into art restoration, or do all kinds of museum work, such as installation, research, administration, or curatorships. In film, I introduce my students to all the positions one sees in the credits of a film, especially production designer, art director, location scout, set photographer, cinematographer, camera assistants, costume designer, set decorator—the list goes on.

Q. What qualities do art students need to be successful in your program?

A. Art students should learn how to read thoughtfully, write clearly, and observe with acuity.

Q. Have certain areas of this field been especially promising in recent years?

A. The whole field of digital technology has provided new avenues for students.

Q. What is the future of your program?

A. To continue to produce well-educated adults with an understanding of history and current cultural trends.

EXPLORE AND GET YOUR FOOT IN THE DOOR

Although courses are very important, they won't teach you everything you need to know about the diverse field of art. Here are some other ways to make the most of your college experience as an art major.

- Try to get an on-campus job that requires artistic skill. Regardless of where you work, whether it's in the yearbook office, drama department, or admissions office, you'll get good experience, help to develop your artistic talent, and help out your school at the same time. You'll also get accustomed to working on a schedule, recording your hours, and (here's the best part) receiving a paycheck.

- Look for opportunities to work in the local community. Some art programs offer work-study arrangements that combine classroom time with actual work in a local establishment. The best jobs are often assistant jobs that will partner you up with a working professional, allowing you to help out a local architect, costume designer, or television editor, depending on your area of interest. Regardless of where you work, the experience will serve you well.

- Get involved in school publications that may need artistic help, such as newspapers, alumni magazines, and yearbooks. If you want to develop your writing skills, offer to write copy or report on campus news. If you're interested in design, volunteer to assist in page layout. If drawing is your thing, ask if you can add illustrations to the publication.

- Because many artists are self-employed, work to develop the skills you will need to run your own business. Join a campus or community organization that encourages entrepreneurial or leadership skills. Colleges may give these clubs different names, such as Young Entrepreneurs or Young Leaders.

The Internet offers some good sites to explore for career information on art. Visit the following sites the next time you're online:

Artist Resource: Job Hunting Advice for Designers, Artists, and Illustrators
http://www.artistresource.org/jobhunt.htm

Career Guide for Studio Art Majors
http://www.utexas.edu/cofa/career/documents/studioguide.pdf

New York Foundation for the Arts
http://www.nyfa.org

PREPARING FOR THE WORKFORCE

As you enter the second half of your undergraduate college years, you need to be concerned with more than just your grades.

Securing a job or steady freelance work is going to take much more than scoring an A on your next art project. Starting to think about and, more importantly, act on your employment prospects now will put you that much further ahead of your competition once you graduate.

There are many things you can do to prepare for the working world. First, maintain good grades and work hard all the way through the end of your senior year. This may be difficult, while at the same time worrying about getting a job, living on your own, and planning your spring break vacation. But it is imperative that you finish your college major as strongly as you started.

Using Your Connections

Take advantage of the art professionals and educators that you have come to know over the past few years. Your professors and advisers are great sources for advice on getting a job and may be able to provide you with contacts or job leads. Besides advice, your college's faculty can provide you with another job necessity: a letter of recommendation. Ask the teacher(s) who know you well and have watched your talents develop.

Internships

Completing an internship is another great way to prepare for a career. Internships are monitored work arrangements in which you have the chance to apply your study of art to actual workplace surroundings. Students may have specific learning goals to meet through the internship, or they may be just want to acquire some basic experience. More often than not, interns are hired for much more than answering the phones or filing. Student interns may sit in on meetings, assist with art projects, and support artists or staff members in any given function. Whether paid or unpaid, full or part time, internships will give you the chance to learn more about your chosen area of art, gain working experience, and make connections in the industry.

According to the National Association of Colleges and Employers, internships often give students the competitive edge that needed to land a job. During times of sluggish economic growth, more highly qualified students are applying for a limited number of jobs. Having an internship on your resume will signal to employers that you have achieved more than just good grades.

The following websites offer information about internships:

American Repertory Theater
http://www.amrep.org/intern

InternshipPrograms.com
http://internships.wetfeet.com

Internships.com
http://www.internships.com

Rising Star Internships
http://www.rsinternships.com

Smithsonian American Art Institute: Fellowships, Internships, and Scholarly Opportunities
http://nmaa-ryder.si.edu

Job Fairs and Corporate Recruiters

In addition to the work contacts you can make through an internship, another good way to explore employers is at a job fair. These may be held at your college campus, a local hotel, or a large exhibition hall. Your college's career center should know of any recruiters that are coming by the college or the nearby area. According to CollegeGrad.com, a job site that focuses on entry-level workers, you should bring the following items to your next career fair:

- Resume: Bring several copies of your resume (spotless and printed on quality paper) to hand out to each employer you meet.

- Letters of recommendation: Those letters from your professors and advisers will come in handy at your next fair. These documents serve as a personal testament to your abilities.

- Portfolio: A 9 x 12 inch leather-bound folder will come in handy to hold examples of your writing or artistic work as well as your resumes and letters of recommendation. It will also be useful to hold any notes taken during your interviews with employers and any information you pick up at the fair.

- Briefcase: Your portfolio may not be big enough to handle the number of pamphlets, booklets, and brochures you will collect at a good career fair.

- Proper attire: Even if the career fair takes place on your college campus, don't dress in typical college fashion. Leave the jeans and sweatshirts at home, and put on a conservative business suit. Because the time spent with employers will be shorter than even a typical office interview, you have to make a good impression. Dressing neatly and conservatively will ensure that the employers' attention is spent on you, not what you are wearing.

After checking with your college's career counselor, check out the following websites to learn more and search for fairs by employer and state:

CareerFairs.com
http://careerfairs.com

CollegeGrad.com
http://www.collegegrad.com

JobWeb Online Career Fair
http://www.jobweb.com/employ/fairs

The Job Fair, Inc.
http://www.thejobfair.com

Information Interviewing

Information interviews present great opportunities to gain contacts and learn more about different facets of the arts. These are different from traditional job interviews in that they are informal conversations with working art professionals, used for the sole benefit of the student. There is no pressure for job competition during information interviews. By talking with working architects, designers, editors, illustrators, and photographers, for example, you can ask questions you may have about their line of work, how they got into their job, what skills are required, and tips on how you can best prepare to enter a similar job.

As you would in a traditional interview, dress and act appropriately and have written questions ready to ask. Have a notepad and pen to write down the subject's answers for future reference. Here are some recommended questions:

- I have done some research on this position, and _____ is what I've found. Can you tell me more about what sort of work is done here?
- What is a typical day like at this job?

- What sort of advancement potential does this career have?
- What do you think is most rewarding about your position? Most challenging?
- Why did you decide to work for this company?
- Who are your major clients? Major competitors?
- How do you suggest that students find jobs in this field?
- If you are in charge of hiring, what do you look for in candidates?
- What additional training or education should I pursue to enhance my potential for finding a position within this field?
- How have you been able to balance the demands of the office with your personal life? Do you often find yourself bringing home additional work that you didn't finish at the office?
- How stressful is your job?
- What don't you like about this career?

Of course, at the end of your interview, thank your subject for his or her time, and then follow up with a written note. These interviewees are not only great sources of information, but they may come in handy as a source for future job leads.

For more details on information interviews and to read sample interviews online, visit the following websites:

About.com: Informational Interviewing
http://jobsearch.about.com/cs/infointerviews

Artist-Entrepreneur Project
http://www.artist-entrepreneurs.com

Artists' Stories
http://www.artistresource.org/stories.htm

Career Key: Information Interviewing
http://www.careerkey.org/english/you/
    information_interviewing.html

Career Research: What Do You Want to Be?
http://www.cyberfilmschool.com/columns/mchugh_18.htm

Quintessential Careers: Informational Interviewing Tutorial
http://www.quintcareers.com/informational_interviewing.html

INTERVIEW: Roscoe Betsill

Roscoe Betsill is a photo stylist specializing in food photography. Betsill spoke to the editors of Top Careers for Art Graduates *about styling photos and the education and training involved.*

Q. Please briefly describe your primary and secondary job duties.

A. My primary job function is to prepare and present food for photography for both editorial and advertising clients. I am responsible for shopping for ingredients, preparing the food according to a recipe or product specifications, and setting up the food so that it will be stable and presentable for photography.

Q. Where do you work? Do you travel for your job?

A. I generally work indoors in photographic studios. I do occasionally work on location, on sites as far flung as country settings and beaches in New York to locations in Europe, in French chateaux and Tuscan villas.

Q. How did you train for this job? What was your college major?

A. I hold a bachelor's degree in communications, radio, television, and film from Northwestern University, where I took several advertising and a number of fine arts courses. More relevant training for my job, however, was in cooking school. I attended LaVarenne in France, where I received the grande diplome.

Q. How/where did you get your first job in this field? What did you do?

A. I got my first job in the field by assisting a freelance photo stylist. I also worked in the test kitchens of *Food and Wine* and *Family Circle* magazines, which helped to jump-start my career.

Q. How does someone break into this field?

A. For those who want to work in food styling, there are a few courses and seminars offered by institutions such as the Culinary Institute of America. To actually break into the field, you need to assist a working photo stylist. It can also be helpful to find work in the test kitchen of a food-oriented magazine or at a food company that tests and develops recipes.

Q. What qualities should a successful photo stylist possess?

A. To succeed in this job, you must be meticulous about your photo subject, paying very careful attention to every detail. You also should be organized, work in a timely manner, and be able to solve problems creatively.

Q. What are some of the pros and cons of your job?

A. Pros: For me, it is very satisfying to have a new set of parameters for each assignment. There is always an element of surprise, even after being in the field for over 15 years. However, this fluid work environment might be a deterrent to some.

Cons: There can be a fair amount of pressure in photo styling. You must perform quickly and efficiently, often before an extremely critical and demanding audience.

Q. What advice would you give aspiring food stylists?

A. Food styling can be a rewarding career, but it's hard to break into this field. You need to be persistent and creative in your job search. Being personable can be nearly as important as being talented in landing some jobs. Having good design sense as well as a diverse knowledge of food preparation is also essential.

CHAPTER 3

TAKING YOUR ART DEGREE TO WORK

If you are a recent college graduate who, diploma in hand, is gazing into the working world like it's the jaws of doom, don't fret. Many new grads lack direction once the graduation cap is thrown and the gown is off. You might ask yourself, what jobs should I seek out? Which companies should I target?

Before answering these questions, you need to do a self-assessment. You may have taken this type of test before in high school or college, whether it was the Myers-Briggs or another such formal test, to decide which classes to take or major to choose (see Chapter 1). As you complete this assessment, focus on your future career. Keeping your art major in mind, write down specific interests and skills that have been proven in your previous schoolwork and work experience. Then think about jobs that will best utilize these strengths and preferences. Are you stronger in technical areas and detailed sketching, or are you more confident in writing and communicating with others? Perhaps it's a combination of both.

After writing down and evaluating your skills and interests, consider some of the following questions:

- Do you enjoy working independently (as a painter, sculptor, photographer, etc.) or as part of a group (as on an editorial staff)?

- Are you good at motivating yourself to get work done, or do you need more interaction and supervision to stay motivated and focused?

- Are financial rewards (such as a higher salary) important to you—either out of necessity or desire? Or are you more concerned with finding a job that fulfills you—regardless of the size of your paycheck?

- Does location of a job matter to you? Do you want to stay close to family and/or friends? Do you prefer a city, suburban, or rural environment? Would you rather work in an office (as a desktop publishing specialist, Internet developer, etc.), outdoors (as a landscape architect, etc.), in a classroom (as an art teacher, college professor, etc.), in another country (as a museum curator, fashion designer, etc.) or in a Hollywood studio (as a cinematographer, costume designer, film editor, etc.)?

■ Do you need or want a flexible work schedule? Would you be willing to work occasional long or irregular hours or on weekends (as an architect, graphic designer, etc.)?

Continue to think of more narrowly focused questions to consider. These answers should help you with the biggest question of them all: What do I want to do with my life? The key is to keep in mind your given strengths and skills—and find a job and work environment that fits.

INTERVIEW: Meghan Lee

Meghan Lee has been a graphic designer for several years, first with a small marketing group, now running her own business. She was kind enough to speak to the editors of Top Careers for Art Graduates *about her experience and share some advice with the readers.*

Q. Describe your primary and secondary job duties as a graphic designer.

A. My primary job duties include conceptualization and design of communication materials such as logos, letterhead packages, brochures, and websites. My secondary duties include project management, production trafficking, and billing.

Q. How did you train for this job? What was your college major?

A. My college major was in graphic design, which was a four-year program. I also minored in journalism to gain exposure and experience writing copy for advertising.

I received the bulk of my job training during my last year of college and at my first job out of college. During this time, I received hands-on computer (Macintosh) training on software programs, design challenges, and production techniques.

Q. What are the most important personal and professional qualities for graphic designers?

A. Personal qualities

- Listen. You should be able to listen to clients to really hear what they like and dislike regarding their design.

- Explain. You need to be able to explain your creative process in layman's terms so that someone without a creative background can appreciate the work that is needed to produce each design.

- Pride with detachment. You need to avoid "too much" personal attachment to your work so that when the client rejects your ideas (and they will at one time or another) you do not take it personally or let it hurt your ego.

Professional qualities

- You need to be able to identify your clients' needs and respond accordingly.

- You should anticipate your clients' reaction before you present something to them to make sure you provide them with the most appropriate design.

- You should be flexible with your designs and show your clients a wide range of creative ideas that can achieve the same result.

Q. What advice would you give to a graphic designer who is just starting out?

A. One of the most important things to learn early on is determining what's appropriate for each client. This means knowing your audience. For example, if the client is one of the Big Four accounting firms, don't design anything for them in neon green. On the other hand, if your client is an alternative rock band, don't show up for a meeting wearing a suit. Let your creativity speak for itself, but make sure you've got your client's best interest in mind with your design. Don't just show off your latest Photoshop techniques.

Q. What is the future employment outlook for graphic design?

A. Everything you read is created by a graphic designer of some position or another—we're certainly not a dying breed. Much of the industry's latest developments has been in online design, however, there still is a place and need for print design as well.

NETWORKING

Once you've narrowed your job interests using questions such as those above, you need to focus on either finding employers that are hiring or, if you decide to work on your own, finding clients that are buying—both tricky tasks, especially during a slower economy. Though many artists want to work for themselves, most artists begin their careers working for an employer to gain credibility and experience. With slow economic growth and sagging profits, most employers are hiring fewer workers than in previous years. As a result, there are more graduates vying for fewer positions—all the more reason for you to focus your energy and fine-tune your job search.

One of the ways to jump-start your job search is through the people you know. You have more contacts for potential job leads than you might realize. Your former professors, academic advisors, family, and friends can give you helpful advice, if not direct leads to employers.

Another source of contacts is your school. Most colleges have alumni departments that track the locations and jobs of recent graduates. Contact your college's alumni director for a list of names of people in your area. In addition, alumni sometimes organize themselves into groups for social and professional reasons, especially in larger cities. Check your college's website, or ask your alumni director if there is an organized alumni group in your area. If you live near a chapter, find out about its next meeting or social gathering and get involved. Not only will you have fun and meet new people, your fellow alumni may work in the arts or in companies in which you are interested.

Previous summer or part-time jobs can also provide you with job contacts. Even if your position wasn't tied directly to art, try contacting old managers and co-workers for advice and suggestions for leads. If you completed an internship during your college years, now is the time to follow up with an email, resume, and/or letter. Even if your previous employer is not hiring at the time, keep in contact with previous managers for other job ideas or advice.

CREATING A RESUME THAT GETS NOTICED

Before you follow up with all these contacts, you need to shape up your resume. The content, length, and format of your resume will depend on the type of job you are seeking. Regardless of the position, the resume and cover letter may be your one chance to grab a potential employer's attention, so be sure they shine.

Resume Advice from Those Who Trash Them

Companies receive resumes by the handful. Make that piles. Or perhaps tons. Especially during times of slow economic growth, the number of resumes that come across a typical hiring manager's desk can be overwhelming. Fortunately for them (but not for the job seekers), there are many glaring errors that applicants commit that send their resume right into the trash bin. According to monster.com, here's a list of the top 10 resume mistakes from the recruiters and hiring managers who see them each and every workday.

1. Problem: Spelling errors, typos, and just plain bad writing.

   Fix: Read your resume over carefully, use spell check, and have friends and family members look it over for mistakes you might have missed.

2. Problem: Too many duties, not enough explanation.

   Fix: Instead of simply listing your previous job descriptions, describe your accomplishments. Employers don't need to know exactly what you did at your last job, but instead, they want to hear about the direct results of your efforts. For example, list any improvements you brought to your previous job or department.

3. Problem: Employment dates are wrong or missing completely.

   Fix: Include time ranges in months or years for all work positions. Explain any gaps in your work history in your cover letter. Employers need dates to verify your experience and gain a sense of your overall work history.

4. Problem: You don't seem to know your name and address.

   Fix: Double-check your contact information each and every time you update your resume. The whole point of the resume is to get a phone call asking for an interview. Employers will not look you up to contact you.

5. Problem: Converted or scanned resume shows formatting errors.

   Fix: If you are emailing your resume, make sure it is saved and sent in plain text (ASCII) format. Even if you send your resume by fax or mail, use plain text because some employers scan resumes for easy browsing. Fancy fonts, boxes, or colors are unnecessary on a professional resume and will only cause problems.

(continues)

Resume Advice from Those Who Trash Them
(continued)

6. Problem: Organized your resume by function.

   Fix: Most employers prefer a chronological resume, where work and school experience is listed by date, over a functional one, where experience is listed by skills or functions performed. Month- or even year-long gaps in employment (which becomes obvious in chronological resumes) are more common now than in previous years and can be filled with volunteer work or continued education.

7. Problem: Too long.

   Fix: Highlight only your work and educational experience that is most prevalent to the job at hand. Recruiters simply don't have the time to read through long resumes.

8. Problem: Too wordy.

   Fix: Similar to #7, pare down your work, school, and other descriptions to include just the most important highlights.

9. Problem: Unqualified.

   Fix: Apply only to jobs for which you are qualified. You're not only wasting the employer's time, you're wasting your own when you apply for positions that require higher degrees or more work experience than you have.

10. Problem: Too personal.

    Fix: Include your fondness for stamp collecting if you are applying to work in the post office. Otherwise, leave it off your resume. In other words, list only information that's pertinent to the employer and the open position. Listed activities and interests should be included only if they are related to the job.

The Content

If you are seeking a job as a visual artist, you resume should list your educational background first, followed by a list of where your art has been viewed, such as literary journals or gallery showings. This section can also include any awards or recognitions you have won for your work. However, for the many art majors looking for jobs outside the arts (such as in the business sector or in academia), resumes should highlight your education and work experience.

Recording your contact information, educational background, and extracurricular activities is the easy part. The challenge is summing up your work experience and job skills to make yourself stand out. The following is a recommended list for tackling this tough part of your resume.

- Write down a list of all the jobs or positions you've held (paid or unpaid) that have led you in your current career direction. Unless you were a manager, leave out your freshman-year job at Taco Bell.

- Record your job responsibilities. Don't worry about using fancy language to describe your jobs just yet; just be sure to list all the tasks that you handled.

- List the skills that you learned from handling these job duties, such as artistic techniques, specific computer programs, or particular organizational skills.

- Take a trip to the library or bookstore and pick up a resume guide. These resources should have examples of quality resumes. Look over the job descriptions that are used, and see if any could be applied to your own experience.

- Return to your list of job duties, and write short sentences using some of the active-language examples found in the resume guide's job descriptions. "Action" words include short, definitive sentence starters like "managed," "organized," and "coordinated." The point here is to be as succinct and effective as possible. Just don't copy verbatim from your resume guide.

The Format

Resumes are usually organized in one of two ways: chronologically or functionally. Look at your resume books and choose the format that you think would work best for you. Even if you're applying for a job as a designer or visual artist, don't make your resume look too stylish or ornate. This will only distract employers from what is really important: your skills.

Keep the layout as clean and uncluttered as possible, and be sure that the type is easy to read (12pt is a standard). Employers sometimes have hundreds of resumes to review for one position, so they won't waste their time trying to decipher a page of small text and long paragraphs. Short bulleted lists offer a concise and easy-to-read format for your work and educational experiences.

Last but not least, feel free to increase the type size on the element you want the employer to remember most: your name!

Share it with Others

Once you're through with this first draft (notice the word "draft"; this should not be your final version), show it to family members, friends, and other connections and ask for suggestions. Write and rewrite until your resume is the best representation of what you have to offer a company.

Create Several Versions

Before sending out your winning resume, take note; the most successful resumes are the ones that are tailor-made to fit a particular position. That means that every time you apply for a job, you should review your resume and adjust skills and experiences that can apply directly to the position. You are much more likely to be considered for a job if you highlight specific ways in which your past education and experiences can be an asset to the hiring employer.

THE COVER LETTER

Always include a cover letter with your resume. As with your resume, the letter must be polished and tailored to the job for which you are applying. Address the cover letter to the individual in charge of hiring. If a name is not included in a job listing, call the company to inquire, or visit the company's website and check the staff listings. If you still can't find what you're looking for, addressing the letter to "Human Resources" should get it into the hands of the right person. The heading of the letter should include your name, address, and phone number, as well as the same for the person to whom you're sending it.

Your cover letter should also be concise. The body of the letter should contain three short paragraphs, as follows:

- The first paragraph should mention the position for which you are applying and where you saw the job listing. Employers like to keep track of how and where their applicants learn about positions. For example, a good first paragraph might simply state, "I am applying for the position of Advertising Assistant, which I saw advertised in *The Daily Bugle* on 22 March 2003." If a friend or associate recommended you for the job, you can mention that here, but only if that person gives you permission to do so.

- In the second paragraph, state briefly why the job interests you and why you will be a valuable addition to the company. Do not restate the contents of your resume here: simply touch on one or two of your strongest skills and what you can bring to the position. Most importantly, write with confidence. Avoid phrases like "I think I would be . . ." or "I feel that I . . ." Rather, state simply, "I will be . . ." and "I am . . . ." Clear and definitive language, as opposed to cluttered equivocation, is more likely to grab the attention of the person reading your cover letter and resume.

- In the third paragraph, encourage the employer to review your resume and provide any additional information that may have been requested in the job listing, such as salary requirements, ability to travel or relocate, etc. Here you can also state that you will follow up on your resume submission, but do this only if you honestly plan to do so by phone or letter. Do not include such a statement if the job listing states that only suitable candidates will be contacted. This is the employer's way of saying, "Don't call us, we'll call you."

If you are applying for a position in academia, you will need to prepare a cover letter that is slightly different than the traditional business cover letter. Visit Academic Cover Letters (http://owl.english.purdue.edu/handouts/pw/p_covseek.html) for more information on creating this type of cover letter.

In addition, hundreds of books and other resources are available for resume assistance, many of which include examples of resumes that work. The following are a few sites to explore for more information:

Art Resumes: What Should They Look Like?
http://www.artistsfoundation.org/html/afa/freeinfo/
artresume.html

Career-Resumes
http://www.career-resumes.com

CollegeGrad.com
http://www.collegegrad.com/resumes

JobStar Central: Resumes
http://jobstar.org/tools/resume

JobWeb Guide to Resumes and Interviews
http://www.jobweb.com/Resumes_Interviews

Susan Ireland's Resume Guide: Artistic and Creative Resume Samples
http://susanireland.com/resumescreative1.htm

APPLYING FOR JOBS ONLINE: SERIOUS INTERNET SURFING

The Internet has revolutionized the way employers and employees find their right match. Not only can you browse jobs online, but you can also apply for them through email. In fact, many employers prefer, if not require, that resumes be submitted by email. According to a survey by the National Association of Colleges and Employers, 90 percent of employers preferred job applicants to respond to jobs online. While it seems that the amount of resume advice available is nearly endless, many students are still left wondering how to prepare their resume for online submission. Here's a quick list of the things to consider before you click the Send button:

- If submitting your resume online, save it as "Text Only" to convert it into ASCII format. This is the only way to guarantee that the recipient of your resume will read it in the manner and format in which you intended. Fonts and automatic formatting that you may have used in a word processing program may not be converted correctly when the resume reaches the desk of an employer. Sending your resume in text-only format also ensures that employers receive your information free from possible attachment viruses. Only send your resume as another type of attachment, such as Microsoft Word, if the ad explicitly states that you should do so.

- Once you save your resume as text, clean up the body of the email, watching out for new line and section breaks. If you used bullets, use asterisks (*) instead. If you used formatted section breaks, use dashes (—) to separate sections.

- When you prepare your email to send to the employer, write your cover letter in the body of the email, then attach the text-only version of your resume. When the employer reads your email, your resume will actually be viewed in the body of the email instead of as a separate attachment.

- Make sure this text-only resume is as clean and error-free as your original. As one recruiter on the monster.com website puts it, "Do you know what we call people who submit electronic resumes with typos? We call them unemployed."

- Be sure to mention the name of the position, any job codes that may have been mentioned in the ad, and the words resume and cover letter in the Subject line of the email. The latter is just in case the employer automatically looks for an attachment and overlooks your cover letter in the body of the email.

Some employers enable you to apply for jobs directly from their company websites. If this is the case, follow the directions on the site very closely, and have your cover letter and resume in plain-text format at the ready.

THE PRESCRIPTION
FOR A PERFECT INTERVIEW

If all goes well, your well-crafted resume and cover letter will score you a few interviews. These one-on-one encounters with employers, gallery owners, or school administrators can be intimidating, to say the least. But there is a lot you can do to prepare yourself before stepping into an office and shaking the hand that may help feed you someday. Follow these tips for a successful interview:

- Do your homework. Research the company, art gallery, museum, etc., before your interview so you can better understand the position for which you are applying. Almost all employers have an online presence. Check out the organization's website and explore its departments, services, locations, and other open positions. This research will not only help you to understand the job, but it will enable you to ask more intelligent questions.
- Listen hard . . . then speak up. When asked a question, carefully consider what was said, think a moment, then answer. This sounds simple, but it is often hard to do when under pressure.
- Ask away. Certainly you will want to be attentive to all the interviewer has to say about the organization's structure and work environment and the specifics of the job. But when the tables are turned and it's your time to ask questions, be sure to do so. Have a list of questions made up beforehand covering issues that the employer may not address. For example: What sort of training will I receive on the job? Who will I be

reporting to? How many people will I be working with? This will show that you are truly interested in the position and in getting to know more about the employer.

■ Dress conservatively. Even if you consider yourself the quirkiest of artists, a conservative suit (in dark blue or black) is recommended for most office interviews. While what you wear shouldn't score you points with an employer, poor, sloppy, or shocking attire can definitely work against you.

■ Be punctual. If you can't make it to an interview on time, how is the interviewer going to think you'll be able to make it in to the office on time every morning?

■ Say thanks. Your mother was right: Be polite. Always thank the interviewer for his or her time, and follow up with a handwritten or emailed note that reiterates your gratitude and (when appropriate) your continued interest in the job.

Tips for the Dining Interview

Many interviews, especially for higher level jobs, occur outside of the workplace. If you find yourself in a lunch or dinner interview, take note:

■ Remember you are there for the interview, not a free meal.

■ Don't arrive famished or full.

■ Order something at a reasonable price. If the interviewer orders first, order something similar in size and price.

■ Never drink at an interview, even if the interviewer orders a cocktail or beer. You are the one in the hot seat, so make sure you have your full faculties intact.

■ Order something safe. Avoid options that are overly spicy, messy, or stinky. (No spaghetti, hot wings, or garlic bread!)

■ Always thank the interviewer for the meal and the interview, regardless of whether or not you liked your meal, the service, or the location. Follow up with a thank-you note in the next week.

A New Breed of Interview: The Situational Interview

When most people think of a job interview, an image comes to mind of a question-and-answer session between a job seeker and a hiring manager. However, a new trend in applicant evaluation has emerged. Some employers, even those at small design firms or local museums, are now looking at an individual's ethics as much as his or her education and job experience. Employers want to hire good people as much as they want to hire skilled people.

In these situational, or behavioral, interviews, applicants are put through real-life job situations (such as being verbally harassed by an upset museum visitor) and then are analyzed based on their gut instincts, actions, words, and even body language. According to the *Handbook of Industrial and Organizational Psychology,* while the traditional sit-down interview is reported to be approximately 7 percent effective in predicting job performance, the situational interview is approximately 54 percent accurate.

The bad news for job seekers is that, unlike standard interviews, these character evaluations are tough to prepare for. The only thing to do is be yourself, think before you speak and act, and hope your responses reflect your years of education and training.

Here are some online resources for more interview advice:

Ask the Interview Coach
http://www.asktheinterviewcoach.com

Collegegrad.com: Interviewing Information
http://www.collegegrad.com/intv

Monster: Interview Center
http://interview.monster.com

Salary.com: Job.interview.net
http://www.job-interview.net

THE PORTFOLIO

Just as the resume is your key to getting an interview, your art portfolio is the key to getting a job. Yes, part of your success will depend on fielding typical interview questions with ease. However, if you come to the interview ready to chat but without samples of your work, chances are the interviewer will kindly ask you to leave. Whether your chosen field is illustration, architecture, or interior design, you will need a portfolio containing work that represents your full range of talent. Because of the portfolio's importance in landing a job, you need to invest time, energy, and a little money to make it neat, complete, and an impressive representation of you as an artist.

According to the Artist Resource website (http://www.artistresource.org), portfolios can be organized in different ways depending on your chosen specialty and career goals. You can arrange samples by technique or method, by chronological order (placing most recent works first), or by complexity (placing most complex work first).

Depending on the size and format of your work, you can use a three-ring binder for written work, illustration, or color slides. You might also use a zippered folder with pockets to hold loose pieces, or even a sturdy box for storing three-dimensional artwork. Whatever type of portfolio you choose, be sure it's made from high-quality materials. If artwork is displayed on pages, pieces should be matted against a muted background that frames the work but does not distract from it in any way.

One of the most common mistakes people make when putting together a portfolio is including too many pieces of work. Quality is much more important than quantity. Only include work that best represents your potential and direction. Show off your originality as well as your technical and artistic knowledge. Most importantly, when applying for a particular job, tailor your portfolio as you tailored your resume to fit the employer's needs. For example, if you are applying for a job as a Web designer, put your work in Web design in the most prominent position of the portfolio: in front. If you also have work and experience in other forms of art, include it in a back section, or, if the art is completely unrelated to the job, leave it out completely.

To learn more about creating a strong portfolio, visit these sites:

Artist Portfolio Guidelines
http://art-support.com/portfolio.htm

Artist Resource: The Professional Portfolio
http://www.artistresource.org/jobhunt.htm#Portfolio

CreativePublic.com: Building Your Portfolio
http://www.creativepublic.com/visitors_area/portfoliotips.html

PapaInk: Young Artist Portfolios
http://www.papaink.org/icurator/portfolio_index.php

Webgrrls International: Building Your Portfolio
http://www.webgrrls.com/wfs.jhtml?/career/advice/
  portfolio.phtml

YOU'VE GOT THE JOB . . . NOW WHAT?

Your resume shined, your interview was flawless, and your portfolio proved impressive: you're hired! Unfortunately, starting a new job can

Confused by Degrees?

What is the difference between a bachelor of fine arts (B.F.A.) degree and a bachelor of arts (B.A.) degree? Both degrees include studies of a broad selection of subjects. However, the B.F.A. focuses more on art and design classes, whereas the B.A. degree concentrates on liberal arts components, such as English or history. According to Artschools.com, approximately two-thirds of the B.F.A. focus is in creating and researching the visual arts. In a B.A. program, approximately two-thirds of the course work covers the liberal arts.

be just as intimidating as job hunting itself. It will take some time to adjust and settle in to the new environment and job duties. Depending on the individual and the position, this could take weeks or even months. During this time, you will learn about your organization's structure, other jobs within the workplace, and how they interact.

After some time, however, most workers desire new duties, responsibilities, and challenges in their work. A bigger paycheck may also be on their mind and in their horizon. In general, workers can advance in one of two ways. Some choose to move laterally, switching to a similar position or level in another department or with another company for more pay. Other workers choose to move vertically, moving to a position of higher authority within a company or with another employer.

THE GRADUATE FACTOR

The working world offers many advancement opportunities to those with a bachelor's degree. However, now more than ever, a graduate degree is becoming commonplace among managers and executives and is required for positions in academia. If you hope to advance to high-level management or may choose to teach someday, you will need to consider graduate school.

Graduate school applications can be lengthy and time consuming. In addition, you will need to sharpen your No. 2 pencil again. Most graduate schools require students to take the Graduate Record Examination (GRE) before applying. Similar to how the SATs and ACTs help evaluate incoming college students, the GRE is used to evaluate graduate school students. This achievement test is composed of verbal, quantitative, and analytical writing sections on various subjects. Visit http://www.gre.org to learn more.

There are as many different graduate degrees as there are art jobs out there. So be sure to do some research, compare your options, and seek out the degree that will increase your chances for advancement and fulfill your career goals.

U.S. News & World Report ranks graduate programs based on degree conferred, from fine art to ceramics to industrial design. For 2004, the magazine gave the highest rating to the following three schools (all of which received the same rating "score") for their master's of fine arts programs: the Rhode Island School of Design, the School of the Art Institute of Chicago, and Yale University in New Haven, Connecticut. Go to http://www.usnews.com/usnews/edu/grad/rankings/art for more details and ratings for other art programs. Also be sure to check out the following online resources:

GradSchools.com: Arts and Fine Arts
http://www.gradschools.com/art_fine.html

Peterson's Graduate Schools and Programs
http://www.petersons.com/GradChannel

Sensebox: Listing of Graphic Design Graduate Schools
http://www.sensebox.com/db1

INTERVIEW: Shannon Leahy

Shannon Leahy has been a visual artist for the past four years working mostly in acrylic paint and ink. She spoke about her experiences and shared some advice with the readers of Top Careers for Art Graduates.

Q. What is your exact job title? In which areas of art do you specialize?

A. I have two job descriptions: I work as a store artist for Trader Joe's, a company of small and successful grocery stores across the country. I'm responsible for creating murals that both illustrate the company's values and add a bit of fun to the shopping experience of its customers. I also am a self-employed, freelance artist, meaning I create my own art and sell it to interested buyers. In my own work, I tend to focus on intuitive/abstract expressionism.

Q. How long have you been an artist?

A. I have always been creatively motivated but didn't receive income from my pursuits until college.

Q. How did you train for this job? What was your college major?

A. I trained for my job by just doing it. Trader Joe's was just opening a new store, and they sought a local artist to do the displays. I had just finished a bachelor of fine arts degree at the School of the Art Institute of Chicago and was a perfect candidate for the position.

Q. Did this major prepare you for your career or, in retrospect, would you pursue another major? If so, what major?

A. I think that I chose the right degree for my specific job. It is my hope to eventually pursue painting as a full-time career, and both my college degree and Trader Joe's are helping make that desire possible.

Q. Did you participate in any internships while you were in college?

A. I interned with two different architectural photographers. I was taught, through these positions, the importance of having a discriminating eye and extreme patience.

Q. What qualities do you need to be a successful artist?

A. To be an artist, one must have perseverance. It can be daunting to want to be a full-time artist, when buyers may be fickle and the market unpredictable. In the real world, few artists right out of school succeed in paying their bills on their art alone. It takes patience, long hours in the studio, and the ability to roll with the punches when things don't go your way. In the end, it is about doing what you love to do, and believing in it.

Art and business don't necessarily mix. It takes patience and self-determination to succeed. Find galleries that are just beginning, or that focus primarily on emerging artists, and talk to them. Established galleries may not welcome a newcomer who has not yet paid his/ her dues. Don't get discouraged! Focus on the work.

Q. What advice can you offer art majors as they graduate and look for jobs?

A. Don't be afraid to try something new. If you learn that you hate some aspect of a job, or the job itself, at least you have learned what job you don't like. If you meet someone whose career interests you, ask questions and find out how you can get involved. Most of my early jobs were discovered by striking up conversations with creative people, and keeping my ears and eyes alert to job openings.

SECTION II

CAREERS

ANTIQUE AND ART DEALERS

QUICK FACTS

School Subjects Art Business Family and consumer science	**Certification or Licensing** None available
	Outlook About as fast as the average
Personal Skills Artistic Leadership/management	**DOT** N/A
Work Environment Primarily indoors Primarily multiple locations	**GOE** N/A
	NOC 0621
Minimum Education Level High school diploma	**O*NET-SOC** N/A
Salary Range $15,000 to $30,000 to $1,000,000+	

OVERVIEW

Antique and art dealers make a living acquiring, displaying, and selling antiques and art. By strict definition, antiques can be defined as items more than 100 years old. However, over the last two decades, the term antique has been applied to furniture, jewelry, clothing, art, household goods, and many other collectibles, dating back to as recently as the 1970s. People collect a wide array of items, from traditional paintings and sculptures to unique period toys and cigar boxes. Many antique and art dealers are self-employed and go into business after developing an interest in collecting pieces. The Antiques and Collectibles Dealer Association (ACDA) estimates there are approximately 200,000 to 250,000 antique dealers in the United States, based in antique shops, antique malls, and on the Internet.

HISTORY

Interest in collecting antiques and art can be traced back to the Renaissance, when people began to admire and prize Greek and Roman antiquities such as coins, manuscripts, sculptures, paintings, and pieces of architecture. In order to fulfill public interest and curiosity, as well as to supply the growing number of private and public collections, many pieces from Egypt, Italy, and Greece were looted and carried off to other countries.

The collectibles market, as it is known today, consists of everyday household objects, furniture, clothing, art, and automobiles, usually from another time period. After World War I, public interest in collectibles grew; many people began to purchase, preserve, and display pieces in their homes. As interest grew, so did the need for antique and art businesses and dealers.

There are different categories of collectibles and different ways and reasons to acquire them. Some people choose to collect pieces from different time periods such as American Colonial or Victorian; others collect by the pattern or brand, such as Chippendale furniture or Coca-Cola memorabilia. Some people collect objects related to their career or business. For example, a physician may collect early surgical instruments, or a pharmacist may collect antique apothecary cabinets. A growing category in the collectibles industry is ephemera, which includes theater programs, postcards, cigarette cards, and food labels, among other items. Ephemera were produced without lasting value or survival in mind. Though many pieces of ephemera can be purchased inexpensively, others, especially items among the first of their kind or in excellent condition, are rare and considered very valuable.

Some larger antique and art dealers specialize and deal only with items from a particular time period or design. However, most dealers collect, buy, and sell most previously owned household items and decor. Such shops will carry items ranging from dining room furniture to jewelry to cooking molds.

The idea of what is worth collecting constantly changes with time and the public's tastes and interests. Tastes in art range from traditional to contemporary, from Picasso to Warhol. Items representing the rock music industry of the 1960s and 1970s, as well as household items and furniture of the 1970s, are highly sought after today. Dealers not only stock their stores with items currently in demand but keep an eye on the collectibles of the future.

THE JOB

For Sandra Naujokas, proprietor of Favorite Things Antique Shop in Orland Park, Illinois, the antiques business is never boring. Twenty-five years ago, she started a collection of English-style china, and she's been hooked on antiques and collecting ever since. Naujokas spends her work day greeting customers and answering any questions they may have. When business slows down, she cleans the store and prices inventory. Sometimes people will bring in items for resale; it's up to Naujokas to carefully inspect each piece and settle on a price. She relies on pricing manuals such as *Kovels' Antiques & Collectibles Price List* and *Schroeder's Antiques Price Guide,* which give guidelines and a suggested price on a wide range of items.

Naujokas also goes on a number of shopping expeditions a year to restock her store. Besides rummage sales and auctions, she relies on buying trips to different parts of the country and abroad to find regional items. At times, she is invited to a person's home to view items for sale. "It's important to be open to all possibilities," Naujokas says.

She also participates in several shows a year to reach customers that normally would not travel to the store's location. "You need to do a variety of things to advertise your wares," Naujokas advises.

She also promotes her business by advertising in her town's travel brochure, the local newspapers, and by direct mail campaigns. Her schedule is grueling, as the store is open seven days a week, but Naujokas enjoys the work and the challenge of being an antique dealer. Besides the social aspect—interacting with all sorts of people and situations—Naujokas loves having the first choice of items for her personal collections. Her advice for people interested in having their own antique store? "You have to really like the items you intend to sell."

REQUIREMENTS
High School

You can become an antique or art dealer with a high school diploma, though many successful dealers have become specialists in their field partly through further education. While in high school, concentrate on history and art classes, to familiarize yourself with the particular significance and details of different periods in time and the corresponding art of the period. Consider studying home economics if you plan to specialize in household items; it can come in handy when distinguishing a wooden rolling pin from a wooden butter paddle, for example.

English and speech classes to improve communication skills are also helpful. Antique and art dealing is a people-oriented business: Dealing efficiently with different types of people and situations is crucial. Operating your own small business will also require skills such as accounting, simple bookkeeping, and marketing, so business classes are recommended.

Postsecondary Training

While a college education is not required, a degree in art or history will give you a working knowledge of the antiques you sell and the historical periods from which they originated. Another option is obtaining a degree in business or entrepreneurship. Such knowledge will help you to run a successful business.

Certification or Licensing

Presently, there are no certification programs available for antique dealers. However, if you plan to open your own antique store, you will need a local business license or permit.

In addition, if you wish to conduct appraisals, it will be necessary to take appraisal courses that are appropriate for your interest or antique specialty. Certification is not required of those interested in working as an appraiser, but it is highly recommended, according to the International Society of Appraisers, which administers an accreditation and certification program to its members. Obtaining accreditation or certification will demonstrate your knowledge and expertise in appraisal and attract customers. To obtain accreditation, candidates must complete three courses in appraisal theory, principles, and practice. In order to become certified, individuals must complete additional training in their specialty area, submit two appraisals for peer review, complete professional development study, and pass a comprehensive examination.

Other Requirements

To be an antique or art dealer, you'll need patience—and lots of it. Keeping your store well stocked with antiques, art, or other collectibles takes numerous buying trips to auctions, estate sales, flea markets, rummage sales, and even to foreign countries. Many times you'll have to sort through boxes of ordinary "stuff" before coming across a treasure. Unless you're lucky enough to have a large staff, you will have to make these outings by yourself. However, most dealers go into the profession because they enjoy the challenge of hunting for valuable pieces.

Tact is another must-have quality for success in this industry. Remember the old adage: One person's trash is another person's treasure.

EXPLORING

If you want to explore this field further, you may want to start by visiting an antique store or art gallery. If you see valuable treasures as opposed to dull paintings, old furniture, outdated books, or dusty collectibles, then chances are this is the job for you.

You can also watch the PBS's *Antiques Roadshow,* in which locals bring family treasures or rummage sale items to be appraised by antique industry experts—very often with surprising results.

EMPLOYERS

Many antique and art dealers and are self-employed, operating their own shops or renting space at a local mall. Others operate solely through traveling art shows or through mail-order catalogues. Some dealers prefer to work as employees of larger antique or art galleries. In general, the more well known the dealer, the more permanent and steady the business. Prestigious auction houses such as Christie's or Sotheby's are attractive places to work, but competition for such jobs is fierce.

STARTING OUT

All dealers have a great interest in antiques or art and are collectors themselves. Often their businesses result from an overabundance of their personal collections. There are many ways to build your collection and create inventory worthy of an antique business. Attending yard sales is an inexpensive way to build your inventory; you'll never know what kind of valuables you will come across. Flea markets, local art galleries, and antique malls will provide great purchasing opportunities and give you the chance to check out the competition. Sandra Naujokas finds that spring is an especially busy time for collecting: As people do their "spring cleaning," many decide to part with household items and décor they no longer want or need.

ADVANCEMENT

For those working out of their homes or renting showcase space at malls or larger shops, advancement in this field can mean opening your own antique shop or art gallery. Besides a business license, dealers that open their own stores need to apply for a seller's permit and a state tax identification number.

At this point, advancement is based on the success of the business. To ensure that their business thrives and expands, dealers need to develop advertising and marketing ideas to keep their business in the public's eye. Besides using the local library or Internet for ideas on opening their own businesses, newer dealers often turn to people who are already in the antique and art business for valuable advice.

EARNINGS

It is difficult to gauge what antique and art dealers earn because of the vastness of the industry. Some internationally known, high-end antique stores and art galleries dealing with many pieces of priceless furniture or works of art may make millions of dollars in yearly profits. However, this is the exception. It is impossible to compare the high-end dealer with the lower end market. The majority of antique and art dealers are comparatively small in size and type of inventory. Some dealers work only part time or rent showcase space from established shops. According to a survey conducted by ACDA, the average showcase dealer earns about $1,000 a month in gross profits. From there, each dealer earns a net profit as determined by the piece or pieces sold, minus overhead and other business costs. Note that annual earnings vary greatly for antique and art dealers due to factors such as size and specialization of the store, location, market, and current trends and tastes of the public.

WORK ENVIRONMENT

Much of antique and art dealers' time is spent indoors. Many smaller antique shops and art galleries do not operate with a large staff, so dealers must be prepared to work alone at times. Also, there may be large gaps of time between customers. Most stores are open at least five days a week and operate during regular business hours, though some have extended shopping hours in the evening.

However, dealers are not always stuck in their store. Buying trips and shopping expeditions give them opportunities to restock their inventory, not to mention explore different regions of the country or world. Naujokas finds that spring is the busiest time for building her store's merchandise, while the holiday season is a busy selling time.

OUTLOOK

According to ACDA, the collectibles industry should enjoy moderate growth in future years. The Internet has quickly become a popular way to buy and sell antiques and art. Though this medium has introduced collecting to many people worldwide, it has also had an adverse affect on the industry, namely for dealers and businesses that sell antiques and art in more traditional settings such as a shop or mall, or at a trade show. However, Jim Tucker, founder and director of the ACDA, predicts that the popularity of websites devoted to selling collectibles will level off due to the face-to-face interaction that is prized in this business.

Though the number of antique art and collectibles—items more than 100 years old—is limited, new items will be in vogue as collectibles. Also, people will be ready to sell old furniture and other belongings to make room for new, modern purchases. It is unlikely that there will ever be a shortage of inventory worthy of an antique shop or art gallery.

FOR MORE INFORMATION

For industry information, antique show schedules, and appraisal information, contact

Antique and Collectible Associations
PO Box 4389
Davidson, NC 28036
Tel: 800-287-7127
Email: info@antiqueandcollectible.com
http://www.antiqueandcollectible.com

For art resources and listings of galleries, contact

Art Dealers Association of America
575 Madison Avenue
New York, NY 10022
Tel: 212-940-8590
Email: adaa@artdealers.org
http://www.artdealers.org

For information about appraising and certification, contact

International Society of Appraisers
Riverview Plaza Office Park
16040 Christensen Road, Suite 102
Seattle, WA 98188-2929

Tel: 206-241-0359
Email: isahq@isa-appraisers.org
http://www.isa-appraisers.org

*For information on collecting, art and antique shows, and collecting clubs,
visit the following website:*
Collectors.org
http://www.collectors.org

ARCHITECTS

QUICK FACTS

School Subjects Art Mathematics	**Certification or Licensing** Required
Personal Skills Artistic Communication/ideas	**Outlook** About as fast as the average
Work Environment Primarily indoors Primarily one location	**DOT** 001
Minimum Education Level Bachelor's degree	**GOE** 05.01.07
Salary Range $30,000 to $55,470 to $132,000+	**NOC** 2151
	O*NET-SOC 17-1011.00

OVERVIEW

Architects plan, design, and observe the construction of facilities used for human occupancy and of other structures. They consult with clients, plan layouts of buildings, prepare drawings of proposed buildings, write specifications, and prepare scale and full-sized drawings. Architects also may help clients to obtain bids, select a contractor, and negotiate the construction contract. They also visit construction sites to ensure that the work is being completed according to specifications. There are approximately 102,000 architects working in the United States.

HISTORY

Architecture began not with shelters for people to live in but with the building of religious structures—from Stonehenge in England and the pyramids in Egypt to pagodas in Japan and the Parthenon in Greece. It was the Romans who developed a new building method—concrete vaulting—that made possible large cities with permanent masonry buildings. As they extended the Roman Empire, they built for public and military purposes. They developed and built apartment buildings, law courts, public baths, theaters, and circuses. During the industrial revolution, with its demand for factories and mills, iron and steel construction developed, which evolved into the steel and glass skyscrapers of today.

Because the history of architecture follows that of human civilization, the architecture of any period reflects the culture of people from that time. Architecture of early periods has influenced that of later centuries, including the work of contemporary architects. The field continues to develop as new techniques and materials are discovered and as architects infuse function with creativity.

THE JOB

The architect normally has two responsibilities: to design a building that will satisfy the client and to protect the public's health, safety, and welfare. This second responsibility requires architects to be licensed by the state in which they work. Meeting the first responsibility involves many steps. The job begins with learning what the client wants. The architect takes many factors into consideration, including local and state building and design regulations, climate, soil on which the building is to be constructed, zoning laws, fire regulations, and the client's financial limitations.

The architect then prepares a set of plans that, upon the client's approval, will be developed into final design and construction documents. The final design shows the exact dimensions of every portion of the building, including the location and size of columns and beams, electrical outlets and fixtures, plumbing, heating and air-conditioning facilities, windows, and doors. The architect works closely with consulting engineers on the specifics of the plumbing, heating, air conditioning, and electrical work.

The architect then assists the client in getting bids from general contractors, one of whom will be selected to construct the building to the specifications. The architect helps the client through the completion of the construction and occupancy phases, making certain the correct materials are used and that the drawings and specifications are faithfully followed.

Throughout the process the architect works closely with a design or project team. This team is usually made up of the following: designers, who specialize in design development; a structural designer, who designs the frame of the building in accordance with the work of the architect; the *project manager* or *job superintendent*, who sees that the full detail drawings are completed to the satisfaction of the architect; and the *specification writer* and *estimator*, who prepare a project manual that describes in more detail the materials to be used in the building, their quality and method of installation, and all details related to the construction of the building.

The architect's job is very complex. He or she is expected to know construction methods, engineering principles and practices, and materials. Architects also must be up to date on new design and construction techniques and procedures. Although architects once spent most of their time designing buildings for the wealthy, they are now more often involved in the design of housing developments, individual dwellings, supermarkets, industrial plants, office buildings, shopping centers, air terminals, schools, banks, museums, churches, and dozens of other types of buildings.

Architects may specialize in any one of a number of fields, including building appraisal, city planning, teaching, architectural journalism, furniture design, lighting design, or government service.

Can't Stand Wearing Ties or High Heels?

Here are a list of jobs catering to those who shudder at the sight of a suit:

- computer programmer
- artist
- writer
- actor
- petroleum engineer
- coach
- philosopher
- zoologist
- anthropologist
- child care worker

From "Top Jobs Matching Your Interests and Needs," Princeton Review (http://www.princetonreview.com)

Regardless of the area of specialization, the architect's major task is that of understanding the client's needs and then reconciling them into a meaningful whole.

REQUIREMENTS
High School

To prepare for this career while in high school, take a college preparatory program that includes courses in English, mathematics, physics, art (especially freehand drawing), social studies, history, and foreign languages. Courses in business and computer science also will be useful.

Postsecondary Training

Because most state architecture registration boards require a professional degree, high school students are advised, early in their senior year, to apply for admission to a professional program that is accredited by the National Architectural Accrediting Board. Competition to enter these programs is high. Grades, class rank, and aptitude and achievement scores count heavily in determining who will be accepted.

Most schools of architecture offer degrees through either a five-year bachelor's program or a three- or four-year master's program. The majority of architecture students seek out the bachelor's degree in architecture, going from high school directly into a five-year program. Though this is the fastest route, you should be certain that you want to study architecture. Because the programs are so specialized, it is difficult to transfer to another field of study if you change your mind. The master's degree option allows for more flexibility but takes longer to complete. In this case, students first earn a liberal arts degree then continue their training by completing a master's program in architecture.

A typical college architecture program includes courses in architectural history and theory, the technical and legal aspects of building design, science, and liberal arts.

Certification or Licensing

All states and the District of Columbia require that individuals be licensed before contracting to provide architectural services in that particular state. Though many work in the field without licensure, only licensed architects are required to take legal responsibility for all work. Using a licensed architect for a project is, therefore, less risky than using an unlicensed one. Architects who are licensed usually take on projects with larger responsibilities and have greater chances to advance to managerial or executive positions.

The requirements for registration include graduation from an accredited school of architecture and three years of practical experience (called an internship) with a licensed architect. After these requirements are met, individuals can take the rigorous four-day Architect Registration Examination. Some states require architects to maintain their licensing through continued education. These individuals may complete a certain number of credits every year or two through seminars, workshops, university classes, self-study courses, or other sources.

In addition to becoming licensed, a growing number of architects choose to obtain certification by the National Council of Architecture Registration Boards. If an architect plans to work in more than one state, obtaining this certification can make it easier to become licensed in different states.

Other Requirements

If you are interested in architecture, you should be intelligent, observant, responsible, and self-disciplined. You should have a concern for detail and accuracy, be able to communicate effectively both orally and in writing, and be able to accept criticism constructively. Although great artistic ability is not necessary, you should be able to visualize spatial relationships and have the capacity to solve technical problems. Mathematical ability is also important. In addition, you should possess organizational skills and leadership qualities and be able to work well with others.

EXPLORING

Most architects will welcome the opportunity to talk with young people interested in entering architecture. You may be able to visit their offices to can gain a firsthand knowledge of the type of work done by architects. You can also visit a design studio of a school of architecture or work for an architect or building contractor during summer vacations. Also, many architecture schools offer summer programs for high school students. Books and magazines on architecture also can give you a broad understanding of the nature of the work and the values of the profession.

EMPLOYERS

Of the 102,000 architects working in the United States, most are employed by architectural firms or other firms related to the construction industry. Nearly three out of every 10 architects, however, are self-employed—the ultimate dream of many people in the profession. A few develop graphic design, interior design, or product specialties. Still others put their training to work in the theater, film, or television fields, or in museums, display firms, and architectural product and materials manufacturing companies. A small number are employed in government agencies such as the Departments of Defense, Interior, and Housing and Urban Development and the General Services Administration.

STARTING OUT

Students entering architecture following graduation start as interns in an architectural office. As interns, they assist in preparing architectural construction documents. They also handle related details, such as administering contracts, coordinating the work of other professionals on the project, researching building codes and construction materials, and writing specifications. As an alternative to working for an architectural firm, some architecture graduates go into allied fields such as construction, engineering, interior design, landscape architecture, or real estate development.

ADVANCEMENT

Interns and architects alike are given progressively more complex jobs. Architects may advance to supervisory or managerial positions. Some architects become partners in established firms, while others take steps to establish their own practice.

EARNINGS

Architects earned a median annual salary of $55,470 in 2001, according to the U.S. Department of Labor. The lowest paid 10 percent earned less than $35,520 annually, while the highest paid 10 percent earned $89,240 or more.

The American Institute of Architects (AIA) reports that the starting annual salary for graduates of schools of architecture working during their internship before licensing was approximately $30,000 in 2002.

Well-established architects who are partners in an architectural firm or who have their own businesses generally earn much more than salaried employees. According to the AIA, partners in very large firms can earn $132,000 or more a year. Most employers offer such fringe benefits as health insurance, sick and vacation pay, and retirement plans.

WORK ENVIRONMENT

Architects normally work a 40-hour week. There may be a number of times when they will have to work overtime, especially when under pressure to complete an assignment. Self-employed architects work less regular hours and often meet with clients in their homes or offices during the evening. Architects usually work in comfortable offices, but they may spend a considerable amount of time outside the office visiting clients or viewing the progress of a particular job in the field. Their routines usually vary considerably.

OUTLOOK

Employment in the field is expected to grow about as fast as the average through 2010, according to the U.S. Department of Labor. The number of architects needed will depend on the volume of construction. The construction industry is extremely sensitive to fluctuations in the overall economy, and a recession could result in layoffs. On the positive side, employment of architects is not likely to be affected by the growing use of computer technologies. Rather than replacing architects, computers are being used to enhance the architect's work.

Competition for employment will continue to be strong, particularly in prestigious architectural firms. Openings will not be newly created positions but will become available as the workload increases and established architects transfer to other occupations or leave the field.

FOR MORE INFORMATION

For information on education, scholarships, and student membership opportunities, contact the following organizations:

American Institute of Architects
1735 New York Avenue, NW
Washington, DC 20006
Tel: 800-AIA-3837
Email: infocentral@aia.org
http://www.aia.org

American Institute of Architecture Students
1735 New York Avenue, NW
Washington, DC 20006
Tel: 202-626-7472
Email: mail@aiasnatl.org
http://www.aiasnatl.org

Association of Collegiate Schools of Architecture
1735 New York Avenue, NW
Washington, DC 20006
Tel: 202-785-2324
Email: vlove@acsa-arch.org
http://www.acsa-arch.org

ARCHIVISTS

QUICK FACTS

School Subjects English Foreign language History	**Certification or Licensing** Voluntary
	Outlook About as fast as the average
Personal Skills Communication/ideas Leadership/management	**DOT** 101
Work Environment Primarily indoors Primarily one location	**GOE** 11.03.03
	NOC 5113
Minimum Education Level Master's degree	**O*NET-SOC** 25-4011.00
Salary Range $18,910 to $34,190 to $63,299+	

OVERVIEW

Archivists contribute to the study of the arts and sciences by analyzing, acquiring, and preserving for research historical documents, organizational and personal records, and information systems that are significant enough to be preserved for future generations. Archivists keep track of artifacts such as letters, contracts, photographs, filmstrips, blueprints, electronic information, and other items of potential historical significance.

HISTORY

For centuries, archives have served as repositories for the official records of governments, educational institutions, businesses, religious organizations, families, and countless other groups. A need for archiving has existed since the first time information was recorded. The evolution of archiving information as we know it today can be traced back to the Middle Ages.

As the feudal system in Europe gave way to nations and a more systematic order of law, precise record keeping became increasingly important to keep track of land ownership and official policy. These records helped governments serve the needs of their nations and protected the rights of the common people in civil matters.

In America, early settlers maintained records using skills they brought from their European homelands. Families kept records of the journey to their new country and saved correspondence with family members still in Europe. Religious institutions kept records of the births, deaths, and marriages of their members. Settlers kept track of their business transactions, such as a land purchases, crop trades, and building constructions.

In the early 18th century, similar to what occurred in Europe in the Middle Ages, civic records in America became more prevalent as towns became incorporated. Leaders needed to maintain accurate records of property ownership and laws made by—and for—citizens.

Although archives have existed for centuries, archivists have established themselves as professionals only in the last 100 years or so. In the past, museums and societies accumulated records and objects rapidly and sometimes indiscriminately, accepting items regardless of their actual merit. Each archive had its own system of documenting, organizing, and storing materials. In 1884, the American Historical Association was formed to develop archival standards and help boost interaction among archivists.

As new scientific discoveries are made and new works are published each year, the need for sifting through and classifying items increases. More advanced computer systems will help archivists catalog archival materials as well as make archives more readily available to users. Advances in conservation techniques will help extend the life of fragile items, allowing them to be available to future generations.

THE JOB

Archivists analyze documents and materials such as government records, minutes of corporate board meetings, letters from famous people, charters of nonprofit foundations, historical photographs, maps, coins, works of art, and nearly anything else that may have historical significance. To determine which documents should be saved, they consider such factors as when each was written, who wrote it, and for whom it was written. In deciding on other items to archive, the archivist needs to consider the provenance, or history of creation and ownership, of the materials. They also take into account the capacity of their organization's archives. For instance, a repository with very little space for new materials may need to decline the gift of a large or bulky item, despite its potential value.

Archives are kept by various organizations, including government agencies, corporations, universities, and museums, and the value of documents is generally dictated by whichever group owns them. For example, the U.S. Army may not be interested in General Motors' corporate charter, and General Motors may not be interested in a Civil War battle plan. Archivists understand and serve the needs of their employers and collect items that are most relevant to their organizations.

Archivists may also be in charge of collecting items of historical significance to the institution for which they work. An archivist at a university, for instance, may collect new copies of the student newspaper to keep historical documentation of student activities and issues up to date. An archivist at a public library may prepare, present, and store annual reports of the branch libraries in order to keep an accurate record of library statistics.

After selecting appropriate materials, archivists help make them accessible to others by preparing reference aids such as indexes, guides, bibliographies, descriptions, and microfilmed copies of documents. These finding aids may be printed up and kept in the organization's stack area, put online so off-site researchers have access to the information, or put on floppy disk or CD-ROM for distribution to other individuals or organizations. Archivists also file and cross-index archived items for easy retrieval when a user wishes to consult a collection.

Archivists may preserve and repair historical documents or send damaged items to a professional conservator. They may also appraise the items based on their knowledge of political, economic, military, and social history, as well as by the materials' physical condition, research potential, and rarity.

Archivists play an integral role in the exhibition programs of their organizations. A university library, for instance, may present an exhibit that honors former Nobel Prize-winning faculty members. Most accomplished faculty leave their notes, research, experiments, and articles to their institution. An exhibition might display first drafts of articles, early versions of experiments, or letters between two distinguished scientists debating some aspect of a project's design. Exhibits allow members of the university and the community to learn about the history of an organization and how research has advanced the field. The archivist helps to sort through archival materials and decide what items would make for an interesting exhibition at the institution.

Many archivists conduct research using the archival materials at their disposal, and they may publish articles detailing their findings. They may advise government agencies, scholars, journalists, and others conducting research by supplying available materials and information. Archivists also act as reference contacts and teachers. An employee doing research at the company archives may have little knowledge of how and where to begin. The archivist may suggest the worker consult specific reference guides or browse through an online catalog. After the employee decides which materials will be of most use, the archivist may retrieve the archives from storage, circulate the collection to the user, and perhaps even instruct the user as to the proper handling of fragile or oversize materials.

Archivists may have assistants who help them with the sorting and indexing of archival collections. At a university library, undergraduate or graduate students usually act as archival assistants. Small community historical societies may rely on trained volunteers to assist the archivist.

Depending on the size of their employing organization, archivists may perform many or few administrative duties. Such duties may include preparing budgets, representing their institutions at scientific or association conferences, soliciting support for institutions, and interviewing and hiring personnel. Some help formulate and interpret institutional policy. In addition, archivists may plan or participate in special research projects and write articles for scientific journals.

REQUIREMENTS
High School

Since it is usually necessary to earn a master's degree to become an archivist, you should select a college preparatory curriculum in high school and plan on going to college. While in high school, you should pay special attention to learning library and research skills. Classes in English, art, history, science, and mathematics will provide you with basic skills and knowledge for university study. Journalism courses will hone your research skills, and political science courses will help you identify events of societal importance. You should also plan on learning at least one foreign language; if you are interested in doing archival work at a religious organization, Latin or Hebrew may be good language options. If you would like to work in a specialized archive, such as a medical school archive, you should also focus on classes in the sciences, such as anatomy, biology, and chemistry.

Postsecondary Training

To prepare for archival work in college, you should get a degree in the liberal arts. You will probably want to study history, library science, or a related field, since there are currently no undergraduate or graduate programs that deal solely with the archival sciences. You should take any specific courses in archival methods that are available to you as an undergraduate. Students who are interested in working in the archives of a museum or related organization often earn an undergraduate degree in art or art history before going on to graduate school. Since many employers prefer to hire archivists with a graduate degree, consider any course load that may help you gain entrance into a program to earn a master's degree in library science, library and information science, or history.

Graduate school will give you the opportunity to learn more specific details about archival work. Over 65 colleges and universities offer classes in the archival sciences as part of other degree programs. These courses will teach you how to do many aspects of archival work, from selecting items and organizing collections to preparing documentation and conserving materials. While in graduate school, you may be able to secure a part-time job or assistantship at your school's archives. Many university archives rely on their own students to provide valuable help maintaining collections, and students who work there gain firsthand knowledge and experience in the archival field.

For many positions, a second master's degree in a specific field or a doctorate is prerequisite. An archivist at a historical society may need a master's degree in history and another master's in library and information science. Candidates with bachelor's degrees may serve as assistants while they complete their formal training.

Certification or Licensing

Although not currently required by most employers, voluntary certification for archivists is available from the Academy of Certified Archivists. Certification is earned by gaining practical experience in archival work, taking requisite courses, and passing an examination on the history, theory, and practice of archival science. Tests are offered each year, usually in conjunction with the annual meeting of the Society of American Archivists. Groups of six or more archivists can petition the organization for an alternate exam location. Archivists need to renew their certification status every five years, usually by examination. Certification can be especially useful to archivists wishing to work in the corporate world.

Other Requirements

Archivists need to have excellent research and organizational skills. They should be comfortable working with rare and fragile materials. They need to maintain archives with absolute discretion, especially in the case of closed archives or archives available only for specific users. Archivists also need to be able to communicate effectively with all types of people that may use the archives, since they will be explaining the research methods and the policies and procedures of their organization. Finally, archivists may be responsible for moving heavy boxes and other awkward materials. An archivist should have the physical capabilities of bending, lifting, and carrying, although requirements may be different for various organizations and archival specialties, and arrangements can often be made for professionals with different abilities.

EXPLORING

If you are interested in archival work, a good way to learn about the field is by using archives for your own research. If you have a report due on Abraham Lincoln, for instance, you could visit an archive near your home that houses some of Lincoln's personal papers and letters. A visit to the archives of a candy manufacturer could help you with an assignment on the history of a specific type of production method. Since institutions may limit access to their collections, be sure to contact the organization about your project before you make the trip.

Getting to know an archivist can give you a good perspective of the field and the specific duties of the professional archivist. You could also see if a professional archival or historical association offers special student memberships or mentoring opportunities.

A personal project might be to construct a "family archive," consisting of letters, birth and marriage certificates, special awards, and any other documents that would help someone understand your family's history.

Another way to gain practical experience is to obtain part-time or volunteer positions in archives, historical societies, or libraries. Many museums and cultural centers train volunteer guides called docents to give tours of their institutions. If you already volunteer for an organization in another capacity, ask to have a personal tour of the archives.

EMPLOYERS

Archivists can find employment in various fields. In 2000, nearly one-third of the nation's archivists were employed in government positions, working for the Department of Defense, the National Archives and Records Administration, and other local, state, and federal repositories. Approximately 18 percent of archivists worked in college and university libraries. Other archivists worked in positions for museums, historical societies, and zoos.

Archivists are also on staff at corporations, religious institutions, and professional associations. Many of these organizations need archivists to manage massive amounts of records that will be kept for posterity, or to comply with state or federal regulations. Some private collectors may also employ an archivist to process, organize, and catalog their personal holdings.

STARTING OUT

There is no best way to become an archivist. Since there is no formal archivist degree, many people working in the field today have had to pave their own way. Daniel Meyer, associate curator of special collections and university archivist at the University of Chicago Library, began by earning a master's degree in history and then a Ph.D. In graduate school, he worked processing collections in his university's archives. By enhancing his educational credentials with practical experience in the field, he gradually moved on to positions with greater degrees of responsibility.

Another archivist approached her career from the other direction: she had a master's degree in French and then went on to earn a library degree, with a concentration in archival management. With her language background and a master's in library science, she was able to begin working in archival positions in several colleges and universities.

Candidates for positions as archivists should apply to institutions for entry-level positions only after completing their undergraduate degrees, usually a degree in history. An archivist going into a particular area of archival work, however, may wish to earn a degree in that field; if you are interested in working in a museum's archives, for instance, you may wish to pursue a degree in art or art history.

Many potential archivists choose to work part time as research assistants, interns, or volunteers in order to gain archival experience. School placement offices are good starting points in looking for research assistantships and internships, and professional librarian and archivist associations often have job listings for those new to the field.

ADVANCEMENT

Archivists usually work in small sections, units, or departments, so internal promotion opportunities are often limited. Promising archivists advance by gaining more responsibility for the administration of the collections. They will spend more time supervising the work of others. Archivists can also advance by transferring to larger repositories and taking more administration-based positions.

Because the best jobs as archivists are contingent upon education, the surest path to the top is to pursue more education. Ambitious archivists should also attend conferences and workshops to stay current with developments in their fields. Archivists can enhance their status by conducting independent research and publishing their findings. In a public or private library, an archivist may move on to a position such as curator, chief librarian, or library director.

Archivists may also move outside of the standard archival field entirely. With their background and skills, archivists may become teachers, university professors, or instructors at a library school. They may also set up shop for themselves as archival consultants to corporations or private collectors.

EARNINGS

Salaries for archivists vary considerably by institution and may depend on education and experience. People employed by the federal government or by prestigious museums generally earn far more than those working for small organizations. The U.S. Department of Labor reported that the average annual salary for an experienced archivist working for the federal government was $63,299 in 2001. The median annual salary for all archivists was $34,190 in 2001. A beginning archivist at a small, nonprofit organization, however, could earn as little as $18,910 per year.

Archivists who work for large corporations, institutions, or government agencies generally receive a full range of benefits, including health care coverage, vacation days, paid holidays, paid sick time, and retirement savings plans. Self-employed archival consultants usually have to provide their own benefits. All archivists have the added benefit of working with rare and unique materials. They have the opportunity to work with history and create documentation of the past.

WORK ENVIRONMENT

Because dirt, sunlight, and moisture can damage the materials they handle, archivists generally work in clean, climate-controlled surroundings with artificial lighting rather than windows. Many archives are small offices, often employing the archivist alone, or with one or two part-time volunteers. Other archives are part of a larger department within an organization; the archives for DePaul University in Chicago, for instance, are part of the special collections department and are managed by the curator. With this type of arrangement, the archivist generally has a number of graduate assistants to help with the processing of materials and departmental support staff to assist with clerical tasks.

Archivists often have little opportunity for physical activity, save for the bending, lifting, and reaching they may need to do in order to arrange collections and make room for new materials. Also, some archival collections include not only paper records but some oversized items as well. The archives of an elite fraternal organization, for example, may house a collection of hats or uniforms that members wore throughout the years, each of which must be processed, cataloged, preserved, and stored.

Most archivists work 40 hours a week, usually during regular, weekday working hours. Depending on the needs of their department and the community they serve, an archive may be open some weekend hours, thus requiring the archivist to be on hand for users. Also, archivists spend some of their time traveling to the homes of donors to view materials that may complement an archival collection.

OUTLOOK

Job opportunities for archivists are expected to increase about as fast as the average over the next decade, according to the U.S. Department of Labor. But since qualified job applicants outnumber the positions available, competition for jobs as archivists is keen. Candidates with specialized training, such as a master's degree in history and in library science, will have better opportunities. A doctorate in history or a related field can also be a boon to job-seeking archivists. Graduates who have studied archival work or records management will be in higher demand than those without that background. Also, many potential archivists can prepare for full-time employment by gaining related work or volunteer experience. As archival work begins to reflect an increasingly digital society, an archivist with extensive knowledge of computers is likely to advance quickly.

Jobs are expected to increase as more corporations and private organizations establish an archival history. Archivists will also be needed to fill positions left vacant by retirees and archivists who leave the occupation. On the other hand, budget cuts in educational institutions, museums, and cultural institutions often reduce demand for archivists. Overall, there will always be positions available for archivists, but the aspiring archivist may need to be creative, flexible, and determined in forging a career path.

FOR MORE INFORMATION

To find out about archival certification procedures, contact
The Academy of Certified Archivists
48 Howard Street
Albany, NY 12207
Tel: 518-463-8644
Email: aca@caphill.com
http://www.certifiedarchivists.org

For information about archival programs, activities, and publications in North America, contact
American Institute for Conservation of Historic and Artistic Works
1717 K Street, NW, Suite 200
Washington, DC 20006
Tel: 202-452-9545
Email: info@aic-faic.org
http://palimpsest.stanford.edu/aic

If you are interested in working with the archives of film and television, contact
Association of Moving Image Archivists
1313 North Vine Street
Hollywood, CA 90028
Tel: 323-463-1500
Email: amia@amianet.org
http://amianet.org

For a list of educational programs and to read So You Want to Be an Archivist: An Overview of the Archival Profession, *visit the SAA's website.*

Society of American Archivists (SAA)
527 South Wells Street, Fifth Floor
Chicago, IL 60607-3922
Tel: 312-922-0140
http://www.archivists.org

For archival programs and activities in Canada, contact
Association of Canadian Archivists
PO Box 2596, Station D
Ottawa, ON K1P 5W6 Canada
Tel: 613-445-4564
Email: aca@magma.ca
http://archivists.ca

For information on archival work and publications in the United Kingdom, contact
Society of Archivists
Prioryfield House
20 Canon Street
Taunton, Somerset, TA1 1SW England
Email: offman@archives.org.uk
http://www.archives.org.uk

ART DIRECTORS

QUICK FACTS

School Subjects Art Business Computer science	**Certification or Licensing** None available
	Outlook About as fast as the average
Personal Skills Artistic Communication/ideas	**DOT** 164
Work Environment Primarily indoors Primarily one location	**GOE** 01.02.03
	NOC 5131
Minimum Education Level Bachelor's degree	**O*NET-SOC** 27-1011.00
Salary Range $31,890 to $60,000 to $113,680+	

OVERVIEW

Art directors play a key role in every stage of the creation of an advertisement or ad campaign, from formulating concepts to supervising production. They are charged with selling to, informing, and educating consumers. They do this by planning and overseeing the presentation of clients' messages in print or on screen, that is, in books, magazines, newspapers, television commercials, posters, and packaging, as well as in film and video and on the World Wide Web.

In publishing, art directors work with artists, photographers, and text editors to develop visual images and generate copy according to a project's marketing strategy. They are responsible for evaluating illustrations, determining presentation styles, layout, and techniques, hiring staff and freelance talent, and preparing budgets.

In films, videos, and television commercials, art directors set the general look of the visual elements and approve the props, costumes, and models. In addition, they are involved in casting, editing, and selecting the music. In film and video, the art director is usually an experienced animator or computer/graphic arts designer who supervises the animators.

Art directors supervise both in-house and off-site staff, handle executive issues, and oversee the entire artistic production process. There are over 147,000 artists and art directors working in the United States.

HISTORY

In illustrating the first books, artists painted their subjects by hand using a technique called "illumination," which required putting egg-white tempera on vellum. Each copy of each book had to be printed and illustrated individually, often by the same person.

Printed illustrations first appeared in books in 1461. Through the years, prints were made through lithography, woodblock, and other means of duplicating images. Although making many copies of the same illustration was now possible, publishers still depended on individual artists to create the original works. Text editors usually decided what was to be illustrated and how, while artists commonly supervised the production of the artwork.

The first art directors were probably staff illustrators for book publishers. As the publishing industry grew more complex, with such new technologies as photography and film, art direction evolved into a more supervisory position and became a full-time job. Publishers and advertisers needed specialists who could acquire and use illustrations. Women's magazines, such as *Vogue* and *Harper's Bazaar,* and photo magazines, such as *National Geographic,* relied so much on illustration that the photo editor and art director began to carry as much power as the text editor.

With the advent of animation, art directors became indispensable. Art directors usually supervised animated short films, such as the early Mickey Mouse cartoons. Walt Disney was the art director on many of his early pictures. As animation evolved into full-length films, the sheer number of illustrations requires more than one art director to oversee the project.

Today's art directors supervise almost every type of visual project produced. Through a variety of methods and media, from television and film to magazines, comic books, and the Internet, art directors communicate ideas by selecting and supervising every element that goes into the finished product.

THE JOB

Art directors are responsible for all visual aspects of printed or on-screen projects. The art director oversees the process of developing visual solutions to a variety of communication problems. He or she helps to establish corporate identities; advertises products and services; enhances books, magazines, newsletters, and other publications; and creates television commercials, film and video productions, and websites. Some art directors with experience or knowledge in specific fields specialize in such areas as packaging, exhibitions and displays, or the Internet. But all directors, even those with specialized backgrounds, must be skilled in and knowledgeable about not only design and illustration but also photography, computers, research, and writing in order to supervise the work of graphic artists, photographers, copywriters, text editors, and other employees.

In print advertising and publishing, art directors may begin with the client's concept or develop one in collaboration with the copywriter and account executive. Once the concept is established, the next step is to decide on the most effective way to communicate it. If a piece is being revised, existing illustrations must be reevaluated.

After deciding what needs to be illustrated, art directors must find sources that can create or provide the art. Photo agencies, for example, have photographs and illustrations on thousands of different subjects. If, however, the desired illustration does not exist, it may have to be commissioned or designed by one of the staff designers. Commissioning artwork means that the art director contacts a photographer or illustrator and explains what is needed. A price is negotiated, and the artist creates the image specifically for the art director.

Once the illustrations have been secured, they must be presented in an appealing manner. The art director supervises (and may help in the production of) the layout of the piece and presents the final version to the client or creative director. Laying out is the process of figuring out where every image, headline, and block of text will be placed on the page. The size, style, and method of reproduction must all be specifically indicated so that the image is recreated as the director intended it.

In broadcast advertising and film and video, the art director has a wide variety of responsibilities and often interacts with an enormous number of creative professionals. Working with directors and producers, art directors interpret scripts or a client concept and create or select settings to convey visually the story or the message.

The art director oversees and channels the talents of set decorators and designers, model makers, location managers, propmasters, construction coordinators, and special effects people. In addition, art directors work with writers, unit production managers, cinematographers, costume designers, and post-production staff, including editors and employees responsible for scoring and titles. The art director is ultimately responsible for all visual aspects of the finished product.

Technology has been playing an increasingly important role in the art director's job. Most art directors, for example, use a variety of computer software programs, including PageMaker, QuarkXPress, CorelDRAW, FrameMaker, Adobe Illustrator, and Photoshop. Many others create and oversee websites for clients and work with other interactive media and materials, including CD-ROM, touch-screens, multidimensional visuals, and new animation programs.

Art directors usually work on more than one project at a time and must be able to keep numerous, unrelated details straight. They often work under pressure of a deadline and yet must remain calm and pleasant when dealing with clients and staff. Because they are supervisors, art directors are often called upon to resolve problems, not only with projects but with employees as well.

Art directors are not entry-level workers. They usually have years of experience working at lower level jobs in the field before gaining the knowledge needed to supervise projects. Depending on whether they work in publishing or film, art directors have to know how printing presses operate or how film is processed; they must also know a variety of production techniques to manipulate images to meet the needs of a project.

REQUIREMENTS
High School

A variety of high school courses will give you both a taste of college-level offerings and an idea of the skills necessary for art directors on the job. These courses include art, drawing, art history, graphic design, illustration, advertising, and desktop publishing.

Math courses are also important. Most of the elements of sizing an image involve calculating percentage reduction or enlargement of the original picture. This must be done with a great degree of accuracy if the overall design is going to work; for example, type size may have to be figured within a thirty-second of an inch for a print project. Errors can be extremely costly and may make the project look sloppy.

Other useful courses that you should take in high school include business, computing, English, technical drawing, cultural studies, psychology, and social science.

Postsecondary Training

A college degree is usually a requirement for art directors, but in some instances, it is not absolutely necessary. According to the American Institute of Graphic Arts, nine out of 10 artists have a college degree. Among them, six out of 10 have majored in graphic design, and two out of 10 have majored in fine arts. In addition, almost two out of 10 have a master's degree. Along with general two- and four-year colleges and universities, a number of professional art schools offer two-, three-, or four-year programs with such classes as figure drawing, painting, graphic design, and other art courses, as well as classes in art history, writing, business administration, communications, and foreign languages.

Courses in advertising, marketing, photography, filmmaking, set direction, layout, desktop publishing, and fashion are also important for those interested in becoming art directors. Specialized courses, sometimes offered only at professional art schools, may be particularly helpful for students who want to go into art direction. These include typography, animation, storyboard, website design, and portfolio development.

Because of the rapidly increasing use of computers in design work, a thorough understanding of how computer art and layout programs work is essential for this type of career.

In addition to course work at the college level, many universities and professional art schools offer graduates or students in their final year a variety of workshop projects, desktop publishing training opportunities, and internships. These programs provide students with opportunities to develop their personal design styles as well as their portfolios.

Other Requirements

The work of an art director requires creativity, imagination, curiosity, and a sense of adventure. Art directors must be able to work with all sorts of specialized materials, including graphic design programs, as well as make presentations on the ideas behind their work.

The ability to work well with different people and organizations is a must for art directors. They must always be up to date on new techniques, trends, and attitudes. And because deadlines are a constant part of the work, an ability to handle stress and pressure well is key.

Accuracy and attention to detail are important parts of the job. When the art is done correctly, the public usually pays no notice. But when a project is done badly or sloppily, many people will notice, even if they have no design training. Other requirements to be an art director include time-management skills and an interest in media and people's motivations and lifestyles.

EXPLORING
High school students can get an idea of what an art director does by working on the staff of the school newspaper, magazine, or yearbook. You might also secure a part-time job assisting the advertising director of the local newspaper or to work at an advertising agency.

Developing your own artistic talent is important, and this can be accomplished through self-training (reading books and practicing) or through courses in painting, drawing, or other creative arts. At the very least, you should develop your "creative eye," that is, your ability to develop ideas visually. One way to do this is by familiarizing yourself with great works, such as paintings or highly creative magazine ads, motion pictures, videos, or commercials.

Students can also become members of a variety of art or advertising clubs around the nation. Check out Paleta: The Art Project (http://www.paletaworld.org) to join a free art club.

EMPLOYERS
Art directors are employed by advertising agencies, publishing houses, museums, packaging firms, photography studios, marketing and public relations firms, desktop publishing outfits, digital pre-press houses, or printing companies. Art directors who oversee and produce on-screen products often work for film production houses, Web designers, multimedia developers, computer games developers, or television stations.

While companies of all sizes employ art directors, smaller organizations often combine the positions of graphic designer, illustrator, and art director. And although opportunities for art direction can be found all across the nation and abroad, many larger firms in such cities as Chicago, New York, and Los Angeles usually have more openings, as well as higher pay scales, than smaller companies.

STARTING OUT
Since an art director's job requires a great deal of experience, it is usually not considered an entry-level position. Typically, a person on

an art-direction career track is hired as an assistant to an established director. Recent graduates wishing to enter advertising should have a portfolio of their work containing 7–10 sample ads to demonstrate their understanding of both the business and the media in which they want to work.

Serving as an intern is a good way to get experience and develop skills. Graduates should also consider taking an entry-level job in a publisher's art department to gain initial experience. Either way, aspiring art directors must be willing to acquire their credentials by working on various projects. This may mean working in a variety of areas, such as advertising, marketing, editing, and design.

College publications offer students a chance to gain experience and develop portfolios. In addition, many students are able to do freelance work while still in school, allowing them to make important industry contacts and gain on-the-job experience at the same time.

ADVANCEMENT

While some may be content with the role of art director once they attain it, many art directors take on even more responsibility within their organizations by becoming television directors, starting their own advertising agencies, creating their own websites, developing original multimedia programs, or launching their own magazines.

Many people who reach the position of art director do not advance beyond the title but move on to work at more prestigious firms. Competition for positions at companies that have national reputations continues to be keen because of the sheer number of talented people interested. At smaller publications or local companies, the competition may be less intense, since candidates are competing primarily against others in the local market.

EARNINGS

The job title of art director can mean many different things, depending on the company at which the director is employed. According to the U.S. Department of Labor, a beginning art director or an art director working at a small firm can expect to make $31,890 or less per year in 2001, with experienced art directors working at larger companies earning more than $113,680. Median annual earnings for art directors employed in the advertising industry (the largest employer of salaried art directors) were $63,510 in 2000. The median annual earnings for art directors working in all industries were $56,880 in 2000. Again, it is important to note that these positions are not entry level; beginning art directors have probably already accumulated several years of experience in the field for which they were paid far less.

According to the American Institute of Graphic Arts' *Aquent Salary Survey 2002*, the median salary for art directors was $60,000. Art directors in the 25th percentile earned $48,000 annually, while those in the 75th percentile made $75,000 per year.

Most companies employing art directors offer insurance benefits, a retirement plan, and other incentives and bonuses.

WORK ENVIRONMENT

Art directors usually work in studios or office buildings. While their work areas are ordinarily comfortable, well lit, and ventilated, they often handle glue, paint, ink, and other materials that pose safety hazards and should therefore exercise caution.

Art directors at art and design studios and publishing firms usually work a standard 40-hour week. Many, however, work overtime during busy periods in order to meet deadlines. Similarly, directors at film and video operations and at television studios work as many hours as required—usually many more than 40 per week—in order to finish projects according to predetermined schedules.

While art directors work independently, reviewing artwork and reading copy, much time is spent collaborating with and supervising a team of employees, often consisting of copywriters, editors, photographers, graphic artists, and account executives.

OUTLOOK

The extent to which art director positions are in demand, like many other positions, depends on the economy in general; when times are tough, people and businesses spend less, and cutbacks are made. When the economy is healthy, employment prospects for art directors will be favorable. The U.S. Department of Labor predicts that employment for art directors will grow about as fast as the average for all other occupations. One area that shows particularly good promise for growth is the retail industry, since more and more large retail establishments, especially catalog houses, will be employing in-house advertising art directors.

In addition, producers of all kinds of products continually need advertisers to reach their potential customers, and publishers always want some type of illustration to enhance their books and magazines. Creators of films and videos also need images in order to produce their programs, and people working with new media are increasingly looking for artists and directors to promote new and existing products and services, enhance their websites, develop new multimedia programs, and create multidimensional visuals. People who can generate new concepts and ideas quickly and creatively will be in high demand.

On the other side of the coin, the supply of aspiring artists is expected to exceed the number of job openings. As a result, those wishing to enter the field will encounter keen competition for salaried, staff positions as well as freelance work. And although the Internet is expected to provide many opportunities for artists and art directors, some firms are hiring employees without formal art or design training to operate computer-aided design systems and oversee work.

FOR MORE INFORMATION

The AAF is the professional advertising association that binds the mutual interests of corporate advertisers, agencies, media companies, suppliers, and academia. For more information, contact

American Advertising Federation (AAF)
1101 Vermont Avenue, NW, Suite 500
Washington, DC 20005-6306
Tel: 202-898-0089
Email: aaf@aaf.org
http://www.aaf.org

This management-oriented national trade organization represents the advertising agency business. For information, contact

American Association of Advertising Agencies
405 Lexington Avenue, 18th Floor
New York, NY 10174-1801
Tel: 212-682-2500
http://www.aaaa.org

For more information on design professionals, contact

American Institute of Graphic Arts
164 Fifth Avenue
New York, NY 10010
Tel: 212-807-1990
http://www.aiga.org

The Art Directors Club is an international, nonprofit organization of direc-tors in advertising, graphic design, interactive media, broadcast design, typography, packaging, environmental design, photography, illustration, and related disciplines. For information, contact
Art Directors Club
106 West 29th Street
New York, NY 10001
Tel: 212-643-1440
Email: info@adcny.org
http://www.adcny.org

For information on the graphic arts, contact
Graphic Artists Guild
90 John Street, Suite 403
New York, NY 10038-3202
Tel: 800-500-2672
http://www.gag.org

BOOK CONSERVATORS

QUICK FACTS

School Subjects
Art
History

Personal Skills
Artistic
Mechanical/manipulative

Work Environment
Primarily indoors
Primarily one location

Minimum Education Level
Some postsecondary training

Salary Range
$19,200 to $33,080 to $61,490+

Certification or Licensing
Voluntary

Outlook
About as fast as the average

DOT
102

GOE
01.06.02

NOC
5112

O*NET-SOC
25-4013.00

OVERVIEW

Book conservators treat the bindings and pages of books and nonbook items to help preserve original materials for future use. Their work often includes removing a book block from its binding, sewing, measuring, gluing, rebinding, and using special chemical treatments to maintain the integrity of the item. Most conservators work in libraries, in museums, or for special conservation centers.

HISTORY

Early books were not bound, but rather rolled, such as ancient Egyptian papyrus rolls and early Christian parchment rolls. Eventually the rolls were cut into a number of flat panels sewn together along one edge, thus allowing for a book that was more convenient, portable, and enduring. Early Latin codex manuscripts were made up of folded sheets gathered into bunches called signatures and were sewn together. Wooden boards were then placed on either side of the sewn signatures. In time, the entire volume was covered with leather or other animal skins to hide the sewing cords and provide protection to the pages. The basic constructional elements of bookbinding have changed little in the past 1,800 years, but the materials and methods used have matured considerably.

Before the invention of the printing press, religious orders were often charged with copying texts by hand. These same monastic groups also assumed the roles of bookbinder and conservator. One of the main goals in creating books is the conservation and dissemination of knowledge.

In order to pass that knowledge on to future generations, many early bookbinders began the legacy of conservation by using high quality materials and excellent craftsmanship; a book that is well-crafted in the first place will need less invasive conservation as the material ages. Historically, then, the people who created the books had the specialized knowledge to conserve them.

Conservators today share many of the same traits of early bookbinders: They have the specialized knowledge of how books have traditionally been crafted, but they use technologically advanced adhesives, papers, and binding techniques to ensure that materials created centuries ago will be around for years to come.

The establishment of book conservation as a career field apart from bookbinding probably began when the first courses in conservation and preservation were taught at a library school, or when a professional library association first addressed the topic. Thus, although early bookbinders dealt with issues of material longevity, conservation as a field has only been around for 100 years or so.

THE JOB

Book conservators work to slow down or stabilize the deterioration of books and other print-based materials. They repair books that have been damaged by misuse, accident, pests, or normal wear and tear; treat items that may have been produced or repaired with inferior materials or methods; and work to ensure that the books will be around for the future.

Before beginning any conservation efforts, book conservators must examine the item to be restored, determine the extent and cause of the deterioration, evaluate their own conservation skills, and decide on a proper course of action. In deciding how to treat an item, the book conservator must first consider the history of the item. When was it made? Book conservators must have a good knowledge of the history of bookmaking in order to serve the needs of the item. A book bound by hand in Italy in 1600 will have different needs than a volume bound by machine in 1980.

The book conservator also needs to consider what other repairs have been made to the book over the years. Sometimes a shoddy repair job in the past can create more work for today's conservator. For example, someone thirty years ago may have taped a torn page to keep it from ripping out entirely. Unfortunately, this hasty action, coupled with tape that will not stand the test of time, could lead to cracked, yellowing tape and stained book pages. When repairing a ripped sheet, book conservators use a pH-neutral (acid-free) adhesive, such as wheat paste, and Japanese paper, or a special acid-free book tape. Since high levels of acidity in papers and materials increase the rate of deterioration, all materials that conservators use must be acid-free and of archival quality.

Book conservators also think about the current and future use of the book. For a common, high-use volume that will be checked out of the library frequently, they may repair the book with cheaper, lower quality materials that will survive being jostled in backpacks and undergoing repeated trips through the return chute. For a textbook that is reprinted each year, for example, a thick piece of tape may be an adequate conservation method. If such a book is falling out of its cover, the conservator may need to remove the bookblock entirely, repair or replace the end sheets and headbands, and re-glue the bookblock back into the cover. If the cover of the book is broken, the conservator may need to fit the text block into a new cover. This involves measuring out the binder's board and book cloth, cutting the materials to size, gluing the cloth onto the board, sizing in the bookblock, gluing, and setting. After the glue is dry, the conservator will inspect the item to ensure that all materials were fitted in properly, and that all problems were corrected.

Rare books that are handled less frequently or only by specially trained and careful users can have less invasive repairs in order to maintain the integrity of the original item. For instance, a conservator may choose to make a box to house a book rather than repair a broken spine. If the conservation work would lessen the value of the book, sometimes it's better to simply stop the deterioration rather than repair the damage.

The historical and monetary value of a book is a key factor in deciding upon treatment. As with any antique, often less restoration is more. On a recent antiques television program, an owner refinished an antique table and thereby reduced its resale value by thousands of dollars. The same can be said for books. Many old and rare books have great value because of the historical materials and methods in evidence.

Sometimes pests are encountered in conservation work. Beetle larvae and other insects may feast upon crumbs left in books, the pulp of the paper, or the adhesive, and make holes in the text. The conservator will assess the extent of the damage and prescribe a treatment. For critter damage to books, the most important thing is to ensure that any infestation is under control. The conservator needs to make sure that all bugs in a book are dead; if not, the items may need to be taken to a professional for fumigation. Once that is complete, the conservator can look at possible repair options. If the damage is under control, the conservator will probably opt for further damage prevention in lieu of repair.

Often conservators treat books for only part of their day. They might also spend much time working on ways to minimize the need for conservation and repair work in the first place. Book conservators who work as part of a large department have other duties, such as dealing with patrons, reference work, security, training assistants, fielding calls from the public, giving seminars, and teaching. Conservators may also serve on groups and committees devoted to preservation, conservation, and the administration of a conservation lab or department.

REQUIREMENTS
High School

You should plan on taking a college preparatory course load while in high school. Classes, such as history, literature, art, foreign languages, chemistry, and mathematics will all help you build a strong background for book conservation. By studying history, you can learn the social and historical contexts of books and knowledge. Understanding the history of an item can give you a better perspective on approaching the material as a conservator. Strong knowledge of literature can help you appraise the potential value of a book. A comprehension of foreign languages allows you to deal with a wider variety of books from around the globe. Chemistry and math will begin to teach you about the composition and measurement of the materials you will be using. Art will teach you how to use your hands to create beautiful works that last.

Postsecondary Training

After high school, you should strongly consider getting a bachelor's degree. Although most employers don't currently require a college degree for book conservator jobs, earning a bachelor's can only help your chances of advancing to positions with more responsibility. A degree in art, art history, or one of the fine arts may help you gain entry into a book conservation apprenticeship or internship program. Your school may offer courses in the book or paper arts, which often include classes in preservation and conservation. You will also need to take courses that help you learn how to select items for conservation, purchase and best utilize your conservation materials, and prepare documentation on the conservation methods and treatments you provide to an item.

Upon earning a bachelor's degree, you may wish to attend library school to earn a master's degree in library science with a concentration in book and document conservation. Again, advanced degrees may not be necessary for some positions, but they can always help you gain more prominent positions—particularly in administration—and perhaps command a higher salary. Additionally, any special skills you gain through advanced education will make you more attractive to potential employers and private clients.

Certification or Licensing

Some book conservators gain certification from their library school or from a special certifying organization. The certification process generally requires a mix of formal study of theory and practice, as well as a certain amount of actual experience in the field. Certification is not officially required by any federal, state, or local agencies, but some employers may request, or require, a certified book conservationist for particular positions or projects. Also, the certifying organization compiles a list of all certified conservators; if someone contacts the organization looking for a conservator, the agency will refer the client to member book conservators in the area.

Other Requirements

Book conservators need be able to think creatively. Conservation projects require the conservator to visualize the end product before beginning work. Conservators should enjoy problem solving and be able to decide the best way to conserve the materials. Having a hands-on nature is key as well, since book conservators spend a majority of their time inspecting materials and making repairs by hand.

Since book conservators routinely work with musty, moldy, and mildewed books, they should not be overly sensitive to odors. They also deal with sharp instruments, such as awls, knives, and paper cutters, so for safety reasons they should have a certain amount of facility with their hands. Book conservators also work with adhesives and chemicals, so they must take care not to spill materials.

Although much of their day is spent working with the materials, many conservators deal with the public as well. Book conservators, therefore, should be able to communicate well, and with a certain measure of tact, with many types of people. They should be able to explain conservation options to clients and to best determine what procedures will meet the needs of the material and the owner.

EXPLORING

If you are interested in becoming a book conservator, you should start out by learning all you can about how books are made. Study the history of books and of binding. Purchase an inexpensive, hardcover book at a used bookstore and take it apart to see how the bookblock is sewn together and how it is connected to the cover. Then try to put the book back together. There are many "how to" bookbinding guides to help you. Check out *Hand Bookbinding: A Manual of Instruction* by Aldren A. Watson (Dover Publications, 1996) or *ABC of Bookbinding* by Jane Greenfield (Oak Knoll Books, 1998) for the history of different styles of bookbinding and definitions of terms used in the field.

Contact the conservation or preservation department at your local library. The department may offer tours of its facilities or workshops on the proper care of books. Contact professional librarian associations; they may have divisions devoted to conservation. Community colleges and art museums often have weekend or evening classes in the conservation and book arts.

Finally, you might try contacting your local park district or community center to suggest sessions about book conservation. Many such groups offer summer day camps or after-school programs and look for input from participants about what types of activities are of interest. Plus, if you have had some conservation experience of your own, you could offer to teach younger students about how they can begin conserving books by taking good care of their own materials and the books they check out of the library.

EMPLOYERS

College and university libraries, public libraries, institutional libraries, and special libraries all employ book conservators. These organizations may have an entire department devoted to the conservation and preservation of materials, or the tasks of conservation may be bestowed upon another division, such as an archival or rare book collection. Museums sometimes have a specific book conservator post, or they may offer such duties to an interested art conservationist. Book conservators also work for companies devoted to material conservation. Binderies may hire a conservationist as a quality control consultant.

A number of book conservators are self-employed, working on a freelance or part-time basis for organizations and private citizens. They may be part of a nationwide network of certified book conservators. Often, potential clients contact book conservators through membership in professional organizations.

STARTING OUT

Book conservation is a field that relies heavily on skill, reputation, and word-of-mouth communication. While earning your bachelor's or master's degree, you should try to get an internship, apprenticeship, or assistantship in conservation or a related field. Take all the courses you can that will help you gain conservation skills.

You may also be able to get a part-time or summer job in your school library's preservation or conservation department. Many part time positions or internships can turn into full-time jobs after the incumbent has proven his or her skills or completed specific educational requirements.

Once you complete a training period, you might consider becoming certified. Certification can be a deciding factor in gaining employment, since certain companies and organizations may require book conservators to have official affirmation of their qualifications from an outside agency.

You should also join a conservator's organization in order to get to know professionals in the field. Since many conservator positions are in libraries, you may wish to join a professional library association as well. Professional organizations often have job listings available to members. They also publish journals and newsletters to keep members up-to-date on new developments in the field.

If you are looking to be a self-employed conservator, you may wish to volunteer your services until you have established yourself. Volunteering to assist nonprofit organizations with their conservation needs will give you good exposure to the book conservator world and the skills that potential clients are seeking.

ADVANCEMENT

Book conservators who demonstrate a high level of skill in their craft can move on to positions with more responsibility. They may be called upon to train assistants in book conservation or to teach conservation techniques at a library school, certification program, or conservation lab.

They may also transfer their skill in dealing with rare and fine materials and work more in the art community as art conservators, appraisers, or artists. With more experience and education, a book conservator can become an archivist, curator, or librarian. Many book conservators prefer to move away from full-time conservation and work on freelance projects instead.

With advanced computer knowledge, book conservators can help bring rare and fragile materials into the digital age. They may learn how to make materials available on the Internet and become virtual curators. They may also move on to actual exhibition work. Knowing how to preserve materials gives them the advantage in knowing how to exhibit them safely.

As book conservators gain more prominent positions, the trend is away from materials and toward administration. Beginning conservators will often spend most of their day dealing directly with the materials to be conserved. Conservators who move on to more advanced positions generally spend more time training others; evaluating materials and methods; dealing with outside suppliers, customers, and associations; attending meetings; and planning for the future of the department and the field.

EARNINGS

It is difficult to say how much the average book conservator makes, since many conservators work part time, are self-employed, or have positions that encompass other duties as well. In general, the salary range for book conservators may fall within the range the U.S. Department of Labor reports for all conservators, archivists, and other museum workers. In 2000 this group of professionals had a median annual income of $33,080. The lowest paid 10 percent earned less than $19,200 yearly, and the highest paid 10 percent made more than $61,490 per year. Often the size of the employer affects how much a conservator earns, with larger employers able to pay more.

In addition, book conservators in major metropolitan areas generally earn more than those in small cities, and those with greater skills also command higher salaries.

Conservators who work for libraries, conservation organizations, large corporations, institutions, or government agencies generally receive a full range of benefits, including health care coverage, vacation days, paid holidays, paid sick time, and retirement savings plans. Self-employed book conservators usually have to provide their own benefits. All conservators have the added benefit of working with rare and unique materials. They have the opportunity to work with history and preserve an artifact for the future.

WORK ENVIRONMENT

Because of the damage that dirt, humidity, and the sun can cause to books, most conservators work in clean, climate-controlled areas away from direct sunlight. Many conservation labs are small offices, which often employ the conservator alone or perhaps with one or two part-time assistants. Other labs are part of a larger department within an organization; the University of Chicago's Regenstein Library, for instance, has a conservation lab within the Special Collections department. With this type of arrangement, the book conservator generally has a few student and nonstudent assistants who work part time to help with some of the conservation duties.

Book conservators are always on the move. They use their hands constantly to measure, cut, and paste materials. They also bend, lift, and twist in order to reach items they work on and make room for new materials. Also, books are not always an easy size or weight to handle. Some oversized items need to be transported on a book truck from the stack area to the conservation area for treatment.

Most book conservators work 40 hours a week, usually during regular, weekday working hours. Depending on the needs of their department and the clientele they serve, book conservators may need to be available some weekend hours. Also, some book conservators may agree to travel to the homes of clients to view materials that may require conservation.

OUTLOOK

The future of book conservation as a profession will most likely grow about as fast as the average through 2010. The U.S. Department of

Labor notes that while the outlook for conservators in general is favorable, there is strong competition for jobs. Book conservators who are graduates of conservation programs and are willing to relocate should have the best opportunities for employment. Those who can use their conservation skills in tandem with other abilities may also find more job openings. Book conservators with an artistic bent, for instance, could bring their conservation skills to an exhibition program at an art museum. Conservators who enjoy public contact could use their practical experience to teach classes in conservation techniques.

Some people are concerned that our increasingly digital society will create fewer opportunities for book conservators. They claim that technologies, such as television, computers, telephones, and the Internet have changed communication styles so drastically that printed books will eventually become obsolete. New technologies will bring new challenges to conservation. These trends will probably increase opportunities for conservators who can mesh traditional conservation efforts with new technologies. For example, a book conservator with excellent computer skills and Web authoring knowledge can work on a project to digitize rare book collections and make them available to people all over the world.

FOR MORE INFORMATION

For information about how to become a conservator, contact

American Institute for Conservation of Historic and Artistic Works
1717 K Street, NW, Suite 200
Washington, DC 20006
Tel: 202-452-9545
Email: info@aic-faic.org
http://aic.stanford.edu

For information about preservation methods, services, and opportunities, contact the following association:

Library of Congress Preservation Directorate
101 Independence Avenue, SE
Washington, DC 20540-4500
Tel: 202-707-5213
Email: preserve@loc.gov
http://lcweb.loc.gov/preserv

For information on internship programs in Canada, contact
Canadian Conservation Institute
1030 Innes Road
Ottawa, ON K1A 0M5 Canada
Tel: 613-741-4390
http://www.pch.gc.ca/cci-icc

For a wealth of information about conservation topics, check out this project of the Preservation Department of Stanford University Libraries:
Conservation OnLine
http://palimpsest.stanford.edu

BOOK EDITORS

QUICK FACTS

School Subjects Art Computer science English Journalism	**Certification or Licensing** None available
	Outlook Faster than the average
Personal Skills Artistic Communication/ideas	**DOT** 132
	GOE 01.01.01
Work Environment Primarily indoors Primarily one location	**NOC** 5122
Minimum Education Level Bachelor's degree	**O*NET-SOC** 27-3041.00
Salary Range $23,090 to $37,550 to $73,460+	

OVERVIEW

Book editors acquire and prepare written material for publication in book form. Such formats include trade books (fiction and nonfiction), textbooks, and technical and professional books (which include reference books). A book editor's duties include evaluating a manuscript, accepting or rejecting it, rewriting, correcting spelling and grammar, researching, and fact checking. Book editors may work directly with printers in arranging for proofs and with artists and designers in arranging for illustration matter and determining the physical specifications of the book.

Approximately 122,000 editors work for newspapers, magazines, and book publishers in the United States. Book editors are employed at small and large publishing houses, book packagers (companies that specialize in book production), associations, and government agencies.

HISTORY

Though the origins of publishing remain unknown, experts have proposed that publishing came into existence soon after people developed written language, perhaps in Sumer in approximately 4000 B.C. After people began to record information in writing, someone needed to decide which information was valuable or worth recording. Technically speaking, the first record keepers were the first publishers and editors. Some of the first things deemed suitable for publication were accounting records, genealogies, laws, and religious rituals and beliefs.

In the early years of European publishing, the works that were published were intended for the small, elite group of educated people who could read and who could afford to buy books. For the most part, these people were clergymen and members of the upper class who had intellectual interests. Publishing was the business of printers, who also often performed what we would now call editorial tasks. Books of that era generally were written and edited in Latin, which was the language of intellectuals. Over time, however, literacy spread and books began to be written in the languages of the countries in which they were published.

Beginning in the 19th century, the various tasks performed by publishing concerns became more specialized. Whereas in early publishing a single person would often perform various functions, in later publishing, employees performed a limited range of tasks. Instead of having a single editor, a publication would have an editorial staff. One person would be responsible for acquisitions, another would copyedit, another would be responsible for editorial tasks that related to production, and so forth.

Editing has also been powerfully affected by technology. Publishing came into existence only after Gutenberg had invented the necessary technology, and it has changed in various ways as technology has developed. The most important recent developments have made it possible to transfer and edit information rapidly and efficiently. The development of the computer has revolutionized editing, making it possible to write and rewrite texts electronically and transmit corrected manuscripts almost instantaneously from one part of the world to another.

THE JOB

The editorial department is generally the heart of any publishing house. Procedures and terminology may vary from one type of publishing house to another, but there is some general agreement about the essentials. Publishers of trade books, textbooks, and reference books all have somewhat different needs for which they have developed different editorial practices.

The editor has the principal responsibility in evaluating the manuscript. The editor responsible for seeing a book through to publication may hold any of several titles. The highest level editorial executive in a publishing house is usually the *editor in chief* or *editorial director*. The person holding either of these titles directs the overall operation of the editorial department. Sometimes an executive editor occupies the highest position in an editorial department. The next level of editor is often the *managing editor*, who keeps track of schedules and deadlines and must know where all manuscripts are at any given time. Other editors who handle copy include the *senior editors, associate editors, assistant editors, editorial assistants*, and *copy editors*.

In a trade-book house, the editor, usually at the senior or associate position, works with manuscripts that he or she has solicited from authors or that have been submitted by known authors or their agents. Editors who seek out authors to write manuscripts are also known as *acquisitions editors*.

In technical/professional book houses, editors commonly do more researching, revising, and rewriting than trade-book editors do. These editors must be skilled in certain subjects. Editors must be sure that the subject is covered comprehensively and organized according to an agreed-upon outline. Editors contract for virtually all of the material that comes into technical/professional book houses. The authors they solicit are often scholars.

Editors who edit heavily or ask an author to revise extensively must learn to be highly diplomatic; the art of author-editor relations is a critical aspect of the editor's job.

When the editor is satisfied with the manuscript, it goes to the copy editor. The copy editor usually does the final editing of the manuscript before it goes to the typesetter. On almost any type of manuscript, the copy editor is responsible for correcting errors of spelling, punctuation, grammar, and usage.

The copy editor marks up the manuscript to indicate where different kinds of typefaces are used and where charts, illustrations, and photos may be inserted. It is important for the copy editor to discover any inconsistencies in the text and to query the author about them. The copy editor then usually acts as a liaison between the typesetter, the editor, and the author as the manuscript is typeset into galley proofs and then page proofs.

In a small house, one editor might do the work of all of the editors described here. There can also be separate fact checkers, proofreaders, style editors (also called line editors), and indexers. An assistant editor could be assigned to do many of the kinds of jobs handled by the senior or associate editors. *Editorial assistants* provide support for the other editors and may be required to proofread and handle some administrative duties.

REQUIREMENTS
High School

If you have an interest in a career as an editor, the most obvious classes that will prepare you include English, literature, and composition classes. You should also become familiar and comfortable working with word processing programs, either through taking a computer science class or through your own schoolwork. Taking journalism classes will give you the opportunity to practice different writing styles, including short feature pieces and long investigative stories. Art classes can also be useful to learn basics of photography and illustration and to learn about elements of design and page appearance. Take advantage of any clubs or extracurricular activities that will give you a chance to write or edit. Joining the school newspaper staff is a great way to explore different tasks in publishing, such as writing, editing, layout, and printing.

Postsecondary Training

A college degree is a requirement for entry into the field of book editing. For general editing, a degree in English or journalism is particularly valuable, although most degrees in the liberal arts are acceptable. Degrees in other fields, such as the arts, history, sciences, psychology, or mathematics can be useful in publishing houses that produce books related to those fields. Textbook and technical/professional book houses in particular seek out editors with strengths in certain subject areas.

Other Requirements

Book editors should have a sharp eye for detail and a compulsion for accuracy (of both grammar and content). Intellectual curiosity, self-motivation, and a respect for deadlines are also important characteristics for book editors. Knowledge of word processing and desktop publishing programs is a requirement.

It goes without saying that if you are seeking a career in book editing, you should not only love to read, but love books for their own sake as well. If you are not an avid reader, you are not likely to go far as a book editor. The craft and history of bookmaking itself is also something in which a young book editor should be interested. A keen interest in any subject, be it a sport, a hobby, or an avocation, can lead you into special areas of book publishing.

EXPLORING

As previously mentioned, joining your school's newspaper staff is a great way to explore editing and writing while in high school. Even if your duties are not strictly editorial, gaining experience by writing, doing layout work, or even securing advertisements will help you to understand how the editing stage relates to the entire field of publishing. Joining your school's yearbook staff or starting your own literary magazine are other ways to gain valuable experience.

You might be able to find a part-time job with a local book publisher or newspaper. You could also try to publish your own magazine or newsletter. Combine one of your other interests with your desire to edit. For example, if you are interested in sports, you could try writing and editing your own sports report to distribute to family and friends.

Since editing and writing are inextricably linked, be sure to keep your writing skills sharp. Outside of any class assignments, try keeping a journal. Try to write something every day and gain practice at reworking your writing until it is as good as you can make it. Explore different kinds of writing, such as short stories, poetry, fiction, essays, comedic prose, and plays.

If you are interested in becoming a book editor, you might consider joining a book club. Check Web Magic's list of book clubs at http://www.literature.com. Other interesting book websites, such as http://www.literarymarketplace.com, may be of interest if you'd like to learn more about publishing companies.

EMPLOYERS

Book editors may find employment with publishing houses, the federal government, and book packagers, or they may be self-employed as freelancers. The major book publishers are located in larger cities, such as New York, Chicago, Los Angeles, Boston, Philadelphia, San Francisco, and Washington, D.C. Publishers of professional, religious, art, business, and technical books are dispersed throughout the country. There are approximately 122,000 editors employed in the United States (including book editors and all other editors).

STARTING OUT

New graduates can find editing positions through their local newspaper or through contacts made in college. College career counselors may be able to assist in finding book publishers to apply for jobs. Another option is to look them up in the Yellow Pages, Internet, and *Literary Market Place* and apply for positions directly. Many publishers will advertise job openings on their corporate Web sites. Starting positions are generally at the assistant level and can include administrative duties in addition to basic editing tasks.

ADVANCEMENT

An editor's career path is dependent on the size and structure of the book publisher. Those who start as editorial assistants or proofreaders generally become copy editors. The next step may be a position as a senior copy editor, which involves overseeing the work of junior copy editors, or as a *project editor*. The project editor performs a wide variety of tasks, including copyediting, coordinating the work of in-house and freelance copy editors, and managing the schedule of a particular project. From this position, an editor may move up to become first assistant editor, then managing editor, then editor in chief. As editors advance, they are usually involved in more management work and decision making. The editor in chief works with the publisher to ensure that a suitable editorial policy is being followed, while the managing editor is responsible for all aspects of the editorial department. Head editors employed by a publisher may choose to start their own editing business and freelance full time.

WORK ENVIRONMENT

Book editors do most of their work on a computer, either in an office setting or at home. When working alone, the environment is generally quiet, which allows the editor to concentrate on the work at hand. Editors also work in teams, allowing for an exchange of ideas and collaboration. They typically work a normal schedule of 40 hours per week, though if a book is near a deadline, they may work longer hours to get assignments done on schedule.

EARNINGS

Earnings for book editors vary based on the size of the employer and the types of books it publishes, geographic location, and experience of the editor. The U.S. Department of Labor reports the median yearly salary for book editors was $37,550 in 2000. For all editors in 2001, the salaries ranged from a low of less than $23,090 to a high of more than $73,460 annually. The median salary for all editors in 2001 was $39,960. In general, editors are paid higher salaries at large companies, in major cities, and on the East and West Coasts.

Publishers usually offer employee benefits that are about average for U.S. industry. There are other benefits, however. Most editors enjoy working with people who like books, and the atmosphere of an editorial department is generally intellectual and stimulating. Some book editors have the opportunity to travel in order to attend meetings, to meet with authors, or to do research.

OUTLOOK

According to the U.S. Department of Labor, employment for writers and editors should grow faster than the average over the next decade, although competition for positions will be strong. The growth of online publishing will increase the need for editors who are Web experts. Other areas where editors may find work include advertising, public relations, and businesses with their own publications, such as company newsletters. Turnover is relatively high in publishing—editors often advance by moving to another firm or by establishing a freelance business. There are many publishers and organizations that operate with a minimal salaried staff and hire freelance editors for everything from project management to proofreading and production.

FOR MORE INFORMATION

The following organization's we site is an excellent source of information about careers in editing. The ACES organizes educational seminars and maintains lists of internships.

American Copy Editors Society (ACES)
3 Healy Street
Huntington, NY 11743
http://www.copydesk.org

For additional information about careers in publishing, contact the following:
Association of American Publishers
71 Fifth Avenue
New York, NY 10003-3004
Tel: 212-255-0200
http://www.publishers.org

Publishers Marketing Association
627 Aviation Way
Manhattan Beach, CA 90266
Tel: 310-372-2732
Email: info@pma-online.org
http://www.pma-online.org

Small Publishers Association of North America
PO Box 1306
425 Cedar Street
Buena Vista, CO 81211
Tel: 719-395-4790
Email: span@spannet.org
http://www.spannet.org

Literary Market Place, *published annually by R. R. Bowker, lists the names of publishing companies in the United States and Canada as well as their specialties and the names of their key personnel.*
Literary Market Place
http://www.literarymarketplace.com

CERAMIC ARTISTS

QUICK FACTS

School Subjects Art History	**Certification or Licensing** Recommended
	Outlook About as fast as the average
Personal Skills Artistic Communication/ideas	**DOT** 779
Work Environment Indoors and outdoors Primarily one location	**GOE** 01.06.02
	NOC 5244
Minimum Education Level Some postsecondary training	**O*NET-SOC** 27-1013.04, 51-9195.05
Salary Range $15,000 to $30,000 to $100,000	

OVERVIEW

Ceramic artists—also known as *potters, ceramists, sculptors,* and *clay artists*—work with clay to make both functional and purely aesthetic objects. They blend basic elements (such as clay and water) and more specialized components (such as texture fillers, colorants, and talc) and form the mixture into shapes. They then use glazing and firing techniques to finish their pieces. Depending on the artists' individual preferences, they use either manual techniques or wheel throwing techniques to create such things as functional pottery (like coffee cups and vases), beads, tiles, architectural installations, and sculptures.

HISTORY

Ceramic arts are part of an historic tradition that is more than 12,000 years old. Ceramics involves using clay to create form and beauty. The word *ceramics* is from the Greek word *keramos,* meaning "potter's clay and ware." Ceramic artistry has always involved the basic method of making clay products permanent by applying heat. The oldest known ceramic objects are from the Near East; these are small models of figures probably used in spiritual ceremonies around 10,000 B.C. The early knowledge of using fire to harden damp clay into ceramic material became widespread about 6,000–4,000 B.C. and afterward the craft of ceramics developed differently in various areas of the world.

As generations of humans evolved, the technique of building up pots with coils eventually developed into the use of some kind of turntable to make it easier to shape the clay into vessel forms. One of the earliest pottery-turning devices found is believed to have been used by a potter in ancient Ur in about 3500 B.C. At a later time the simple stone turntable evolved into a true potter's wheel. This technological development was so important that the Egyptians believed a god had invented the potter's wheel.

Whatever techniques or tools were used to shape early clay objects, all pieces had to be treated by heat to become hardened, permanent ceramics. The earliest method involved heating objects in open fire pits, often also burning straw inside the pottery to dry and warm it. By about 3000 B.C., in the region now known as Israel, potters were building enclosed kilns; in China, kilns were being made that had tunnels leading to beehive-shaped chambers, thus creating forced drafts and improved use of fuel; and in Mesopotamia, kilns had domed roofs and perforated floors. Using kilns, potters came to have more control over the fire, and wind was less of a problem than when open firing methods were used.

Today's ceramic artists continue to use modern adaptations of the early potter's wheel when they make such container vessels as pots, cups, and vases. For making functional pottery, what has always mattered is the emptiness that is created when a pot is "thrown on the wheel"; the hole becomes just as important as the shape of the pottery itself. Modern artists also use adaptations of early firing methods (although old methods of open firing are still used today in certain villages in Fiji, Africa, the Middle East, and the southwestern United States). But today's ceramics technology—including the use of knowledge based on chemistry, space, and computer-controlled kilns—provides artists with so many more techniques and tools to work with their craft. The vision and focus of today's ceramic artist is much wider than that of the ancient sculptor of fertility figurines.

Many pottery companies began to produce "art pottery" around the turn of the century, and this was influenced by art movements in the United States and Europe. For example, at Rookwood Pottery in

Cincinnati, Ohio, artists designed and produced Standard Ware, which eventually became quite popular. In the early 20th century, Adelaine Alsop Robineau cast her own ware and learned to throw her forms on the wheel; she often worked for hundreds of hours on individual pieces, carving intricate designs and raised patterns. George Ohr was an innovative potter of the early 1900s who made vases and pots that expressed his unique personality. Rookwood Pottery, Robineau, and Ohr are just three representatives of the ceramic artistry that led to what is being done today. The U.S. architect Louis Sullivan influenced architectural ceramics by using clay to decorate his metal-framed buildings. The Moravian Pottery and Tile Works in Pennsylvania influenced the tile-making niche and is still producing tiles today. The work of artists such as Maija Grotell, Laura Anderson, Bernard Leach, and Shoji Hamada continue to influence students in the ceramic arts.

Artists make simple works such as delicate porcelain vases, but they also experiment and explore diverse forms like large architectural creations, odd-shaped sculptural vessels, and environmental installations. The artist's vision has new sources of imagery (history, mythology, social concern, autobiography) with which to work, all leading back to hands working with clay.

THE JOB

The particular properties of clay influence artists' decisions about what they are going to make—be it functional or purely aesthetic—and how they are going to make it. For some ceramic artists, shape and form are all important. For others, throwing on the wheel is what matters most. In any case, clay is the basis. Different types of clay—like ball clay, earthenware clay, and stoneware clay—are dug from deposits in a soft and pliable form. To become hard and permanent after shaping, each type of clay needs to be fired to a certain temperature in an open fire or a kiln. The variations in the size of the clay particles and the different temperatures at which clays reach their maturity (correct hardness) produce the differences in texture and appearance among different pieces. For instance, earthenware clay is fired at low temperatures and does not become as dense as clays like porcelain and stoneware, which are fired at higher temperatures.

Although each artist works the clay in a unique way, there are some basic methods that can be used to define the nature of an artist's work. Some ceramic artists build their objects almost completely by hand, not using a potter's wheel; others use a wheel to mold their forms; others make molds and pour clay into them. Handbuilding allows a potter to build free-form art, while the potter's wheel aids in making symmetrically shaped works. In both cases, one must prepare the clay by wedging, which involves throwing the clay body down hard against a flat surface or simply kneading it. Wedging removes air bubbles and provides a consistent level of moisture throughout the clay.

In handbuilding, an artist uses either the coil or the slab method. The coil method entails forming long rods of clay, coiling the rods into a desired shape, and blending the coils to create a smooth surface. With slabs, one simply joins pieces of clay together to make a pot or other shape. Before actually joining the slabs or coiling, the artist must score the adjoining edges—that is, lightly nick them to create a rough surface—and add watery clay, which is known as slip. This process helps the clay pieces stick together.

When using a potter's wheel, one places a wedged piece of clay in the middle of the wheel, centers the clay body so that a symmetrical shape can be formed, and pushes down the center of the solid clay body to begin forming walls. Shaping a pot involves skilled hand movements that cause the clay to bend and constrict as desired.

Once a pot is taken off the wheel, it is left to dry until it is leather hard. At that time, the artist places the clay body back on the wheel to trim off any uneven edges and form a base. The artist can paint the body or apply slip to add texture at this point. When the body is bone dry, it is placed into an open fire or a kiln for several hours. Afterward, the artist applies glaze and fires the body again.

Pouring clay into a mold and throwing it on a wheel is called jiggering; mass-produced objects like sinks and jars are often made this way. But many potters and sculptors create single objects by pressing or pouring clay into molds without using the wheel. They use hump molds (any material over which you can press clay), plaster press molds, polystyrene foam molds, or other creative types of molds (one artist used a shark's head; another used a motorcycle guard).

A *production potter* is a ceramic artist who makes a full series of household ware. The production potter also often makes what is called studio pottery—vases, bowls, and other pieces made more for display than for everyday use. These potters might work alone in a studio or with one or two colleagues or helpers, or they might set up a large workshop employing several people.

Other artists concentrate on specific niches in which they enjoy producing objects considered both functional and artful, such as bead making, tile making, and the making of architectural ceramics. Architectural ceramists work on such things as tile-decorated subway stations, ceramic-clad building columns, and other types of sculptural installations in public settings like museums, shopping malls, and parks.

The ceramic sculptor creates works of art rather than functional pottery. Using clay and often other types of art media, sculptors handbuild more than they throw on the wheel.

REQUIREMENTS
High School

In high school, you should take pottery classes and other art classes, such as drawing and painting. It may also be helpful to take art history classes, so you can learn how architectural forms have evolved and how art styles are influenced.

Postsecondary Training

To further prepare yourself to become a ceramic artist, it is common to attend a postsecondary art program with a focus in ceramic art and design. You can choose from specialized art schools (the Art Institute of Chicago and the Maine College of Art, for example) or a number of general universities and colleges. It traditionally takes four years to get a bachelor of fine arts degree with a major in ceramic art. Courses include specifics like earthenware and stoneware. Design aspects of functional forms, such as plates, pitchers, and lidded containers, are explored in addition to learning how to get your pieces ready for the kiln and how to fire your work.

Although many artists have followed this traditional educational path, there certainly are exceptions. Some ceramic artists are self-taught. Others get involved with apprenticeships or internships at potters' studios.

Other Requirements

If you really want to be a ceramic artist, you can't be squeamish about getting up to your elbows in wet clay. Ceramics can be a messy endeavor: work clothes get splotched, caked, and stiff, and your hands get covered in clay.

You must have artistic talent and patience to succeed in this career. As a ceramic artist, your imagination is always on call.

EXPLORING

Before exploring work opportunities in ceramic art, explore clay itself, perhaps beginning with a high school ceramics class. Also, many colleges, universities, and community schools offer art programs for high school students to prepare them for art programs at higher levels. Look for summer camps that offer art programs; these usually include some type of ceramics courses. There might even be a potter's studio in your own neighborhood or town; if there is, visit and ask if you can watch the work. Ask about workshops the studio might offer. You can also learn to design and show ceramics pieces in contests through a local 4-H club. To learn more, visit http://www.4-h.org.

EMPLOYERS

As for all other artists, it is difficult to earn a living by selling your pieces. Ceramic artists may have an advantage if they are able to produce functional objects as well as artistic pieces. Still, it's most likely that you will have to supplement your income by working another job.

Many artists go into teaching. Those who want to teach at a high school or university level should have a good background in other craft media because entry-level teaching positions often include assignments in more than one medium. You can also teach small workshops in your own studio, inviting people from different backgrounds and with different goals to learn ceramics. Another avenue for teaching is in art therapy, which involves working with patients on a level that includes artistic creation as a way to help the healing process; it is likely that you'll have to take courses in psychology and health before being qualified as a ceramic arts therapist.

STARTING OUT

Being an artist doesn't necessarily mean you have to have a job practicing your art or have to sell your art. Many would say that once you've finished your studies in ceramic arts and have been working with your style of creativity for a while, you can consider yourself an artist whether you have a job in ceramics or not.

However, if you want to be involved in the community of ceramic artists, you will probably want to find work first with an established pottery studio or individual artist who is already showing his or her work and has some kind of reputation as an artist. You could perhaps find work at a local art gallery or a ceramics studio. Volunteering your time is not a bad idea because it shows that you're interested in learning.

It is also recommended that you enter your work in competitions and art shows. You can do this both in school and outside. Many events are held that invite young artists to submit their work for display and to be judged by established artists. If you are successful enough to win some awards, this will do good things for your reputation as an artist. Whether you win or not, the experience itself is valuable.

Once you've finished your studies in an art program or with an established artist, you can begin to set up your own studio or work with a few others to set up a collaborative works pace. Don't forget, though, that this could be a slow process. You should probably expect to spend a lot of time and effort developing your artistic reputation.

ADVANCEMENT

Ceramic artists who want to work on their own will have to consider renting studio space and showing their work somehow. Perhaps a gallery owner will want to include their pieces in his or her shop; maybe the school they attended will have a show and put their pieces on display there; or maybe someone will come into their studio one day and fall in love with what they're making. These are just a few possibilities for having work shown, appreciated, and bought.

Many artists feel that their goals lie in simply being able to work at their art, in whatever environment. They might not be especially concerned about whether their pieces sell to the public; they might be more satisfied to know that a limited group of people enjoy their work. Others want specifically to have their own studios, produce many pieces, and become famous in the art world. It depends on their desires, their own personality, and their concern with what brings fulfillment in their life's work.

EARNINGS

To most artists, earnings come in different forms, not just monetary wealth. Of course many would like to be successful in terms of how many pieces they sell and how much money they make, but this doesn't happen with every ceramic artist. A ceramic artist might work hundreds of hours on one piece of sculpture, and finally realize that they don't want to part with it at all. They might be tremendously inspired, quickly throw an unusually good pot on the wheel, and immediately offer it for sale.

Ceramic artists who want to earn steady pay would be wise to work for an established potter or a large ceramics manufacturer. This type of job might pay at least $15,000 to $25,000 per year, and the artist will get a paycheck every few weeks. For many, being an artist is more satisfying than having a good income. Setting up one's own studio, being able to get involved in the creative process whenever inspiration strikes, working with clay—this type of living is what many artists strive for. Ceramic artists who are self-employed will have to provide their own health insurance, paid vacations, and other fringe benefits. An extremely talented artist might earn more than $100,000 per year. However, it is also possible that this artist's pieces will lose popularity, and he or she will make $20,000 the next year.

WORK ENVIRONMENT

The life of an artist can be hugely rewarding, fulfilling, and enlightening. For all ceramic artists, the creative process must central to their existence. Whether they are a functional potter, a sculptor, or a tile maker, this creative process is the most significant condition of their work.

The life of a professional ceramic artist is like that of other artists—the work is personally rewarding but perhaps difficult, with earned money and recognition often out of proportion to the training, time, and effort involved. Perhaps the most difficult task for the potter wanting his or her own studio is to be practical. They must consider costs for such things as the clay, kiln, fuel, chemicals, and the rental of studio space and utilities.

Their work space might be a studio at school, a potter's workshop, or their basement or garage. An artist's work area often reflects the activity done there, the personality of the artist, and the techniques used to create the ceramic pieces. An artist's studio space doesn't have to be elaborate, but certain things—like spaciousness, ventilation, and lighting—should be considered. Health and safety issues should be considered as well; a studio should have a filter vacuum cleaner, venting system, and fire extinguisher.

OUTLOOK

It is very hard to predict whether ceramic artists will enjoy success and recognition in the near future. Within the broader art world—

which includes painting, architecture, and sculpture—ceramic art and design is quite new. Ceramics instruction is widespread today, but as late as the 1930s ceramics wasn't really considered much of an art. People today still debate whether it is a craft or an art.

However, there are good signs that ceramics as an art form has the potential to become well recognized. The last decade has produced many books, videos, and magazines on the subject, along with workshops, conferences, and competitions throughout the world. Ceramic artists gather to show their work, work together, and teach others. Many ceramic artists have made prominent names for themselves in the art world.

FOR MORE INFORMATION
For general information on ceramic arts study, contact
National Art Education Association
1916 Association Drive
Reston, VA 20191-1590
Tel: 703-860-8000
Email: naea@dgs.dgsys.com
http://www.naea-reston.org

This association supports established and emerging artists and arts organizations. For information on art programs, contact your state agency or the following:
National Assembly of State Arts Agencies
1029 Vermont Avenue, NW, 2nd Floor
Washington, DC 20005
Tel: 202-347-6352
Email: nasaa@nasaa-arts.org
http://www.nasaa-arts.org

For education information, contact
National Council on Education for the Ceramic Arts
77 Erie Village Square, #280
Erie, CO 80516
Tel: 866-266-2322
Email: programs@nceca.net
http://www.nceca.net

CINEMATOGRAPHERS AND DIRECTORS OF PHOTOGRAPHY

QUICK FACTS

School Subjects Art English	**Certification or Licensing** None available
Personal Skills Artistic Technical/scientific	**Outlook** Faster than the average
	DOT 143
Work Environment Indoors and outdoors Primarily multiple locations	**GOE** 10.02.03
Minimum Education Level Bachelor's degree	**NOC** 5131
Salary Range $14,730 to $28,980 to $62,090+	**O*NET-SOC** 27-4031.00

OVERVIEW

The *cinematographer*, also known as the director of photography or DP, is instrumental in establishing the mood of a film by putting the narrative aspects of a script into visual form. The cinematographer is responsible for every shot's framing, lighting, color level, and exposure—elements that set the artistic tone of the film.

HISTORY

Motion picture cameras were invented in the late 1800s. In 1903, Edwin Porter made *The Great Train Robbery*, the first motion picture that used modern filmmakers' techniques to tell a story. Porter filmed the scenes out of sequence, then edited and spliced them together to make the film, as is done today.

In the early years of film, the director handled the camera and made the artistic decisions that today are the job of the director of photography. The technical sophistication and artistic choices that are part of today's filming process had not yet emerged; instead, directors merely filmed narratives without moving the camera. Lighting was more for functional purposes of illumination than for artistic effect. Soon, however, directors began to experiment. They moved the camera to shoot from different angles and established a variety of editing techniques.

In the 1950s, the dominance of major studios in film production was curbed by an antitrust court decision, and more independent films were made. Changes in the U.S. tax code made independent producing more profitable. New genres and trends challenged the director and artistic staff of a production. Science fiction, adventure, mystery, and romance films grew in popularity. By the late 1960s, university film schools were established, where students could study directing, cinematography, and other film topics.

New developments in technologies and equipment have continued to influence both how films are made and how they look. The end of the 20th century and the beginning of the 21st saw the production of movies incorporating such elements as computer graphics, digital imaging, and digital color. Films such as *Titanic, Gladiator, Lord of the Rings,* and "prequel" episodes of *Star Wars* presented new visual challenges for filmmakers because of the large number of special effects they required. DPs lead the way in understanding and using new technologies to push the art of filmmaking into a new, digital era.

THE JOB

Cinematographers consider how the "look" of a film helps to tell its story. How can the look enhance the action, the emotions expressed, or the characters' personalities? Should the scene be filmed from across the room or up close to the actors? Should the lighting be stark or muted? How does the angle of the camera contribute to the scene? These are just some of the questions DPs must answer when composing a shot. DPs have both the artistic and technical knowledge that makes them an integral member of the production team. They work in both film and television, helping directors to interpret a script and bring it to life.

At the beginning of a project, the DP reads the script and talks to the director about how to film each scene. Together they determine how to achieve the desired effects by deciding on camera angles and movement, lighting, framing, and the filters to use. By manipulating effects, DPs help determine the mood of a scene. For example, to raise the level of tension and discomfort in an argument, the DP can tell a camera operator to film at an unusual angle or move around the actors as they speak. The director may choose to film a scene in more than one way and then decide which best suits the project. With good collaboration between the director and the DP, decisions will be made quickly and successfully.

DPs are responsible for assembling the camera crew and telling crew members how to film each scene. They must be knowledgeable about all aspects of camera operation, lighting, filters, and types of film. There are multiple ways an effect can be approached, and DPs must be aware of them in order to make suggestions to the director and to capture the mood desired. For small, low-budget films, some of the crew's roles may be combined. For example, the DP may operate a camera in addition to overseeing the crew.

In a large production, the crew's roles will be more specialized. The camera operator either operates the camera physically or controls it remotely, using a control panel. The first assistant camera operator helps with focus, changes lenses and filters, sets the stop for film exposure, and makes sure the camera is working properly. Focus is extremely important and is not entrusted to vision; the first assistant carries a measuring tape and measures all the key positions of the actors to ensure correct focus. The second assistant camera operator, also called the loader, loads film magazines, keeps track of how much film stock is left, and keeps camera reports. Camera reports record which shots the director likes and wants to have printed. A gaffer leads the electrical crew, and the grips handle the dollies and cranes to move the cameras.

When shooting begins, cinematographers take a series of test shots of film locations to determine the lighting, lenses, and film stock that will work best. Once filming starts, they make adjustments as necessary. They may also film screen tests of actors so the director can be sure they are right for their parts.

Richard Shore, A.S.C., has had a career that extends over 40 years, 20 countries, and 200 films. His feature work includes *Bang the Drum Slowly,* a film that Robert DeNiro credits as starting his career. Currently, Shore is a lecturer at the New York Film Academy (NYFA), where he teaches basic and advanced courses in filmmaking and works one-on-one with students. He teaches classes in cinematography, lighting, scripts, and other aspects of filmmaking.

One of Shore's early filmmaking jobs was making training films for the U.S. Army during the Korean War. "After the war," he says,

"I got work making travel films, documentaries, industrial films. I also made TV commercials." This eventually led to a career filled with awards, including two Oscars, three Emmys, and induction into the American Society of Cinematographers (ASC).

Different projects have different demands—for one of the films for which he won an Oscar, a short film about poet Robert Frost, Shore was involved in many aspects of the filmmaking process beyond the duties of DP. For one of the Emmy-winning projects, Shore worked as a director. While working on a documentary about French president Francois Mitterand, Shore traveled extensively, spending two months with Mitterand in Paris, then flying with him to Washington, D.C., to meet with President Reagan. "In the film industry," Shore says, "you have experiences you can't get anywhere else."

REQUIREMENTS
High School
You should take courses that will prepare you for college, such as math, English, government, and foreign language. Courses in English composition and literature will give you a background in narrative development, and art and photography courses can help you understand the basics of lighting and composition. A broadcast journalism or media course may give you some hands-on experience in camera operation and video production.

Postsecondary Training
A bachelor's degree in liberal arts or film studies provides a good background for work in the film industry, but practical experience and industry connections will provide the best job opportunities. Upon completing an undergraduate program, you may wish to enroll in a master's program or master's of fine arts program at a film school. Schools offering well-established programs include the School of Visual Arts in New York, New York University, and the University of Southern California. These schools have film professionals on their faculties and provide a very visible stage for student talent, being located in the two film business hot spots—California and New York. Film school offers overall formal training, providing an education in fundamental skills by working with student productions. Such education is rigorous, but in addition to teaching skills it provides you with peer groups and a network of contacts with students, faculty, and guest speakers that can be of help after graduation.

An alternative to film school is the New York Film Academy (NYFA). By immersing students in film production in an intensive six-week course, allowing students access to cameras and editing tables, the NYFA gives students an idea of the demands of the career. Students will also have made three short films of their own. (Contact information for all schools is listed at the end of this article.)

"A lot of people want to make films," Richard Shore says, "but there is really no direct route to entering the film industry. All production companies care about is what you can show them that you've done. You need to make a short film and submit it to a festival. If it's shown and gets recognition, that's your entrée."

Other Requirements

You'll need to keep abreast of technological innovations while working in the industry. You must be comfortable with the technical as well as artistic aspects of the profession. You also must be a good leader who can make decisions and direct a crew effectively.

"You really have to want it," Shore says about the work of a DP. "It's almost like a calling. You can't go into it half-way." Shore says it's also helpful to have your own original story ideas when embarking on a film career. "Film is a story-telling art, a narrative art. Someone with the ideal background is someone interested in literature, particularly the novel."

EXPLORING

With cable television, videos, and DVDs, it is much easier to study films today than it was 25 years ago. And it's likely to become easier as the Internet might someday allow you to download any film you choose. You should take full advantage of the availability of great films and study them closely for the styles of the filmmakers. The documentary *Visions of Light: The Art of Cinematography,* directed by Arnold Glassman, Todd McCarthy, and Stuart Samuels is a good introduction to some of the finest cinematography in the history of film. You can also experiment with composition and lighting if you have access to a 16-millimeter camera, a camcorder, or a digital camera. Check with your school's media center or journalism department about recording school events. Your school's drama club can also introduce you to the elements of comedy and drama and may involve you with writing and staging your own productions.

You should subscribe to *American Cinematographer* magazine or read selected articles at the magazine's website (http://www.theasc.

com/magazine). Other industry magazines such as *Variety* (http://www.variety.com), Hollywood Reporter (http://www. hollywoodreporter.com), and *Cinefex* (http://www.cinefex.com) can also give you insight into filmmaking.

EMPLOYERS
Motion picture studios, production companies, independent producers, and documentary filmmakers all employ DPs, either as salaried employees or as freelancers. The U.S. Department of Labor reports that 25 percent of all camera operators work on a freelance basis. Most freelancers are responsible for finding their own projects to work on, but a few are represented by agents who solicit work for them.

STARTING OUT
Internships are a very good way to gain experience and become a marketable job candidate. Since local television stations and lower budget film productions operate with limited funds, they may offer internships for course credit or experience instead of a salary. You should check with your state's film commission to learn of productions in your area and volunteer to work in whatever capacity needed. Many production opportunities are also posted on the Web. By working on productions, you'll develop relationships with crew members and production assistants, and you'll be able to build a network of industry connections.

Before working as a DP, you'll likely work as a camera assistant or production assistant. You can gain some experience in camera work with a college broadcasting station or a local TV crew or advertising agency.

Camera operators may choose to join a union because some film studios will hire only union members. The principal union for this field is the International Alliance of Theatrical Stage Employees, Moving Picture Technicians, Artists, and Allied Crafts of the United States and Canada (IATSE). Union members work under a union contract that determines their work rules, pay, and benefits.

ADVANCEMENT
The position of cinematographer is in itself an advanced position. Richard Shore says securing a job as a DP "takes years and years of training. You must work your way up from first assistant, to camera operator, to DP. It's not a union thing, it's a way of learning. You learn from watching cinematographers work."

Those wanting to be DPs must get a foot in the door by making short films and getting them seen by producers. "Not only do you need skills, but you must make connections with people," Shore explains.

Camera operators may have opportunities to work as cinematographers on some projects. As they continue to develop relationships with filmmakers and producers, their DP work may increase, leading to better paying, high-profile film projects. Once a DP has begun working in the industry, advancement may come as the DP develops a reputation for excellent, innovative work. Directors and producers may then request to work with that particular DP, which can also lead to higher pay.

EARNINGS

Many DPs do freelance work or have jobs under union contracts. They may work for a variety of employers ranging from major studios producing films with multimillion-dollar budgets to small, independent producers who are financing a film with their credit cards. As a result, their earnings vary widely.

When starting out as a camera operator, an individual may volunteer for a job, without pay, simply to get experience. At the other end of the earnings scale, a well-established DP working on big-budget productions can make well over a million dollars a year. The IATSE establishes minimum wage scales for DPs who are union members, based on the nature of a film shoot. For feature film studio shoots, a cinematographer is paid about $520 a day. For location shoots, the wage is about $670 a day. Special provisions are also made for holiday and overtime work.

For an idea of what the average cinematographer may make in a year, consider government findings. The U.S. Department of Labor, which categorizes DPs with all camera operators, reports the median annual earnings for those working in motion picture production were $28,980 in 2001. The lowest paid 10 percent of camera operators, including those working in television and video, made less than $14,730. At the high end, 10 percent earned more than $62,090.

Freelancers must pay for their own benefits, such as health insurance, and they usually must buy their own equipment, which can be quite expensive.

WORK ENVIRONMENT

Conditions of work will vary depending on the size and nature of the production. In television production and in movies, DPs may work both indoors and outdoors. Indoors, conditions can be cramped, while outdoors there may be heat, cold, rain, or snow. DPs may need to travel for weeks at a time while a project is being shot on location, and some locations, such as the middle of a desert, may mean staying miles from civilization. Hours can be long and the shooting schedule rigorous, especially when a film is going over budget. DPs work as members of a team, instructing assistants while also taking instruction from directors and producers. Those making a film with a small budget may be required to oversee many different aspects of the production.

Filming challenges, such as how to shoot effectively underwater, in the dark, or in public areas are a normal part of the job. DPs need patience in setting up cameras and preparing the lighting, as well as in dealing with the variety of professionals with whom they work.

"If you can get into film," Richard Shore says, "it's a wonderful career." One reason DPs enjoy their work so much is that they work with talented, artistic, and skillful professionals. "There's a camaraderie among film crew members," Shore says.

OUTLOOK

The U.S. Department of Labor predicts employment for camera operators to grow faster than the average over the next decade. More opportunities, though, will be available for those willing to work outside of the film industry at, for example, advertising agencies and TV broadcasting companies. The department anticipates that other types of programming, such as Internet broadcasts of music videos, sports, and general information shows, will provide job openings in this field.

However, competition for work will be fierce because so many people are attracted to this business. "There are so many more qualified people than there are jobs," Richard Shore says. "It's impossible to guarantee success." Nevertheless, those with the right connections, strong samples of their work, and some luck are likely to find opportunities.

DPs of the future will be working more closely with special effects houses, even on films other than science fiction, horror, and other genres typically associated with special effects. Digital technology is used to create crowd scenes, underwater images, and other effects more efficiently and economically. DPs will have to approach a film with an understanding of which shots can be produced digitally and which will require traditional methods of filmmaking.

FOR MORE INFORMATION

For information about education and training workshops for television and film production and to read about events in the industry, visit the AFI website.

American Film Institute (AFI)
2021 North Western Avenue
Los Angeles, CA 90027
Tel: 323-856-7600
http://www.afi.com

The ASC website has information on the ASC, articles from American Cinematographer magazine, industry news, and a student section with grants and fellowship information. The ASC online store sells many helpful publications covering aspects of film production.

American Society of Cinematographers (ASC)
PO Box 2230
Hollywood, CA 90036
Tel: 800-448-0145
Email: info@theasc.com
http://theasc.com

For information on membership benefits, contact

International Alliance of Theatrical Stage Employees, Moving Picture Technicians, Artists, and Allied Crafts of the United States and Canada (IATSE)
1430 Broadway, 20th Floor
New York, NY 10018
Tel: 212-730-1770
http://www.iatse-intl.org

To read about programs at several schools, visit the following websites:

New York Film Academy
http://www.nyfa.com

New York University
http://www.nyu.edu

School of Visual Arts
http://schoolofvisualarts.edu

University of Southern California
http://www.usc.edu

COLLEGE PROFESSORS

QUICK FACTS

School Subjects
English
History
Speech

Personal Skills
Communication/ideas
Helping/teaching

Work Environment
Primarily indoors
Primarily one location

Minimum Education Level
Master's degree

Salary Range
$35,790 to $60,000 to
$108,000+

Certification or Licensing
None available

Outlook
Faster than the average

DOT
090

GOE
11.02.01

NOC
4121

O*NET-SOC
25.1031.00, 25-1061.00,
25-1062.00, 25-1081.00,
25-1121.00, 25-1122.00,
25-1123.00, 25-1124.00,
25-1125.00, 25-1126.00,
25-1191.00, 25-1194.00

OVERVIEW

College professors instruct undergraduate and graduate students in specific subjects at colleges and universities. They are responsible for lecturing classes, leading small seminar groups, and creating and grading examinations. They also may conduct research, write for publication, and aid in administration. Approximately 1.3 million postsecondary teachers are employed in the United States.

HISTORY

The concept of colleges and universities goes back many centuries. These institutions evolved slowly from monastery schools, which trained a select few for certain professions, notably theology.

Outside of academia, the terms *college* and *university* have become virtually interchangeable in America, although originally they designated two very different kinds of institutions.

Two of the most notable early European universities were the University of Bologna in Italy, thought to have been established in the 12th century, and the University of Paris, which was chartered in 1201. These universities were considered to be the models after which other European universities were patterned. Oxford University in England was probably established during the 12th century. Oxford served as a model for early American colleges and universities and today is still considered one of the world's leading institutions.

Harvard, the first U.S. college, was established in 1636. Its stated purpose was to train men for the ministry; the early colleges were all established for religious training. With the growth of state-supported institutions in the early 18th century, the process of freeing the curriculum from ties with the church began. The University of Virginia established the first liberal arts curriculum in 1825, and these innovations were later adopted by many other colleges and universities.

Although the original colleges in the United States were patterned after Oxford University, they later came under the influence of German universities. During the 19th century, more than 9,000 Americans went to Germany to study. The emphasis in German universities was on the scientific method. Most of the people who had studied in Germany returned to the United States to teach in universities, bringing this objective, factual approach to education and to other fields of learning.

In 1833, Oberlin College in Oberlin, Ohio became the first college founded as a coeducational institution. In 1836, the first women-only college, Wesleyan Female College, was founded in Macon, Georgia.

The junior college movement in the United States has been one of the most rapidly growing educational developments. Junior colleges first came into being just after the turn of the 20th century.

THE JOB

College and university faculty members teach at junior colleges or at four-year colleges and universities. At four-year institutions, most faculty members are *assistant professors, associate professors,* or *full professors.* These three types of professorships differ in status, job responsibilities, and salary. Assistant professors are new faculty members who are working to get tenure (status as a permanent professor); they seek to advance to associate and then to full professorships.

College professors perform three main functions: teaching, advising, and research. Their most important responsibility is to teach students. Their role within a college department will determine the level of courses they teach and the number of courses per semester. Most professors work with students at all levels, from college freshmen to graduate students. They may head several classes a semester or only a few a year. Some of their classes will have large enrollment, while graduate seminars may consist of only 12 or fewer students. Though college professors may spend fewer than 10 hours a week in the actual classroom, they spend many hours preparing lectures and lesson plans, grading papers and exams, and preparing grade reports. They also schedule office hours during the week to be available to students outside of the lecture hall, and they meet with students individually throughout the semester. In the classroom, professors lecture, lead discussions, administer exams, and assign textbook reading and other research. In some courses, they rely heavily on laboratories to transmit course material.

Another important professorial responsibility is advising students. Not all faculty members serve as advisers, but those who do must set aside large blocks of time to guide students through the program. College professors who serve as advisers may have any number of students assigned to them, from fewer than 10 to more than 100, depending on the administrative policies of the college. Their responsibility may involve looking over a planned program of study to make sure the students meet requirements for graduation, or it may involve working intensively with each student on many aspects of college life.

The third responsibility of college and university faculty members is research and publication. Faculty members who are heavily involved in research programs sometimes are assigned a smaller teaching load. College professors publish their research findings in various scholarly journals. They also write books based on their research or on their own knowledge and experience in the field. Most textbooks are written by college and university teachers. In arts-based programs, such as master's of fine arts programs in painting, writing, and theater, professors practice their craft and exhibit their art work in various ways. For example, a painter or photographer will have gallery showings, while a poet will publish in literary journals.

Publishing a significant amount of work has been the traditional standard by which assistant professors prove themselves worthy of becoming permanent, tenured faculty. Typically, pressure to publish is greatest for assistant professors. Pressure to publish increases again if an associate professor wishes to be considered for a promotion to full professorship.

In recent years, some liberal arts colleges have recognized that the pressure to publish is taking faculty away from their primary duties to the students, and these institutions have begun to place a decreasing emphasis on publishing and more on performance in the classroom. Professors in junior colleges face less pressure to publish than those in four-year institutions.

Some faculty members eventually rise to the position of *department chair*, where they govern the affairs of an entire department, such as English, mathematics, or biological sciences. Department chairs, faculty, and other professional staff members are aided in their myriad duties by *graduate assistants*, who may help develop teaching materials, conduct research, give examinations, teach lower level courses, and carry out other activities.

Some college professors may also conduct classes in an extension program. In such a program, they teach evening and weekend courses for the benefit of people who otherwise would not be able to take advantage of the institution's resources. They may travel away from the campus and meet with a group of students at another location. They may work full time for the extension division or may divide their time between on-campus and off-campus teaching.

Distance learning programs give professors the opportunity to use today's technologies to remain in one place while teaching students who are at a variety of locations simultaneously. The professor's duties, like those when teaching correspondence courses conducted by mail, include grading work that students send in at periodic intervals and advising students of their progress. Computers, the Internet, email, and video conferencing, however, are some of the technology tools that allow professors and students to communicate in "real time" in a virtual classroom setting. Meetings may be scheduled during the same time as traditional classes or during evenings and weekends. Professors who do this work are sometimes known as *extension work, correspondence,* or *distance learning instructors.* They may teach online courses in addition to other classes or may have distance learning as their major teaching responsibility.

The *junior college instructor* has many of the same kinds of responsibilities as the teacher in a four-year college or university. Because junior colleges offer only a two-year program, they teach only undergraduates.

REQUIREMENTS

High School

Your high school's college preparatory program likely includes courses in English, science, foreign language, history, math, and government. In addition, you should take courses in speech to get a sense of what it will be like to lecture to a group of students. Your school's debate team can also help you develop public speaking skills, along with research skills.

Postsecondary Training

At least one advanced degree in your field of study is required to be a professor in a college or university. The master's degree is considered the minimum standard, and graduate work beyond the master's is usually desirable. If you hope to advance in academic rank above instructor, most institutions require a doctorate.

In the last year of your undergraduate program, you'll apply to graduate programs in your area of study. Standards for admission to a graduate program can be high and the competition heavy, depending on the school. Once accepted into a program, your responsibilities will be similar to those of your professors—in addition to attending seminars, you'll research, prepare articles for publication, and teach some undergraduate courses.

You may find employment in a junior college with only a master's degree. Advancement in responsibility and in salary, however, is more likely to come if you have earned a doctorate.

Other Requirements

You should enjoy reading, writing, and researching. Not only will you spend many years studying in school, but your whole career will be based on communicating your thoughts and ideas. People skills are important because you'll be dealing directly with students, administrators, and other faculty members on a daily basis. You should feel comfortable in a role of authority and possess self-confidence.

EXPLORING

Your high school teachers use many of the same skills as college professors, so talk to your teachers about their careers and their college experiences. You can develop your own teaching experience by volunteering at a community center, working at a day care center, or working at a summer camp. Also, spend some time on a college campus to get a sense of the environment. Write to colleges for their admissions brochures and course catalogs (or check them out online); read about the faculty members and the courses they teach. Before visiting college campuses, make arrangements to speak to professors who teach courses that interest you. These professors may allow you to sit in on their classes and observe. Also, make appointments with college advisers and with people in the admissions and recruitment offices. If your grades are good enough, you might be able to serve as a teaching assistant during your undergraduate years, which can give you experience leading discussions and grading papers.

EMPLOYERS

Employment opportunities vary based on area of study and education. Most universities have many different departments that hire faculty. With a doctorate, a number of publications, and a record of good teaching, professors should find opportunities in universities all across the country. There are more than 3,800 colleges and universities in the United States. Professors teach in undergraduate and graduate programs. The teaching jobs at doctoral institutions are usually better paying and more prestigious. The most sought-after positions are those that offer tenure. Teachers that have only a master's degree will be limited to opportunities with junior colleges, community colleges, and some small private institutions. There are approximately 1.3 million postsecondary teachers employed in the United States.

STARTING OUT

You should start the process of finding a teaching position while you are in graduate school. The process includes developing a curriculum vitae (a detailed, academic resume), writing for publication, assisting with research, attending conferences, and gaining teaching experience and recommendations. Many students begin applying for teaching positions while finishing their graduate program. For most positions at four-year institutions, you must travel to large conferences where interviews can be arranged with representatives from the universities to which you have applied.

Because of the competition for tenure-track positions, you may have to work for a few years in temporary positions, visiting various schools as an *adjunct professor*. Some professional associations maintain lists of teaching opportunities in their areas. They may also make lists of applicants available to college administrators looking to fill an available position.

ADVANCEMENT

The normal pattern of advancement is from instructor to assistant professor, to associate professor, to full professor. All four academic ranks are concerned primarily with teaching and research. College faculty members who have an interest in and a talent for administration may be advanced to chair of a department or to dean of their college. A few become college or university presidents or other types of administrators.

The instructor is usually an inexperienced college teacher. He or she may hold a doctorate or may have completed all the Ph.D. requirements except for the dissertation. Most colleges look upon the rank of instructor as the period during which the college is trying out the teacher. Instructors usually are advanced to the position of assistant professors within three to four years. Assistant professors are given up to about six years to prove themselves worthy of tenure, and if they do so, they become associate professors. Some professors choose to remain at the associate level. Others strive to become full professors and receive greater status, salary, and responsibilities.

Most colleges have clearly defined promotion policies from rank to rank for faculty members, and many have written statements about the number of years in which instructors and assistant professors may remain in grade. Administrators in many colleges hope to encourage younger faculty members to increase their skills and competencies and thus to qualify for the more responsible positions of associate professor and full professor.

EARNINGS

Earnings vary depending on the departments professors work in, the size of the school, the type of school (for example, public, private, or women's only), and by the level of position the professor holds. In its 2000–01 salary survey, the American Association of University Professors (AAUP) reported the average yearly income for all full-time faculty was $60,000. It also reports that professors averaged the following salaries by rank: full professors, $78,912; associate professors, $57,380; assistant professors, $47,358; and instructors, $35,790. Full professors working in disciplines such as law, business, health professions, computer and information sciences, and engineering have the highest salaries. Lower paying disciplines include visual and performing arts, agricultural studies, education, and communications. The American Association for the Advancement of Science reports that, according to findings from its member salary survey, the median earnings for full professors in the life science fields were approximately $108,000 in 2001. Associate professors in life sciences earned a median of $72,000 that same year.

According to a study by the College and University Professional Association for Human Resources, the average salary in all fields at public institutions was $60,893 for 2001–02. At private colleges, the average was $60,289. Law professors earned top salaries of $107,696 at private colleges, and library science faculty members were near the bottom of the salary scale, earning $44,206 per year.

Many professors try to increase their earnings by completing research, publishing in their field, or teaching additional courses. Professors working on the west coast and the east coast of the United States and those working at doctorate-granting institutions tend to have the highest salaries.

Benefits for full-time faculty typically include health insurance and retirement funds and, in some cases, stipends for travel related to research, housing allowances, and tuition waivers for dependents.

WORK ENVIRONMENT

A college or university is usually a pleasant place in which to work. Campuses bustle with all types of activities and events, stimulating ideas, and a young, energetic population. Much prestige comes with success as a professor and scholar; professors have the respect of students, colleagues, and others in their community.

Depending on the size of the department, college professors may have their own office, or they may have to share an office with one or more colleagues. Their department may provide them with a computer, Internet access, and research assistants. College professors are also able to do much of their office work at home. They can arrange their schedule around class hours, academic meetings, and the established office hours when they meet with students. Most college teachers work more than 40 hours each week. Although college professors may teach only two or three classes a semester, they spend many hours preparing for lectures, examining student work, and conducting research.

OUTLOOK

The U.S. Department of Labor predicts faster than average employment growth for college and university professors over the next several years. College enrollment is projected to grow due to an increased number of 18- to 24-year-olds, an increased number of adults returning to college, and an increased number of foreign-born students. Additionally, opportunities for college teachers will be good in areas such as engineering, business, computer science, and health science, which offer strong career prospects in the world of work. Retirement of current faculty members will also provide job openings. However, competition for full-time, tenure-track positions at four-year schools will be very strong.

A number of factors threaten to change the way colleges and universities hire faculty. Some university leaders are developing more business-based methods of running their schools, focusing on profits and budgets. This can affect college professors in a number of ways. One of the biggest effects is in the replacement of tenure-track faculty positions with part-time instructors. These part-time instructors include adjunct faculty, visiting professors, and graduate students. Organizations such as the AAUP and the American Federation of Teachers are working to prevent the loss of these full-time jobs, as well as to help part-time instructors receive better pay and benefits. Other issues involve the development of long-distance education departments in many schools. Though these correspondence courses have become very popular in recent years, many professionals believe that students in long-distance education programs receive only a second-rate education. A related concern is about the proliferation of computers in the classroom. Some courses consist only of instruction by computer software and the Internet. The effects of these alternative methods on the teaching profession will be offset somewhat by the expected increases in college enrollment in coming years.

FOR MORE INFORMATION
To read about the issues affecting college professors, contact the following organizations:

American Association of University Professors
1012 14th Street, NW, Suite 500
Washington, DC 20005
Tel: 202-737-5900
Email: aaup@aaup.org
http://www.aaup.org

American Federation of Teachers
555 New Jersey Avenue, NW
Washington, DC 20001
Tel: 202-879-4400
Email: online@aft.org
http://www.aft.org

CONSERVATORS AND CONSERVATION TECHNICIANS

QUICK FACTS

School Subjects
Art
Chemistry

Personal Skills
Mechanical/manipulative
Technical/scientific

Work Environment
Primarily indoors
Primarily one location

Minimum Education Level
Bachelor's degree

Salary Range
$19,200 to $33,080 to
$61,490+

Certification or Licensing
None available

Outlook
About as fast as the average

DOT
102

GOE
01.06.02

NOC
5212

O*NET-SOC
25-4013.00

OVERVIEW

Conservators are professionals with specialized education and training who analyze and assess the condition of artifacts and art objects, plan collections' care, and carry out conservation treatments and programs. Conservators may be in private practice or work for museums, historical societies, or state institutions. Conservation professionals must select methods and materials that do not endanger artifacts, but rather preserve specimens and retain the original integrity of each piece. To do this conservators must have a sound sense of the objects in their care, which may be natural objects, such as bones and fossils, or man-made objects, such as paintings, sculpture, paper, and metal. They must also have a solid working knowledge of chemistry and scientific technique. *Conservation technicians* work under the supervision of conservators and complete maintenance work on the collection.

HISTORY

Conservation is the youngest of all museum disciplines. The word "conservation" has been used in reference to works of art only since approximately 1930. For at least a century before 1930, museums may have employed restorers, or restoration specialists, but the philosophy that guided their work was much different than the ideas and values held by conservators today. Early conservators were often tradespeople, artists, or framers called upon to restore a damaged work of art to an approximate version of its original condition. They repainted, varnished, or patched objects as they saw fit, working independently and experimenting as necessary to achieve the desired results. Conservators today use highly scientific methods and recognize the need both to care for works of art before deterioration occurs and to treat objects after damage has been done.

The first regional conservation laboratory in the United States, known as the Intermuseum Conservation Association (ICA), was created in 1952, in Oberlin, Ohio, when several smaller museums joined to bring their skills together.

Thanks to increasingly precise cleaning methods and scientific inventions such as thermal adhesives, the science of conservation has advanced. Today, the field is highly specialized and those who work in it must face demanding standards and challenges.

THE JOB

Conservation professionals generally choose to specialize in one area of work defined by medium, such as in the preservation of books and paper, architecture, objects, photographic materials, paintings, textiles, or wooden artifacts. There are also conservators who specialize in archaeology or ethnographic materials. Many are employed by museums, while others provide services through private (individual or group) practice. Conservation activities include carrying out technical and scientific studies on art objects, stabilizing the structure and reintegrating the appearance of cultural artifacts, and establishing the environment in which artifacts are best preserved. A conservator's responsibilities also may include documenting the structure and condition through written and visual recording, designing programs for preventive care, and executing conservation treatments. A conservator's tools can include microscopes and cameras, including equipment for specialized processes such as infrared and ultraviolet photography, and X-ray processes.

Conservation technicians assist conservators in preserving or restoring artifacts and art objects. To do this, they study descriptions and information about the object, and may perform chemical and physical tests as specified by the conservator. If an object is metal, a technician may be instructed to clean it by scraping or by applying chemical solvents. Statues can sometimes be washed with soap solutions, and furniture and silver can often be polished.

When a repair is necessary, conservation technicians may be asked to reassemble the broken pieces using glue or solder, then buff the object when the repair is complete. They may repaint objects where the original paint is faded or missing, using paint of the same chemical composition and color as the original. Technicians may also make and repair picture frames and mount paintings in frames.

A *conservation scientist* is a professional scientist whose primary focus is in developing materials and knowledge to support conservation activities. Some specialize in scientific research into artists' materials, such as paints and varnishes. *Conservation educators* have substantial knowledge and experience in the theory and practice of conservation, and have chosen to direct their efforts toward teaching the principles, methodology, and technical aspects of the profession. *Preparators* supervise the installation of specimens, art objects, and artifacts, often working with design technicians, curators, and directors to ensure the safety and preservation of items on display.

REQUIREMENTS
High School
Good conservation work comes from a well-balanced formulation of art and science. To prepare for a career in conservation, high school students should concentrate on doing well in all academic subjects, including courses in chemistry, natural science, history, and the arts.

Postsecondary Training
In the past, many conservation professionals earned their training solely through apprenticeship to esteemed conservators. Today you will need a bachelor's degree to find work as a conservation technician, and in all but the smallest institutions you will need a master's degree to advance to conservator. Because graduate programs are highly selective, you should consider embarking on a carefully planned academic future.

At the undergraduate level, you should take coursework in the sciences, including inorganic and organic chemistry, the humanities (art history, archaeology, and anthropology), and studio art. Some graduate programs will consider work experience and gained expertise in conservation practice as comparable to coursework when screening applicants, and most graduate programs recognize a student's participation in apprenticeship or internship positions while also completing coursework as indicative of the applicant's commitment to the career.

Other Requirements

Conservation can be physically demanding. Conservators and conservation technicians need to be able to concentrate on specific physical and mental tasks for long periods of time. Endurance, manual dexterity, and patience are often needed to complete projects successfully.

EXPLORING

If you are considering a career in the conservation of art or artifacts, try contacting local museums or looking for local art conservation laboratories that may allow tours or interviews. Also, read trade or technical journals to gain a sense of the many issues addressed by conservators, and contact professional organizations, such as the American Institute for Conservation of Historic and Artistic Works, for directories of training and conservation programs.

Because this is a highly professional and competitive field and because employment in the field even at entry levels most often entails the handling of precious materials and cultural resources, you should do your best to be fairly well informed before contacting professionals to request either internship or volunteer positions. You should demonstrate a high level of academic achievement and a serious interest in the career.

EMPLOYERS

Museums, libraries, historical societies, private conservation laboratories, and state and federal agencies that run public archives hire conservators and conservation technicians. Institutions with small operating budgets sometimes hire part-time specialists to perform conservation work. This is especially common when curators need extra help in preparing items for display. Antique dealers may also seek the expertise of an experienced conservator for merchandise restoration, identification, and appraisal purposes.

STARTING OUT

Most often students entering the field of art conservation have completed high school and undergraduate studies, and many are contemplating graduate programs. At this point a student is ready to seek a position (often unpaid) as an apprentice or intern with either a private conservation company or a museum to gain a practical feel for the work. Training opportunities are scarce and in high demand. Prospective students must convince potential trainers of their dedication to the highly demanding craft of conservation, and often professionals will want to be assured that the student is planning to return to an academic program before moving into practice. The combination of academic or formal training along with hands-on experience and apprenticeship is the ideal foundation for entering a future in the career.

ADVANCEMENT

Due to rapid changes in each conservation specialty, practicing conservators find it essential to keep abreast with advances in technology and methodology. Knowledge and skills are expanded through reading publications, attending professional meetings, and enrolling in short-term workshops or courses.

An experienced conservator wishing to move into another realm of the field may become a private consultant, an appraiser of art or artifacts, a conservation educator, a curator, or a museum registrar.

EARNINGS

Salaries for conservators vary greatly depending on the level of experience, chosen specialty, region, job description, and employer. The U.S. Department of Labor classifies conservators with curators, museum technicians, and archivists and reports the median annual earnings for this group as $33,080 in 2000. The lowest paid 10 percent of this group earned less than $19,200, and the highest paid 10 percent made more than $61,490. According to the American Institute for Conservation of Historic & Artistic Works, a first year conservator can expect to earn approximately $20,000 annually. Conservators with several years of experience report annual earnings between $35,000 and $40,000. The American Institute for Conservation of Historic and Artistic Works also notes that senior conservators have reported earnings between $50,000 and $60,000 annually.

Fringe benefits, including paid vacations, medical and dental insurance, sick leave, and retirement plans, vary according to each employer's policies.

WORK ENVIRONMENT
Conservation work may be conducted indoors, in laboratories, or in an outdoor setting. Conservators typically work 40–60 hours per week depending on exhibit schedules and deadlines, as well as the amount and condition of unstable objects in their collections. Many conservation tasks and techniques involve the use of chemicals, some of which are toxic, and for this reason laboratories are equipped with ventilation systems. At times a conservator may find it necessary to wear a mask and possibly even a respirator when working with particularly harsh chemicals or varnishes. Most of the work requires meticulous attention to detail, a great deal of precision, and manual dexterity.

The rewards of the conservation profession are the satisfaction of preserving artifacts that reflect the diversity of human achievements; being in regular contact with art, artifacts, and structures; enjoying a stimulating work place; and the creative application of expertise to the preservation of artistically and historically significant objects.

OUTLOOK
The U.S. Department of Labor predicts the employment of archivists, curators, and museum technicians (which includes conservators and technicians) will grow about as fast as average through 2010. Competition for these desirable positions, however, will be strong.

Society's developing interest in cultural material of all forms will contribute to art conservation and preservation as a growing field. New specialties have emerged in response to the interest in collections maintenance and preventive care. Conservation, curatorial, and registration responsibilities are intermingling and creating hybrid conservation professional titles, such as collections care, environmental monitoring, and exhibits specialists.

Despite these developments, however, recent changes in federal funding will most likely lead to changes regarding employment and educational opportunities. For example, decreased funds available through the National Endowment for the Arts have eliminated funding formerly available to assist students through unpaid internships. As museums experience a tightening of federal funds, many may choose to decrease the number of paid conservators on staff and instead may rely on a small staff augmented by private conservation companies that can be contracted on a short-term basis as necessary. Private industry and for-profit companies will then continue to grow, while federally funded nonprofit museums may experience a reduction of staff.

FOR MORE INFORMATION

To receive additional information on conservation training, contact

American Institute for Conservation of Historic and Artistic Works
1717 K Street, NW, Suite 200
Washington, DC 20006
Tel: 202-452-9545
Email: info@aic-faic.org
http://aic.stanford.edu

International Institute for Conservation of Historic and Artistic Works
6 Buckingham Street
London WC2N 6BA England
Email: iicon@compuserve.com
http://www.iiconservation.org

For information on internships and other learning opportunities in Canada, contact

Canadian Conservation Institute
1030 Innes Road
Ottawa, ON K1A 0M5 Canada
Tel: 613-998-3721
http://www.cci-icc.gc.ca

COSTUME DESIGNERS

QUICK FACTS

School Subjects
Family and consumer science
Theater/dance

Personal Skills
Artistic
Following instructions

Work Environment
Primarily indoors
One location with some travel

Minimum Education Level
High school diploma

Salary Range
$12,480 to $17,500 to $21,090

Certification or Licensing
None available

Outlook
Little change or more slowly than the average

DOT
346

GOE
01.06.02

NOC
5243

O*NET-SOC
39-3092.00

OVERVIEW

Costume designers plan, create, and maintain clothing and accessories for all characters in a stage, film, television, dance, or opera production. Designers custom fit each character and either create a new garment or alter an existing costume.

HISTORY

Costume design has been an important part of the theater since the early Greek tragedies, when actors generally wore masks and long robes with sleeves. By the time of the Roman Caesars, stage costumes had become very elaborate and colorful.

After the fall of Rome, theater disappeared for some time, but later returned in the form of Easter and Nativity plays. Priests and choirboys wore their usual robes with some simple additions, such as veils and crowns. Plays then moved from the church to the marketplace, and costumes again became important to the production.

During the Renaissance, costumes were designed for the Italian pageants, the French *ballets de coeur,* and the English masques by such famous designers as Torelli, Jean Berain, and Burnacini. From 1760 to 1782, Louis-Rene Boquet designed costumes using wide paniers, forming a kind of elaborate ballet skirt. But by the end of the 18th century, there was a movement toward more classical costumes on the stage.

During the early 19th century, historical costumes became popular, and period details were added to contemporary dress. Toward the end of the 19th century, realism became important, and actors wore the dress of the day, often their own clothes. Because this trend resulted in less work for the costume designers, they turned to musical and opera productions to express their creativity.

In the early 20th century, Diaghilev's Russian Ballet introduced a nonnaturalism in costumes, most notably in the designs of Leon Bakst. This trend gave way to European avant-garde theater, in which costumes became abstract and symbolic.

Since the 1960s, new materials, such as plastics and adhesives, have greatly increased the costume designer's range. Costume design is less likely to conform to trends.

THE JOB

Costume designers generally work as freelancers. After they have been contracted to provide the costumes for a production, they read the script to learn about the theme, location, time period, character types, dialogue, and action. They meet with the director to discuss his or her feelings on the plot, characters, period and style, time frame for the production, and budget.

For a play, designers plan a rough costume plot, which is a list of costume changes by scene for each character. They research the history thoroughly. They plan a preliminary color scheme and sketch the costumes, including details such as gloves, footwear, hose, purses, jewelry, canes, fans, bouquets, and other props. The costume designer or an assistant collects swatches of fabrics and samples of various accessories.

After completing the research, final color sketches are painted or drawn and mounted for presentation. Once the director approves the designs, the costume designer solicits bids from contractors, creates or rents costumes, and shops for fabrics and accessories.

Measurements of all actors are taken. Designers work closely with drapers, sewers, hairstylists, and makeup artists in the costume shop. They supervise fittings and attend all dress rehearsals to make final adjustments and repairs.

Costume designers work in films, television, and videos, aiming to provide the look that will highlight characters' personalities. Aside from working with actors, they may also design and create costumes for performers such as figure skaters, ballroom dance competitors, circus members, theme park characters, rock artists, and others who routinely wear costumes as part of a show.

REQUIREMENTS

High School

Costume designers need at least a high school education. It is helpful to take classes in art, home economics, and theater and to participate in drama clubs or community theater. English, literature, and history classes help students learn how to analyze a play and research the clothing and manner of various historical periods. Marketing and business-related classes will be helpful, as most costume designers work as freelancers. Familiarity with computers can also prove useful, as many designers work with computer-aided design (CAD) programs.

While in high school, consider starting a portfolio of design sketches. Practicing in a sketchbook is a great way to get ideas and designs out on paper and organized for future reference. You can also get design ideas through others; watch theater, television, or movie productions and take note of the characters' dress. Sketch them on your own for practice. Looking through fashion magazines can also give you ideas to sketch.

Postsecondary Training

A college degree is not a requirement, but in this highly competitive field, it gives a sizable advantage. Most costume designers today have a bachelor's degree. Many art schools, especially in New York and Los Angeles, have programs in costume design at both the bachelor's and master's degree level. A liberal arts school with a strong theater program is also a good choice.

Other Requirements

Costume designers need sewing, draping, and patterning skills, as well as training in basic design techniques and figure drawing.

Aside from being artistic, designers must also be able to work with people because many compromises and agreements must be made between the designer and the production's director.

Costume designers must prepare a portfolio of their work, including three or four dozen photographs and sketches from two or three shows. Some theatrical organizations require membership in United Scenic Artists, a union that protects the interests of designers on the job and sets minimum fees. Beginning designers become members by passing an exam. More experienced designers must also submit a portfolio for review.

EXPLORING

If you are interested in costume design, consider joining a theater organization, such as a school drama club or a community theater. School dance troupes or film classes also may offer opportunities to explore costume design.

The Costume Designer's Handbook: A Complete Guide for Amateur and Professional Costume Designers, by Rosemary Ingham and Elizabeth Covey (Heinemann, 1992), is an invaluable resource for beginning or experienced costume designers. The book explains in detail the various steps in the costume design process. You can practice designing on your own, by drawing original sketches or copying designs from television, films, or the stage. Practice sewing and altering costumes from sketches for yourself, friends and family.

EMPLOYERS

Costume designers are employed by production companies that produce works for stage, television, and film. Most employers are located in New York and Los Angeles, although most metropolitan areas have community theater and film production companies that hire designers.

STARTING OUT

Most high schools and colleges have drama clubs and dance groups that need costumes designed and made. Community theaters, too, may offer opportunities to assist in costume production. Regional theaters hire several hundred costume technicians each year for seasons that vary from 28 to 50 weeks.

Many beginning designers enter the field by becoming an assistant to a designer. Established designers welcome newcomers and can be generous mentors.

Finding an Art Scholarship

Regardless of the program you choose, art school can be expensive. But take heart: There are thousands of scholarships that can help you fund your education. The key is knowing where to look for them. First ask your high school art teacher and guidance counselor for any advice or leads. Then in the phone book for professional associations, schools, community groups, and national organizations in your area that support the arts. You should also search for such groups on the Internet, though keep in mind that many smaller groups do not host websites.

Here are possible scholarship leads to start your search.

Professional Groups

American Institute of Architects (http://www.aia.org)

American Society of Interior Designers (http://www.asid.org)

Graphic Arts Technical Foundation (http://www.gain.net)

National Sculpture Society (http://www.nationalsculpture.org)

Stained Glass Association of America (http://www.stainedglass.org)

National Foundations

Liberace Foundation for the Performing and Creative Arts (http://www.liberace.com/liberace/foundation.cfm)

National Art Education Association (http://www.naea-reston.org)

National Endowment for the Arts (http://www.nea.gov)

National Foundation for the Advancement in the Arts (http://www.nfaa.org)

Community Groups

Boys and Girls Club of America (http://www.bgca.org)

National 4-H Headquarters (http://www.national4-hheadquarters.gov)

National PTA Organization (http://www.pta.org)

Rotary International (http://www.rotary.org)

Corporate Sponsors of the Arts

Hallmark Corporate Foundation (http://www.hallmark.com)

Target (http://target.com)

Source: Alleback, Ward. *The Art Scholarship Guide* (http://www.artschools.com)

Some beginning workers start out in costume shops, which usually requires membership in a union. However, nonunion workers may be allowed to work for short-term projects. Some designers begin as *shoppers*, who swatch fabrics, compare prices, and buy yardage, trim, and accessories. Shoppers learn where to find the best materials at reasonable prices and often establish valuable contacts in the field. Other starting positions include milliner's assistant, craft assistant, or assistant to the draper.

Schools with bachelor's and master's programs in costume design may offer internships that can lead to jobs after graduation. Another method of entering costume design is to write to regional theaters directly and send your resume to the theater's managing director.

Before you become a costume designer, you may want to work as a freelance design assistant for a few years to gain helpful experience, a reputation, contacts, and an impressive portfolio.

ADVANCEMENT

Beginning designers must show they are willing to do a variety of tasks. The theater community is small and intricately interconnected, so those who work hard and are flexible with assignments can gain good reputations quickly. Smaller regional theaters tend to hire designers for a full season to work with the same people on one or more productions, so opportunities for movement may be scarce. Eventually, costume designers with experience and talent can work for larger productions, such as films, television, and videos.

EARNINGS

Earnings vary greatly in this business depending on factors such as how many outfits the designer completes, how long they are employed during the year, and the amount of their experience. Although the U.S. Department of Labor does not give salary figures for costume designers, it does report that the related occupational group of tailors, dressmakers, and custom sewers had a median hourly wage of $10.14 in 2000. For full-time work, this hourly wage translates into a yearly income of approximately $21,090. However, those just starting out and working as assistants earned as little as $6 an hour, translating into an annual salary of approximately $12,480.

Costume designers who work on Broadway or for other large stage productions are usually members of the United Scenic Artists union, which sets minimum fees, requires producers to pay into pension and welfare funds, protects the designer's rights, establishes rules for billing, and offers group health and life insurance.

According to the union, an assistant for a Broadway show earns about $775 for the duration of the production. A costume designer for a Broadway musical with a minimum of 36 actors earns around $17,500. For opera and dance companies, salary is usually by costume count.

For feature films and television, costume designers earn daily rates for an eight-hour day or a weekly rate for an unlimited number of hours. Designers sometimes earn royalties on their designs.

Regional theaters usually set individual standard fees, which vary widely, beginning around $200 per week for an assistant. Most of them do not require membership in the union.

Most costume designers work freelance and are paid per costume or show. Costume designers can charge $90–$500 per costume, but some costumes, such as those for figure skaters, can cost thousands of dollars. Freelance costume designers often receive a flat rate for designing costumes for a show. For small and regional theaters, this rate may be in the $400–$500 range; the flat rate for medium and large productions generally starts at around $1,000. Many costume designers must take second part-time or full-time jobs to supplement their income from costume design.

Freelancers are responsible for their own health insurance, life insurance, and pension plans. They do not receive holiday, sick, or vacation pay.

WORK ENVIRONMENT

Costume designers put in long hours at painstaking detail work. It is a demanding profession that requires flexible, artistic, and practical workers. The schedule can be erratic—a busy period followed by weeks of little or no work. Though costumes are often a crucial part of a production's success, designers usually get little recognition compared to the actors and director.

Designers meet a variety of interesting and gifted people. Every play, film, or concert is different and every production situation is unique, so there is rarely a steady routine. Costume designers must play many roles: artist, sewer, researcher, buyer, manager, and negotiator.

OUTLOOK

The U.S. Department of Labor predicts employment for tailors, dressmakers, and skilled sewers to decline through 2010, and costume designers may not fair much better. The health of the entertainment business, especially theater, is very dependent on the overall economy and public attitudes. Theater budgets and government support for the arts in general have come under pressure in recent years and have limited employment prospects for costume designers. Many theaters, especially small and nonprofit theaters, are cutting their budgets or doing smaller shows that require fewer costumes. Additionally, people are less willing to spend money on tickets or go to theaters during economic downturns or times of crisis, such as immediately after the 2001 terrorist attacks on the World Trade Center in New York City. Following these attacks numerous shows closed and many theater-related workers lost their jobs.

Nevertheless, opportunities for costume designers exist. As more cable television networks create original programming, demand for costume design in this area is likely to increase. Costume designers are able to work in an increasing number of locations as new regional theaters and cable television companies operate throughout the United States. As a result, however, designers must be willing to travel.

Competition for designer jobs is stiff and will remain so throughout the next decade. The number of qualified costume designers far exceeds the number of jobs available. This is especially true in smaller cities and regions, where there are fewer theaters.

FOR MORE INFORMATION

This union represents costume designers in film and television. For information on the industry and to view costume sketches in their online gallery, contact or check out the following website:

Costume Designers Guild
4730 Woodman Avenue, Suite 430
Sherman Oaks, CA 91423
Tel: 818-905-1557
Email: cdgia@earthlink.net
http://www.costumedesignersguild.com

This organization provides a list of schools, scholarships, and a journal. College memberships are available with opportunities to network among other members who are professionals in the costume field.

Costume Society of America
55 Edgewater Drive
PO Box 73
Earleville, MD 21919
Tel: 800-272-9447

Email: national.office@costumesocietyamerica.com
http://www.costumesocietyamerica.com

For additional information, contact the following organizations:
National Costumers Association
6914 Upper Trail Circle
Mesa, AZ 85207-0943
Tel: 800-622-1321
http://www.costumers.org

United States Institute for Theater Technology
6443 Ridings Road
Syracuse, NY 13206-1111
Tel: 800-938-7488
Email: info@office.usitt.org
http://www.usitt.org

CREATIVE ARTS THERAPISTS

QUICK FACTS

School Subjects Art Music Theater/dance	**Certification or Licensing** Required by all states
	Outlook About as fast as the average
Personal Skills Artistic Helping/teaching	**DOT** 076
Work Environment Primarily indoors Primarily one location	**GOE** 10.02.02
	NOC 3144
Minimum Education Level Master's degree	**O*NET-SOC** N/A
Salary Range $15,000 to $35,000 to $81,000	

OVERVIEW

Creative arts therapists treat and rehabilitate people with mental, physical, and emotional disabilities. They use the creative processes of music, art, dance/movement, drama, psychodrama, and poetry in their therapy sessions to determine the underlying causes of problems and to help patients achieve therapeutic goals. Creative arts therapists usually specialize in one particular type of therapeutic activity. The specific objectives of the therapeutic activities vary according to the needs of the patient and the setting of the therapy program.

HISTORY

Creative arts therapy programs are fairly recent additions to the health care field. Although many theories of mental and physical therapy have existed for centuries, it has been only in the last 70 years or so that health care professionals have truly realized the healing powers of music, art, dance, and other forms of artistic self-expression.

Art therapy is based on the idea that people who can't discuss their problems with words must have another outlet for self-expression. In the early 1900s, psychiatrists began to look more closely at their patients' artwork, realizing that there could be links between the emotional or psychological illness and the art. Sigmund Freud even did some preliminary research into the artistic expression of his patients.

In the 1930s, art educators discovered that children often expressed their thoughts better with pictures and role playing than they did through verbalization. Children often don't know the words they need to explain how they feel or how to make their needs known to adults. Researchers began to look into art as a way to treat children who were traumatized by abuse, neglect, illness, or other physical or emotional disabilities.

During and after World War II, the Department of Veterans Affairs (VA) developed and organized various art, music, and dance activities for patients in VA hospitals. These activities had a dramatic effect on the physical and mental well-being of the World War II veterans, and creative arts therapists began to help treat and rehabilitate patients in other health care settings.

Because of early breakthroughs with children and veterans, the number of arts therapists has increased greatly over the past few decades, and the field has expanded to include drama, psychodrama, and poetry, in addition to the original areas of music, art, and dance. Today, creative arts therapists work with diverse populations of patients in a wide range of facilities, and they focus on the specific needs of a vast spectrum of disorders and disabilities. Colleges and universities offer degree programs in many types of therapies, and national associations for registering and certifying creative arts therapists work to monitor training programs and to ensure the professional integrity of the therapists working in the various fields.

THE JOB

Similar to dreaming, creative arts therapy taps into the subconscious and gives people a mode of expression in an uncensored environment. This is important because before patients can begin to heal, they must first identify their feelings. Once they recognize their feelings, they can begin to develop an understanding of the relationship between their feelings and their behavior.

The main goal of a creative arts therapist is to improve the client's physical, mental, and emotional health. Before therapists begin any treatment, they meet with a team of other health care professionals. After determining the strength, limitations, and interests of their client, they create a program to promote positive change and growth. The creative arts therapist continues to confer with the other health care workers as the program progresses and alters the program according to the client's progress. How these goals are reached depends on the unique specialty of the therapist in question.

"It's like sitting in the woods waiting for a fawn to come out." That is how Barbara Fish, former Director of Activity Therapy for the Illinois Department of Mental Health and Developmental Disabilities, Chicago Metropolitan and Adolescent Services, describes her experience as she waits patiently for a sexually abused patient to begin to trust her. The patient is extraordinarily frightened because of the traumatic abuse she has suffered. This may be the first time in the patient's life that she is in an environment of acceptance and support. It may take months or even years before the patient begins to trust the therapist, "come out of the woods," and begin to heal.

In some cases, especially when the clients are adolescents, they may have become so detached from their feelings that they can physically act out without consciously knowing the reasons for their behavior. This detachment from their emotions creates a great deal of psychological pain. With the help of a creative arts therapist, clients can begin to communicate their subconscious feelings both verbally and nonverbally. They can express their emotions in a variety of ways without having to name them.

Creative arts therapists work with all age groups: young children, adolescents, adults, and senior citizens. They can work in individual, group, or family sessions. The approach of the therapist, however, depends on the specific needs of the client or group. For example, if an individual is feeling overwhelmed by too many options or stimuli, the therapist may give him or her only a plain piece of paper and a pencil to work with that day.

Fish has three ground rules for her art therapy sessions with disturbed adolescents: respect yourself, respect other people, and respect property. The therapy groups are limited to five patients per group. She begins the session by asking each person in the group how he or she is feeling that day. By carefully listening to their responses, a theme may emerge that will determine the direction of the therapy. For example, if there is recurring anger in their statements, Fish may ask the patients to draw a line down the center of a piece of paper. On one side, she will ask them to draw how anger looks and on the other side how feeling sad looks. Then, once the drawing is complete, she will ask them to compare the two pictures and see that their anger may be masking their feelings of sadness, loneliness, and disappointment. As patients begin to recognize their true feelings, they develop better control of their behavior.

To reach their patients, creative arts therapists can use a variety of mediums, including visual art, music, dance, drama, or poetry or other kinds of creative writing. Creative arts therapists usually specialize in a specific medium, becoming a music therapist, drama therapist, dance therapist, art therapist, or poetry therapist. "In my groups we use poetry and creative writing," Fish explains. "We do all kinds of things to get at what is going on at an unconscious level."

Music therapists use musical lessons and activities to improve a patient's self-confidence and self-awareness, to relieve states of depression, and to improve physical dexterity. For example, a music therapist treating a patient with Alzheimer's might play songs from the patient's past in order to stimulate long- and short-term memory, soothe feelings of agitation, and increase a sense of reality.

Art therapists use art in much the same manner. The art therapist may encourage and teach patients to express their thoughts, feelings, and anxieties via sketching, drawing, painting, or sculpting. Art therapy is especially helpful in revealing patterns of domestic abuse in families. Children involved in such a situation may depict scenes of family life with violent details or portray a certain family member as especially frightening or threatening.

Dance/movement therapists develop and conduct dance/movement sessions to help improve the physical, mental, and emotional health of their patients. Dance and movement therapy is also used as a way of assessing a patient's progress toward reaching therapeutic goals.

There are other types of creative arts therapists as well. *Drama therapists* use role-playing, pantomime (the telling of a story by the use of expressive body or facial movements), puppetry, improvisation, and original scripted dramatization to evaluate and treat patients. *Poetry therapists* and *bibliotherapists* use the written and spoken word to treat patients.

REQUIREMENTS
High School
To become a creative arts therapist, you will need a bachelor's degree, so take a college preparatory curriculum while in high school. You should become as proficient as possible with the methods and tools related to the type of creative arts therapy you wish to pursue. When therapists work with patients they must be able to concentrate completely on the patient rather than on learning how to use tools or techniques. For example, if you want to become involved in music therapy, you need to be familiar with musical instruments as well as music theory. A good starting point for a music therapist is to study piano or guitar.

In addition to courses such as drama, art, music, and English, you should consider taking an introductory class in psychology. Also, a communication class will give you an understanding of the various ways people communicate, both verbally and nonverbally.

Postsecondary Training
To become a creative arts therapist you must earn at least a bachelor's degree, usually in the area in which you wish to specialize. For example, those studying to be art therapists typically have undergraduate degrees in studio art, art education, or psychology with a strong emphasis on art courses as well.

In most cases, however, you will also need a graduate degree before you can gain certification as a professional or advance in your chosen field. Requirements for admission to graduate schools vary by program, so contact the graduate programs you are interested in to find out about their admissions policies. For some fields you may be required to submit a portfolio of your work along with the written application. Professional organizations can be a good source of information regarding high-quality programs. For example, both the American Art Therapy Association and the American Music Therapy Association provide lists of schools that meet their standards for approval. (Contact information for both associations are listed at the end of this article.)

In graduate school, you will conduct in-depth studies of psychology and the arts field in which you are interested. Classes for someone seeking a master's degree in art therapy, for example, may include group psychotherapy, foundation of creativity theory, assessment and treatment planning, and art therapy presentation. In addition to classroom study you will also complete an internship or supervised practicum (that is, work with clients). Depending on your program, you may also need to write a thesis or present a final artistic project before receiving your degree.

Certification or Licensing

Typically, the nationally recognized association or certification board specific to your field of choice offers registration and certification. For example, the Art Therapy Credentials Board (ATCB) offers registration and certification to art therapists, and the American Dance Therapy Association offers registration to dance therapists. In general, requirements for registration include completing an approved therapy program and having a certain amount of experience working with clients. Requirements for higher levels of registration or certification generally involve having additional work experience and passing a written exam.

For a specific example, consider the certification process for an art therapist: An art therapist may receive the designation art therapist registered (ATR) from the ATCB after completing a graduate program and having some experience working with clients. The next level, then, is to become an art therapist registered-board certified (ATR-BC) by passing a written exam. To retain certification status, therapists must complete a certain amount of continuing education.

Many registered creative arts therapists also hold additional licenses in other fields, such as social work, education, mental health, or marriage and family therapy. In some states, creative arts therapists need licensing depending on their place of work. For specific information on licensing in your field, you will need to check with your state's licensing board. Creative arts therapists are also often members of other professional associations, including the American Psychological Association, the American Association of Marriage and Family Therapists, and the American Counseling Association.

Other Requirements

To succeed in this line of work, you should have a strong desire to help others seek positive change in their lives. All types of creative arts therapists must be able to work well with other people—both patients and other health professionals—in the development and implementation of therapy programs. You must have the patience and the stamina to teach and practice therapy with patients for whom progress is often very slow because of their various physical and emotional disorders. A therapist must always keep in mind that even a tiny amount of progress might be extremely significant for some patients and their families. A good sense of humor is also a valuable trait.

EXPLORING

There are many ways to explore the possibility of a career as a creative arts therapist. Write to professional associations for information on therapy careers. Talk with people working in the creative arts therapy field and perhaps arrange to observe a creative arts therapy session. Look for part-time or summer jobs or volunteer at a hospital, clinic, nursing home, or any of a number of health care facilities.

A summer job as an aide at a camp for disabled children, for example, may help provide insight into the nature of creative arts therapy, including both its rewards and demands. Such experience can be very valuable in deciding if you are suited to the inherent frustrations of a therapy career.

EMPLOYERS

Creative arts therapists usually work as members of an interdisciplinary health care team that may include physicians, nurses, social workers, psychiatrists, and psychologists. Although often employed in hospitals, therapists also work in rehabilitation centers, nursing homes, day treatment facilities, shelters for battered women, pain and stress management clinics, substance abuse programs, hospices, and correctional facilities. Others maintain their own private practices. Many creative arts therapists work with children in grammar and high schools, either as therapists or art teachers. Some arts therapists teach or conduct research in the creative arts at colleges and universities.

STARTING OUT

After earning a bachelor's degree in a particular field, you should complete your certification, which may include an internship or assistantship. Unpaid training internships often can lead to a first job in the field. Graduates can use the placement office at their college or university to help them find positions in the creative arts therapy field. Many professional associations also compile lists of job openings to assist their members.

Creative arts therapists who are new to the field might consider doing volunteer work at a nonprofit community organization, correctional facility, or neighborhood association to gain some practical experience. Therapists who want to start their own practice can host group therapy sessions in their homes. Creative arts therapists may also wish to associate with other members of the alternative health care field in order to gain experience and build a client base.

ADVANCEMENT

With more experience, therapists can move into supervisory, administrative, and teaching positions. Often, the supervision of interns can resemble a therapy session. The interns will discuss their feelings and ask questions they may have regarding their work with clients. How did they handle their clients? What were the reactions to what their clients said or did? What could they be doing to help more? The supervising therapist helps the interns become competent creative arts therapists.

Many therapists have represented the profession internationally. Barbara Fish was invited to present her paper, "Art Therapy with Children and Adolescents," at the University of Helsinki. Additionally, Fish spoke in Finland at a three-day workshop exploring the use and effectiveness of arts therapy with children and adolescents. Raising the public and professional awareness of creative arts therapy is an important concern for many therapists.

EARNINGS

A therapist's annual salary depends on experience, level of training, and education. Working on a hospital staff or being self-employed also affects annual income. According to the American Art Therapy Association (AATA), entry-level art therapists earn annual salaries of approximately $25,000. Median annual salaries range from $28,000 to $38,000, and AATA reports that top earnings for salaried administrators ranged from $40,000 and $60,000 annually. Those who have Ph.D.'s and are licensed for private practice can earn between $75 and $90 per hour, according to AATA; however, professional expenses such as insurance and office rental must be paid by those in private practice.

The American Music Therapy Association reported average annual salaries for music therapists as $34,893 in 2000. Salaries varied from that average by region, most by less than $2,000 a year, with the highest average salaries reported in the New England states at $41,600. Salaries reported by its members ranged from $15,000 to $81,000. The average annual earnings for music therapists with more than 20 years of professional experience was $43,306 in 2000.

The annual salary for therapists working for the government is determined by the agency they work for, their level of education and experience, and their responsibilities. An August 2002 job posting by the Delaware Department of Health & Social Services, for example, advertised an opening for a certified creative arts therapist that offered the salary range of $26,094 to $32,618, based on the applicant's qualifications.

Benefits depend on the employer but generally include paid vacation time, health insurance, and paid sick days. Those who are in private practice must provide their own benefits.

WORK ENVIRONMENT

Most creative arts therapists work a typical 40-hour, five-day workweek; at times, however, they may have to work extra hours. The number of patients under a therapist's care depends on the specific employment setting. Although many therapists work in hospitals, they may also be employed in such facilities as clinics, rehabilitation centers, children's homes, schools, and nursing homes. Some therapists maintain service contracts with several facilities. For instance, a therapist might work two days a week at a hospital, one day at a nursing home, and the rest of the week at a rehabilitation center.

Most buildings are pleasant, comfortable, and clean places in which to work. Experienced creative arts therapists might choose to be self-employed, working with patients in their own studios. In such a case, the therapist might work more irregular hours to accommodate patient schedules. Other therapists might maintain a combination of service contract work with one or more facilities in addition to a private caseload of clients referred to them by other health care professionals. Whether therapists work on service contracts with various facilities or maintain private practices, they must deal with all of the business and administrative details and worries that go along with being self-employed.

OUTLOOK

The American Art Therapy Association notes that this is a growing field. Demand for new therapists is created as medical professionals and the general public become aware of the benefits gained through art therapies. Although enrollment in college therapy programs is increasing, new graduates are usually able to find jobs. In cases where an individual is unable to find a full-time position, a therapist might obtain service contracts for part-time work at several facilities.

Job openings in facilities such as nursing homes should continue to increase as the elderly population grows over the next few decades. Advances in medical technology and the recent practice of early discharge from hospitals should also create new opportunities in managed care facilities, chronic pain clinics, and cancer care facilities. The demand for therapists of all types should continue to increase as more people become aware of the need to help disabled patients in creative ways. Some drama therapists and psychodramatists are also finding employment opportunities outside of the usual health care field. Such therapists might conduct therapy sessions at corporate sites to enhance the personal effectiveness and growth of employees.

FOR MORE INFORMATION
For more detailed information about your field of interest, contact the following organizations:

American Art Therapy Association
1202 Allanson Road
Mundelein, IL 60060-3808
Tel: 888-290-0878
Email: info@arttherapy.org
http://www.arttherapy.org

American Dance Therapy Association
2000 Century Plaza, Suite 108
10632 Little Patuxent Parkway
Columbia, MD 21044
Tel: 410-997-4040
Email: info@adta.org
http://www.adta.org

American Music Therapy Association
8455 Colesville Road, Suite 1000
Silver Spring, MD 20910
Tel: 301-589-3300
Email: info@musictherapy.org
http://www.musictherapy.org

American Society of Group Psychotherapy and Psychodrama
301 North Harrison Street, Suite 508
Princeton, NJ 08540
Tel: 609-452-1339
Email: asgpp@asgpp.org
http://www.asgpp.org

National Association for Drama Therapy
733 15th Street, NW, Suite 330
Washington, DC 20005
Tel: 202-966-7409
Email: info1@nadt.org
http://www.nadt.org

National Association for Poetry Therapy
12950 Fifth Street, NW
Pembroke Pines, FL 33028
Tel: 866-844-NAPT
Email: info@poetrytherapy.org
http://www.poetrytherapy.org

For an overview of the various types of art therapy, visit the NCATA website.
National Coalition of Arts Therapies Associations (NCATA)
c/o AMTA
8455 Colesville Road, Suite 1000
Silver Spring, MD 20910
Tel: 201-224-9146
http://www.ncata.com

DESKTOP PUBLISHING SPECIALISTS

QUICK FACTS

School Subjects
Art
Computer science
English

Personal Skills
Artistic
Communication/ideas

Work Environment
Primarily indoors
Primarily one location

Minimum Education Level
Some postsecondary training

Salary Range
$17,980 to $31,200 to
$52,360+

Certification or Licensing
Voluntary

Outlook
Much faster than the
average

DOT
979

GOE
01.06.01

NOC
1423

O*NET-SOC
43-9031.00

OVERVIEW

Desktop publishing specialists prepare reports, brochures, books, cards, and other documents for printing. They create computer files of text, graphics, and page layout. They work with files others have created, or they compose original text and graphics for clients. There are approximately 38,000 desktop publishing specialists working in the printing industry, either as freelancers or for corporations, service bureaus, and advertising agencies.

HISTORY

Johannes Gutenberg's invention of movable type in the 1440s was a major technological advancement. Up until that point, books were produced entirely by hand by monks, every word written in ink on vellum. Although print shops flourished all across Europe with this invention, inspiring the production of millions of books by the 1500s, there was no other major change in the technology of printing until the 1800s. By then, cylinder presses were churning out thousands of sheets per hour, and the Linotype machine allowed for easier, more efficient plate-making. Offset lithography (a method of applying ink from a treated surface onto paper) followed and gained popularity after World War II. Phototypesetting was later developed, involving creating film images of text and pictures to be printed. At the end of the 20th century, computers caused another revolution in the industry. Laser printers now allow for low-cost, high-quality printing, and desktop publishing software is credited with spurring sales and use of personal home computers.

THE JOB
If you've ever used a computer to design and print a page in your high school paper or yearbook, then you've had some experience in desktop publishing. Not so many years ago, the prepress process (the steps to prepare a document for the printing press) involved metal casts, molten lead, light tables, knives, wax, paste, and a number of different professionals from artists to typesetters. With computer technology, these jobs are becoming more consolidated.

Desktop publishing specialists have artistic talents, proofreading skills, sales and marketing abilities, and a great deal of computer knowledge. They work on computers converting and preparing files for printing presses and other media, such as the Internet and CD-ROM. Much of desktop publishing is called prepress, when specialists typeset, or arrange and transform, text and graphics. They use the latest in design software; programs such as PhotoShop, Illustrator, PageMaker (all from software designer Adobe), and QuarkXPress, are the most popular. Some desktop publishing specialists use computer-aided design (CAD) technology, allowing them to create images and effects with a digitizing pen.

Once they've created the file to be printed, desktop publishing specialists either submit it to a commercial printer or print the pieces themselves. Whereas traditional typesetting costs over $20 per page, desktop printing can cost less than a penny a page. Individuals hire the services of desktop publishing specialists for creating and printing invitations, advertising and fundraising brochures, newsletters, flyers, and business cards. Commercial printing involves catalogs, brochures, and reports, while business printing encompasses products used by businesses, such as sales receipts and forms.

Typesetting and page layout work entails selecting font types and sizes, arranging column widths, checking for proper spacing between letters, words, and columns, placing graphics and pictures, and more. Desktop publishing specialists choose from the hundreds of typefaces available, taking the purpose and tone of the text into consideration when selecting from fonts with round shapes or long shapes, thick strokes or thin, serifs or sans serifs.

Editing is also an important duty of a desktop publishing specialist. Articles must be updated, or in some cases rewritten, before they are arranged on a page. As more people use their own desktop publishing programs to create print-ready files, desktop publishing specialists will have to be even more skillful at designing original work and promoting their professional expertise to remain competitive.

Darryl Gabriel and his wife Maree own a desktop publishing service in Australia. The Internet has allowed them to publicize the business globally. They currently serve customers in their local area and across Australia and are hoping to expand more into international Internet marketing. The Gabriels use a computer ("But one is not enough," Darryl says), a laser printer, and a scanner to create business cards, pamphlets, labels, books, and personalized greeting cards. Though they must maintain computer skills, they also have a practical understanding of the equipment. "We keep our prices down by being able to re-ink our cartridges," Darryl says. "This takes a little getting used to at first, but once you get a knack for it, it becomes easier."

Desktop publishing specialists deal with technical issues, such as resolution problems, colors that need to be corrected, and software difficulties. A client may come in with a hand-drawn sketch, a printout of a design, or a file on a diskette, and he or she may want the piece ready to be posted on the Internet or to be published in a high-quality brochure, newspaper, or magazine. Each format presents different issues, and desktop publishing specialists must be familiar with the processes and solutions for each. They may also provide services such as color scanning, laminating, image manipulation, and poster production.

Customer relations are as important as technical skills. Darryl Gabriel encourages desktop publishing specialists to learn how to use equipment and software to their fullest potential. He also advises them to know their customers. "Try and be as helpful as possible to your customers," he says, "so you can provide them with products that they are happy with and that are going to benefit their businesses." He says it's also very important to follow up, calling customers to make sure they're pleased with the work. "If you're able to relate to what the customers want, and if you encourage them to be involved in the initial design process, then they'll be confident they're going to get quality products."

REQUIREMENTS
High School
Classes that will help you develop desktop publishing skills include computer classes and design and art classes. Computer classes should include both hardware and software, since understanding how computers function will help you with troubleshooting and

Top 20 Graduate Schools for an M.F.A.

U.S. News and World Report prepares annual ranking lists for graduate school programs. The following list shows the top ranked schools for a master of fine arts (M.F.A.) degree.

1. Rhode Island School of Design
   http://www.risd.edu

2. School of the Art Institute of Chicago
   http://www.artic.edu/saic

3. Yale University (Conn.)
   http://www.yale.edu/art

4. California Institute of the Arts
   http://www.calarts.edu

5. Cranbrook Academy of Art (Mich.)
   http://www.cranbrook.edu/art

6. New York State College of Ceramics at Alfred University
   http://nyscc.alfred.edu

7. Art Center College of Design (Calif.)
   http://www.artcenter.edu

8. University of California at Los Angeles
   http://www.arts.ucla.edu

9. Virginia Commonwealth University
   http://www.vcu.edu/graduate

10. Carnegie Mellon University (Pa.)
    http://www.cmu.edu/cfa

(continues)

Top 20 Graduate Schools for an M.F.A.

(continued)

11. School of Visual Arts (N.Y.)
    http://www.schoolofvisualarts.edu

12. University of Iowa
    http://www.uiowa.edu/~art

13. Arizona State University
    http://www.asu.edu/graduate

14. California College of Arts and Crafts
    http://www.ccac-art.edu

15. Indiana University at Bloomington
    http://www.iub.edu

16. Maryland Institute College of Art
    http://www.mica.edu

17. Pratt Institute (N.Y.)
    http://www.pratt.edu

18. College of Imaging Arts and Sciences at Rochester Institute
    of Technology (N.Y.)
    http://www.rit.edu/~660www

19. San Francisco Art Institute
    http://www.sfai.edu

20. University of Wisconsin at Madison
    http://www.education.wisc.edu/art

Source: *U.S. News & World Report* (Ranked in 2003)

knowing a computer's limits. Through photography classes you can learn about composition, color, and design elements. Typing, drafting, and print shop classes, if available, will also provide you with the opportunity to gain some indispensable skills. Working on the school newspaper or yearbook will train you on desktop publishing skills as well, including page layout, typesetting, composition, and working under a deadline.

Postsecondary Training

Although a college degree is not a prerequisite, many desktop publishing specialists have at least a bachelor's degree. Areas of study range anywhere from English to graphic design. Some two-year colleges and technical institutes offer programs in desktop publishing or related fields. A growing number of schools offer programs in technical and visual communications, which may include classes in desktop publishing, layout and design, and computer graphics. Four-year colleges also offer courses in technical communications and graphic design. You can enroll in classes related to desktop publishing through extended education programs offered through universities and colleges. These classes, often taught by professionals in the industry, cover basic desktop publishing techniques and advanced lessons on Adobe Photoshop or QuarkXPress.

A number of professional organizations and schools offer scholarship and grant opportunities. The Graphic Arts Education and Research Foundation and the Research and Engineering Council of the Graphic Arts Industry can provide information on scholarship opportunities and research grants. Other organizations that offer financial awards and information on scholarship opportunities include the Society for Technical Communication, the International Prepress Association, the Printing Industries of America, and the Graphic Arts Technical Foundation.

Certification or Licensing

Certification is not mandatory; currently there is only one certification program offered in desktop publishing. The Association of Graphic Communications has an Electronic Publishing Certificate designed to set industry standards and measure the competency levels of desktop publishing specialists. The examination is divided into a written portion and a hands-on portion. During the practical exam, candidates receive files on a disk and must manipulate images and text, make color corrections, and perform whatever tasks are necessary to create the final product. Applicants are expected to be knowledgeable in print production, color separation, typography and font management, computer hardware and software, image manipulation, page layout, scanning and color correcting, prepress and preflighting, and output device capabilities.

Other Requirements

Desktop publishing specialists are detail-oriented, possess problem-solving skills, and have a sense of design and artistic skills. "People tell me I have a flair for graphic design and mixing the right color with the right graphics," Darryl Gabriel says.

A good eye and patience are critical, as well as endurance to see projects through to the finish. You should have an aptitude for computers, the ability to type quickly and accurately, and a natural curiosity. In addition, a calm temperament comes in handy when working under pressure and constant deadlines. You should be flexible and be able to handle more than one project at a time.

EXPLORING

Experimenting with your home computer, or a computer at school or the library, will give you a good idea as to whether desktop publishing is for you. Play around with various graphic design and page layout programs. If you subscribe to an Internet service, take advantage of any free Web space available to you and design your own home page. Join computer clubs and volunteer to produce newsletters and flyers for school or community clubs. Volunteering is an excellent way to try new software and techniques as well as gain experience troubleshooting and creating final products. Part-time or summer employment with printing shops and companies that have in-house publishing or printing departments are other great ways to gain experience and make valuable contacts.

EMPLOYERS

Desktop publishing specialists work for individuals and small business owners, such as publishing houses, advertising agencies, graphic design agencies, and printing shops. Some large companies also contract with desktop publishing services rather than hire full-time designers. Government agencies hire desktop publishing specialists for the large number of documents they publish. The U.S. Government Printing Office has a Digital Information Technology Support Group that provides desktop and electronic publishing services to federal agencies.

Desktop publishing specialists deal directly with their clients, but in some cases they may be subcontracting work from printers, designers, and other desktop publishing specialists. They may also work as consultants, working with printing professionals to help solve particular design problems.

STARTING OUT

To start your own business, you must have a great deal of experience with design and page layout and a careful understanding of the computer design programs you'll be using. Before starting out on your own, you may want to gain experience as a full-time staff member of a large business. Most desktop publishing specialists enter the field through the production side or the editorial side of the industry. Those with training as a designer or artist can easily master the finer techniques of production. Printing houses and design agencies are places to check for production artist opportunities. Publishing companies often hire desktop publishing specialists to work in-house or as freelance employees. Working within the industry, you can make connections and build up a clientele.

You can also start out by investing in computer hardware and software, and volunteering your services. By designing logos, letterhead, and restaurant menus, for example, your work will gain quick recognition, and word of your services will spread.

ADVANCEMENT

The growth of Darryl and Maree Gabriel's business is requiring that they invest in another computer and printer. "We want to expand," Darryl says, "and develop with technology by venturing into Internet marketing and development. We also intend to be a thorn in the side of the larger commercial printing businesses in town."

In addition to taking on more print projects, desktop publishing specialists can expand their business into Web design and page layout for Internet magazines.

EARNINGS

There is limited salary information available for desktop publishing specialists, most likely because the job duties of desktop publishing specialists can vary and often overlap with other jobs. The average wage of desktop publishing specialists in the prepress department generally ranges from $15 to $50 an hour. Entry-level desktop publishing specialists with little or no experience generally earn minimum wage. Freelancers can earn from $15 to $100 an hour.

According to the U.S. Department of Labor, median annual earnings of desktop publishing specialists were $31,200 in 2001. Salaries ranged from less than $17,980 to more than $52,360 a year. Wage rates vary depending on experience, training, region, and size of the company.

WORK ENVIRONMENT

Desktop publishing specialists spend most of their time working in front of a computer, whether editing text, or laying out pages. They need to be able to work with other prepress operators, and deal with clients. Hours may vary depending on project deadlines at hand. Some projects may take just a day to complete, while others may take weeks or months. Projects range from designing a logo for letterhead, to preparing a catalog for the printer, to working on a file for a company's website.

OUTLOOK

According to the U.S. Department of Labor, employment for desktop publishing specialists is projected to grow much faster than the average through the next decade, even though overall employment in the printing industry is expected to decline slightly. This is due in part because electronic processes are replacing the manual processes performed by paste-up workers, photoengravers, camera operators, film strippers, and platemakers.

As technology advances, the ability to create and publish documents will become easier and faster, thus influencing more businesses to produce printed materials. Desktop publishing specialists will be needed to satisfy typesetting, page layout, design, and editorial demands. With new equipment, commercial printing shops will be able to shorten the turnaround time on projects and in turn can increase business and accept more jobs. For instance, digital printing presses allow printing shops to print directly to the digital press rather than printing to a piece of film, and then printing from the film to the press. Digital printing presses eliminate an entire step and should appeal to companies who need jobs completed quickly.

QuarkXPress, Adobe PageMaker, Macromedia FreeHand, Adobe Illustrator, and Adobe Photoshop are some programs often used in desktop publishing. Specialists with experience in these and other software will be in demand.

FOR MORE INFORMATION

For information on the Electronic Publishing Certificate, contact
Association of Graphic Communications
330 Seventh Avenue, 9th Floor
New York, NY 10001-5010
Tel: 212-279-2100
Email: info@agcomm.org
http://www.agcomm.org

This organization is a source of financial support for education and research projects designed to promote careers in graphic communications. For more information, contact
Graphic Arts Education and Research Foundation
1899 Preston White Drive
Reston, VA 22091-4367
Tel: 866-381-9839
Email: gaerf@npes.org
http://www.gaerf.org

For career brochures and other information about grants, scholarships, and educational programs, contact the following organizations:
Graphic Arts Technical Foundation
200 Deer Run Road
Sewickley, PA 15143
Tel: 412-741-6860
Email: info@gatf.org
http://www.gain.net

Printing Industries of America
100 Daingerfield Road
Alexandria, VA 22314
Tel: 703-519-8100
Email: gain@printing.org
http://www.gain.net

Research and Engineering Council of the Graphic Arts Industry, Inc.
PO Box 1086
White Stone, VA 22578-1086
Tel: 804-436-9922
Email: recouncil@rivnet.net
http://www.recouncil.org

Society for Technical Communication
901 North Stuart Street, Suite 904
Arlington, VA 22203-1822
Tel: 703-522-4114
Email: stc@stc.org
http://www.stc.org

EDUCATION DIRECTORS AND MUSEUM TEACHERS

QUICK FACTS

School Subjects
English
History
Speech

Personal Skills
Communication/ideas
Helping/teaching

Work Environment
Primarily indoors
One location with some
travel

Minimum Education Level
Bachelor's degree

Salary Range
$18,000 to $32,000 to
$60,000+

Certification or Licensing
None available

Outlook
Little change or more slowly
than the average

DOT
099

GOE
11.07.03

NOC
5124

O*NET-SOC
N/A

OVERVIEW

People visit museums, zoos, and botanical gardens to learn and observe. *Education directors,* or *curators of education,* are responsible for helping these people enrich their visits. Education directors plan, develop, and administer educational programs at museums and other similar institutions. They plan tours, lectures, and classes for individuals, school groups, and special interest groups.

Museum teachers also provide information, share insight, and offer explanations of exhibits. Direct communication ranges from informal explanations at staff previews of a new exhibit, to addressing corporate donor groups, to aiding groups of schoolchildren. Museum teachers may write exhibit labels, prepare catalogs, or contribute to multimedia installations. Museum teachers also teach by demon-stration, by conducting studio classes, or by leading field trips.

HISTORY

In early times, churches displayed art and furnishings for wor-shipers to view. The early equivalents of education directors were the priests or laypeople who developed expertise in the collections. As public museums grew, so did the need for education directors. When Europeans began to encourage the idea of universal educa-tion, museums began to draw in uneducated visitors who needed to be taught about their collections.

Similarly, zoos and arboretums, which were originally organized to exhibit their animals and plants to experts, began to teach others about their collections. Education directors were hired to plan pro-grams and tours for visitors.

In the United States, early museums displayed objects relating to colonial history. Some were in former homes of wealthy colonists and others were established at the first U.S. universities and colleges. In these early museums *curators* or *archivists* maintained the collec-tions and also explained the collections to visitors. As the collections grew and more visitors and groups of visitors came, education direc-tors were hired by the curators to coordinate educational programs.

THE JOB

Education directors carry out the educational goals of a museum, zoo, botanical garden, or other similar institution. The educational goals of most of these institutions include nurturing curiosity and answering questions of visitors, regardless of age or background. Education directors work with administrators and museum or zoo boards to determine the scope of their educational programs. Large museums may offer full schedules of classes and tours, while smaller ones may only provide tours or lectures at the request of a school or other group.

Education directors plan schedules of courses to be offered through the zoo or museum. They may hire lecturers from local colleges or uni-versities as well as regular educational staff members to lead tours or discussion groups. Education directors are usually responsible for training the staff members and may also work with professionals or university faculty to determine the content of a particular lecture, class, or series of lectures. They prepare course outlines and establish the credentials necessary for those who will teach the courses.

In smaller institutions the education director may do much of the teaching, lecturing, or tour leading. In zoos, the education director can arrange for small children to watch cows being milked or for the children to pet or feed smaller animals such as goats. In museums, the education director's job often depends on the museum's collection. In art museums, visitors are often older than in natural history museums, and the education director may plan programs that allow older children to explore parts of the collection at their own pace.

Education directors often promote their programs on local radio or television or in newspapers. They may speak to community or school groups about the museum's education department and encourage the groups to attend. Sometimes, education directors deliver lectures or offer classes away from the museum or zoo.

The education director is responsible for the budget for all educational programs. Directors prepare budgets and supervise the records of income and spending. Often, schools or other groups are charged lower rates for tours or classes at museums or zoos. Education directors work with resource coordinators to establish budgets for resource materials. These need to be updated regularly in most institutions. Even in natural history museums, where the collections may change less than in other museums, slide collections may need to be updated or presentations altered if new research has led to different interpretations of the objects. The education director may also prepare grant proposals or help with fund-raising efforts for the museum's educational program. Once a grant has been received or a large gift has been offered to the education department, the education director plans for the best use of the funds within the department.

Education directors often work with exhibit designers to help create displays that are most effective for visitors. They may also work with illustrators to produce illustrations or signs that enhance exhibits. Zoos, for example, often display maps near the animals to show their countries of origin.

Education directors train their staff members as well as volunteers to work with individual visitors and groups. Some volunteers are trained to assist in presentations or to help large groups on tours. It is the responsibility of the education director to see that the educational program is helpful and interesting to all of the people who visit the museum or zoo.

Education directors plan special activities that vary widely depending on the institution. Film programs, field trips, lectures, and full-day school programs may be offered weekly, monthly, or annually. Some zoos and arboretums have ongoing tours offered daily, while others may only give tours for prearranged groups.

In larger museums, education directors may have a staff of educators. Museum teachers may serve as *docents* or *interpreters* who interact directly with visitors. Docents also give prepared talks or provide information in a loosely structured format, asking and answering questions informally. Good content knowledge is required, as well as sensitivity to visitor group composition and the ability to convey information to different types of audiences. Scholarly researchers, for example, have a different knowledge base and attention span than children.

Other museum teachers, such as *storytellers,* may be self-employed people who contract with a museum to provide special programs a few times a year. Many teachers are volunteers or part-time workers.

Education specialists are experts in a particular field, which may be education itself or an area in which the museum has large holdings, such as Asian textiles, North American fossils, or pre-Columbian pottery. Education specialists divide their time between planning programs and direct teaching. They may supervise other teachers, conduct field trips, or teach classes in local schools as part of joint programs of study between museums and schools.

Educational resource coordinators are responsible for the collection of education materials used in the educational programs. These may include slides, posters, videotapes, books, or materials for special projects. Educational resource coordinators prepare, buy, catalog, and maintain all of the materials used by the education department. They sometimes have a lending library of films, videos, books, or slides that people may borrow. Resource coordinators keep track of the circulation of materials. They may also lead tours or workshops for educators or school personnel to teach them about the collection of the museum or zoo and to keep them apprised of new materials the educators may use in their tours or in their own classrooms. Resource coordinators and directors attend conventions and teachers' meetings to promote their institution's educational program and to encourage participation in their classes or tours.

REQUIREMENTS
High School

As an education director or a museum professional, you will need a diverse educational background to perform well in your job. At the high school level, you should follow a well rounded college preparatory curriculum, including courses in creative writing, literature, history of world civilizations, American history, science, foreign language, art, and speech. These courses will give you general background knowledge you can use to interpret collections, write letters to school principals, design curriculum materials, develop multicultural education, and lecture to public audiences. You should also develop strong math and computer skills. You will use these skills when preparing budgets and calculating the number of visitors that can fit in an exhibit space, and when writing grants or asking corporations and federal agencies for program funding.

Postsecondary Training

In order to be an education director, you must have a bachelor's degree. Many museums, zoos, and botanical gardens also require a master's degree. The largest zoos and museums prefer to hire education directors who have doctoral degrees.

Some colleges in the United States offer programs of instruction leading to a degree in museology (the study of museums). Most education directors work in museums that specialize in art, history, or science. These directors often have degrees in fields related to the museum's specialty. Those who work in zoos usually have studied biology or zoology or have worked closely with animals. Education directors who work in more specialized museums often have studied such specialized fields as early American art, woodcarvings, or the history of circuses. As an education director, you must have a good working knowledge of the animals, plants, or artifacts in the collection.

Museum teachers and education specialists must also have a bachelor's degree in an academic discipline or in education.

Other Requirements

Excellent communication skills are essential in this field. Your primary responsibility will be to interpret and present collections to a broad public audience. The ability to motivate and teach many individuals from a wide range of cultural backgrounds, age groups, and educational levels is necessary. You should also be organized and flexible. You will be at a great advantage if you know a foreign language, sign language, and/or CPR.

EXPLORING

If you are interested in becoming an education director or museum teacher, you can easily obtain volunteer experience: Most zoos and museums need and have student volunteers. You can request a position in the education department, where you may help with elementary school tours, organize files or audiovisual materials, or assist a lecturer in a class.

College-preparatory courses are important if you are interested in this field. Apply to colleges or universities with strong liberal arts programs. Courses in art, history, science, and education are recommended if you want to work at museums. Courses in biology, zoology, botany, and education are beneficial if you wish to work at zoos or botanical gardens. Some larger zoos and museums offer internships to college students who are interested in the field.

The American Association of Museums publishes an annual museum directory, a monthly newsletter, and a bimonthly magazine. It also publishes *Museum Careers: A Variety of Vocations*. This report is helpful for anyone considering a career in the museum field. *Introduction to Museum Work*, published by the American Association for State and Local History, discusses the educational programs at various museums. In addition, the American Association of Botanical Gardens and Arboreta publishes a directory of over 500 internships offered through public gardens each year.

EMPLOYERS

Institutions with a primary goal to educate the public about their collections hire education directors. Depending on each institution's monetary resources, most museums (large and small), zoos, botanical gardens, and occasionally historical societies employ education directors to ensure public access to their collections. Institutions with small operating budgets or limited visitor access sometimes hire part-time educators or rely on volunteer support.

STARTING OUT

Your first job in a museum or zoo will likely be as a teacher or resource coordinator working in the education department. With a few years of experience and improved understanding of the institution's collection, you may enter competition for promotion to education director. Many people in the field transfer from one museum to another or from one zoo to another, in order to be promoted to the position of education director.

ADVANCEMENT

Once in the education department, most people learn much of their work on the job. Experience in working with different people and groups becomes very important. Education directors must continually improve their understanding of their own institution's collection so that they can present it to school and other groups in the best way possible. Some education directors work for the federal government in specific subject areas such as aeronautics, philately (stamp collecting), or branches of science and technology. They must be proficient in these fields as well as in education.

Museum teachers with experience and appropriate academic or teaching credentials may become content specialists in one area of the museum's collection or may become a director of education, assuming responsibility for the departmental budget, educational policies and community outreach programs, and training and supervision of numerous staff and volunteer workers. Advancement may depend on acquisition of an advanced degree in education or in an academic field. Because professional supervisory positions are few in comparison to the large corps of teachers, museum teachers desiring advancement may need to look beyond their home institution, perhaps accepting a smaller salary at a smaller museum in return for a supervisory title.

Teachers who leave museum work are well positioned to seek employment elsewhere in the nonprofit sector, especially with grant-funding agencies involved in community-based programs. In the for-profit sector, excellent communication skills and the ability to express an institution's philosophy both in writing and in interviews are skills valued by the public relations departments of corporations.

EARNINGS

Salaries for education directors vary widely depending on the size, type, and location of the institution, as well as the education and experience of the director. The average beginning salary for education directors with bachelor's degrees plus one year of related experience or equivalent advanced education is $30,000. Those with master's degrees may earn starting salaries of $35,000 to $45,000. Salaries can range from as little as $6,000 for a part-time position at a small museum to $60,000 at a large institution. Salary.com reports that a typical education manager working in the United States is expected to earn a median base salary of $52,996. According to Wall

Street Journal's Career Journal, the 2001 median annual salary for an education director at a nonprofit institution was $59,817.

Educational assistants and museum teachers can expect to earn from $18,000 to $22,000 to start. Those with experience earn from $25,000 to $32,000.

Fringe benefits, including medical and dental insurance, paid vacations and sick leave, and retirement plans, vary according to each employer's policies.

WORK ENVIRONMENT

Most people who choose to be education directors like to be in museums, botanical gardens, or zoos. They also enjoy teaching, planning activities, organizing projects, and carrying a great deal of responsibility. Those in zoos usually enjoy animals and like being outdoors. Those in museums like the quiet of a natural history museum or the energy and life of a science museum aimed at children. Education directors should enjoy being in an academic environment where they work closely with scholars, researchers, and scientists.

Education directors in larger institutions usually have their own offices where they do planning and other administrative work, but they spend the majority of their time in other parts of the museum and at other locations where they lead education programs.

Most museum teachers have a base of operation in the museum but may not have a private office, since the bulk of their work is carried out in exhibit areas, in resource centers or study rooms within the museum, in classrooms outside of the museum, or in the field. Permanent staff work a normal workweek, with occasional weekend or evening assignments.

Museum teaching varies from day to day and offers innovative teachers a chance to devise different programs. However, museum teaching is different from conventional classroom teaching where educators have the benefit of more time to convey ideas and facts.

OUTLOOK

The employment outlook for education directors and museum teachers is expected to increase more slowly than average through the next decade, according to the U.S. Department of Labor. Budget cutbacks have affected many museums and other cultural institutions, which have in turn reduced the size of their education departments. Museums in the United States have seen significant reduction in the number of visitors, which is directly related to the slowdown in the travel industry.

Many educators with specialties in sciences, the arts, or zoology are interested in becoming education directors at museums and zoos. Competition is especially intense for positions in large cities and those with more prestigious reputations. Some smaller museums and botanical gardens may cut out their education director position altogether until the economic climate improves, or they may get by with part-time education directors.

FOR MORE INFORMATION

For information about publications, meetings, seminars, and workshops, contact

American Association for State and Local History
1717 Church Street
Nashville, TN 37203-2991
Tel: 615-320-3203
Email: history@aaslh.org
http://www.aaslh.org

For a directory of internships offered through public gardens, contact

American Association of Botanical Gardens and Arboreta
100 West 10th Street, Suite 614
Wilmington, DE 19801
Tel: 302-655-7100
Email: membership@aabga.org
http://www.aabga.org

For a directory of museums and other information, contact

American Association of Museums
1575 Eye Street, NW, Suite 400
Washington, DC 20005
Tel: 202-289-1818
http://www.aam-us.org

EXHIBIT DESIGNERS

QUICK FACTS

School Subjects
Art
English
History
Mathematics

Personal Skills
Communication/ideas
Helping/teaching

Work Environment
Primarily indoors
One location with some travel

Minimum Education Level
Some postsecondary training

Salary Range
$16,250 to $33,460 to $59,350+

Certification or Licensing
None available

Outlook
Faster than the average

DOT
142

GOE
01.02.03

NOC
5243

O*NET-SOC
27-1027.00, 27-1027.02

OVERVIEW

Exhibit designers plan, develop, and produce physical displays for exhibitions at museums and similar institutions. Designers work closely with museum directors, educators, curators, and conservators to create educational exhibits that focus on portions of the museum's collection while maintaining safe environmental conditions for the objects on display. Exhibit designers prepare both temporary and permanent exhibitions for a broad range of museum audiences. There are approximately 12,000 set and exhibit designers working in the United States.

HISTORY

The very first museum prototypes housed the "muses" of books and documents. Museums evolved from these ancient libraries to storage areas for private collections. Eventually, ambitious private collectors began to organize the objects in their collections, first by type (for instance, placing all baskets together), and then by the manufacturing culture. Private collections became notable if they contained objects that no other collection contained. For as long as unique objects have been cherished, the display of objects has been a necessary practice for satisfying natural human curiosity.

Charles Willson Peale was responsible for opening the first natural history museum intended for public use. As Peale performed all the duties necessary to run his home-based museum, he may also be credited with developing the first exhibit designs in the United States. He exhibited his specimens in natural settings (comparable to modern-day dioramas) in order to present visitors with contextual information about his collections. As curious visitors began to explore his museum, he realized the need to protect his specimens from environmental damage. He placed the more valuable items in cabinets to protect them from careless hands and reduce the effects of everyday wear and tear.

Peale's home museum grew to become the Philadelphia Museum and with its development came techniques and theories about exhibiting art and cultural artifacts that remain useful today.

THE JOB

Exhibit designers play a key role in helping museums and similar institutions achieve their educational goals. Museums are responsible for providing public access and information about their collections to visitors and scholars. They accomplish their mission by presenting exhibits that display objects and contain contextual information. Because museum visits are interactive experiences, exhibit designers have a responsibility to provide the visiting public with provocative exhibitions that contain visual, emotional, and intellectual components. To achieve this transfer of information, designers must create a "conversation" between exhibits and observers.

The decision to construct a new exhibit is made in collaboration with museum curators, educators, conservators, exhibit designers, and the museum director. After a budget has been set, exhibit designers must meet regularly with curators, educators, and conservators throughout the exhibit planning stages. The purpose of each exhibit production is educational, and the exhibit team plans each exhibition so that it tells a story. A successful exhibit brings meaning to the objects on display through the use of informative labels, the logical placement of objects, and the construction of display areas that help to place the objects in proper context.

Planning, designing, and producing a new exhibit is a costly as well as a mentally and emotionally challenging project. Exhibit designers must work creatively during the planning and design stages while remaining flexible in their ideas for the exhibition. On many occasions, designers must compromise artistic integrity for the sake of object safety and educational quality. During exhibit installation, designers work closely with the production team, which consists of other designers, technicians, electricians, and carpenters. Lead designers oversee the exhibit installation and attend to last-minute preparations. Most permanent exhibits are planned four years in advance while most temporary exhibits are allowed between six to 18 months for production.

Exhibit designers have additional responsibilities that include researching exhibit topics and new exhibit theories. Designers must also attend conventions of professional associations and contribute to the advancement of their field by writing scholarly articles about new display techniques.

REQUIREMENTS
High School

Exhibit designers, like the majority of museum professionals, need diverse educational backgrounds to perform well in their jobs. In addition, designers must develop their creative and artistic skills and master mathematics courses. At the high school level, you should take courses in English, history, the sciences, art, and foreign language. These courses will give you general background knowledge you can use to define educational components of exhibitions. Solid geometry, algebra, advanced math, and physics are essential courses for future designers. Exhibit plans must be drawn to scale (often using the metric system) and the measurements must be precise. Designers must also work within a budget, and these courses are necessary for developing good mathematical skills. Computer skills are equally necessary as many designers use computer-aided drafting when planning exhibits. Finally, courses in studio art and drawing introduce you to the hands-on nature of exhibit work.

Postsecondary Training

Some postsecondary training, including college-level math, art, and design courses, is necessary, but most museums expect candidates for the position of exhibit designer to hold a bachelor's degree. Designers are at a greater advantage to be hired by a museum or similar institution if they specialize in a design-related subject and continue further study in the museum's specialty, such as art, history, or science.

Those who desire a director position in a museum's design department should consider acquiring an advanced degree.

Other Requirements

Excellent communication skills are essential. Exhibit designers must be able to clearly express their ideas to both museum staff members who collaborate on exhibit projects and to visitors through the display medium. Designing exhibits is mentally challenging and can be physically demanding. Exhibit designers should be artistic, creative, and knowledgeable about preparing safe display environments that accommodate valuable and fragile objects.

EXPLORING

The best way to learn more about exhibit design is to consult with a professional in the field. Contact your local museum, historical society, or related institution to interview and possibly observe the designer at work. Remain informed of the many new challenges and theories that influence an exhibit designer's work. Joining a professional association, reading industry publications such as the American Association of Museum's *Museum News* and *Aviso*, or volunteering in a museum or art gallery are all excellent ways to explore this career.

Experience with design in other settings can also contribute to developing the skills needed by exhibit designers. You should consider taking studio classes from a local art guild, offer to design school bulletin boards, or design stage sets for the school drama club or local theater company.

EMPLOYERS

Museums and private companies that display collections hire exhibit designers. Historical societies, state and federal agencies with archives, and libraries also employ exhibit designers because of their specialized skills in developing thoughtful displays while considering object safety. Exhibit designers may also find work with private design firms as well as exhibition companies that create and distribute both temporary and permanent exhibits throughout the world.

STARTING OUT

Students who wish to become exhibit designers should supplement their design courses with an internship in a museum or a related institution. Some museums offer full- or part-time positions to qualified candidates when they complete their internship hours. Newsletters such as *Aviso,* which is published monthly, contain classified advertisements for available museum positions. Contacting other professional associations for job listings is also an acceptable method of starting out. Museum positions are highly competitive, and a proven history of experience is invaluable. Keep a portfolio of your design examples to show to potential employers.

ADVANCEMENT

Experienced exhibit designers with appropriate academic credentials and a history of creating and producing educational as well as visitor-friendly displays are well situated to move into supervisory positions with greater responsibility and design freedom. Exhibit designers may choose to acquire advanced degrees in specialties such as architecture or graphic design in order to achieve the director of exhibitions position. Appropriately educated exhibit designers wishing to move into another area of the museum field may learn to assist conservators, become museum educators, collections managers, curators, or registrars. Exhibit designers who leave museum work are well positioned to seek employment in private design firms.

EARNINGS

Salaries for exhibit designers vary widely depending on the size, type, and location of the institution, as well as the education, expertise, and achievements of the designer. A recent survey conducted by the Association of Art Museum Directors reported that the average salary of a chief exhibit preparer is roughly $33,000. The average salary of an exhibit designer ranges from $36,000 to $53,000. Some larger or better funded museums, historical societies, and related institutions pay significantly more, while others may hire on a contractual basis for a predetermined design and installation fee.

The U.S. Department of Labor reports that median annual earnings for set and exhibit designers were $33,460 in 2001. Salaries ranged from less than $16,250 to more than $59,350.

Fringe benefits, including medical and dental insurance, paid vacations and sick leave, and retirement plans, vary according to each employer's policies.

WORK ENVIRONMENT

Exhibit designers typically work 40 hours per week. Continual challenges and strict deadlines make an exhibit designer's work both creative and demanding. Flexibility in working hours may be a requirement of employment as exhibition installment frequently occurs after museum hours when visitors are not present.

Exhibit designers usually have an office or studio in a private area of the museum, but often must work on the exhibit floors during design planning, installation, and tear down periods. Designers must collaborate with curators, museum educators, and conservators throughout the exhibit planning stages to ensure the educational integrity of the exhibition as well as the safety of the objects.

The rewards for designing in a museum environment include a stimulating workplace where the design medium changes continually, the creative application of design expertise, and the satisfaction of educating visitors through the display of artistically and historically significant objects.

OUTLOOK

The *Occupational Outlook Handbook* reports that the employment rate of all designers will grow faster than the average through the next decade, but there is strong competition for museum jobs, which will go to those with many years of experience. Employment of museum technicians is expected to grow as fast as the average through the next decade. As museums continue to address budget difficulties, many may choose to contract with independent exhibition and design companies when there is the need to install a new exhibit instead of retaining a staff of in-house designers. Private industry and for-profit companies have continued to grow while nonprofit museums and similar institutions may be experiencing a reduction of staff or limited hiring of new employees.

FOR MORE INFORMATION

For information on museum careers, education, and internships, contact
American Association of Museums
1575 Eye Street, NW, Suite 400
Washington, DC 20005
Tel: 202-289-1818
http://www.aam-us.org

For publications and recent news about art museums, contact
Association of Art Museum Directors
41 East 65th Street
New York, NY 10021
Phone: 212-249-4423
http://www.aamd.org

The following organization has workshops, salary information, job listings, and a quarterly journal. For information, contact
New England Museum Association
Boston National Historic Park
Charlestown Navy Yard
Boston, MA 02129
Tel: 617-242-2283
http://www.nemanet.org

FASHION DESIGNERS

QUICK FACTS

School Subjects
Art
Family and consumer
science

Personal Skills
Artistic
Communication/ideas

Work Environment
Primarily indoors
One location with some
travel

Minimum Education Level
Some postsecondary
training

Salary Range
$24,710 to $48,530 to
$150,000+

Certification or Licensing
None available

Outlook
Faster than the average

DOT
141

GOE
01.02.03

NOC
5243

O*NET-SOC
27-1022.00

OVERVIEW

Fashion designers create or adapt original designs for clothing for men, women, and children. Most specialize in one particular type of clothing, such as women's dresses or men's suits. Most designers work for textile, apparel, and pattern manufacturers. Some designers are self-employed and develop a clientele of individual customers or manufacturers. Others work for fashion salons, high-fashion department stores, and specialty shops. A few work in the entertainment industry, designing costumes. There are approximately 16,000 fashion designers employed in the United States.

HISTORY

Originally, people wore garments to help them maintain body temperature rather than for style. Clothing usually was handmade at home. Dress design became a profession around the 1600s. Before the invention of the sewing machine in 1846 by Elias Howe, all garments were made by hand. One of the first designers was Rose Bertin, a French milliner who dressed Marie Antoinette and influenced women's fashions during the French Revolution.

Women dominated dress design until 1858, when Charles Frederick Worth, an English tailor and couturier of Empress Eugenie, consort of Napoleon III, opened a salon, or fashion house, in Paris. There, he produced designs for actresses and other wealthy clients, the only individuals with enough time and money to have clothing created specifically for them. Worth was the first designer to make garments from fabrics he had selected; until that time, dressmakers had used fabrics provided by patrons. Worth also was the first designer to display his creations on live models. Today, French designers continue to dominate the field. However, the U.S. garment industry has assumed a position of leadership in clothing design and production in the last 40 years, and London and Milan also have become important fashion centers.

THE JOB

Fashion designers create designs for almost anything that is a part of the costume of men, women, or children. They may design both outer and inner garments or hats, purses, shoes, gloves, costume jewelry, scarves, or beachwear, or they may specialize in certain types of clothing such as bridal gowns or sportswear. People in this profession range from the few top haute couture designers, who produce one-of-a-kind designs for high-fashion houses that cater to a high-priced market, to the thousands of designers who work in the American garment industry creating fashions for mass production and sale to millions of Americans. Most fashion designers are followers rather than originators of fashion, adapting styles to meet the price requirements of customers. Many fashion designers are self-employed; some work on a freelance basis.

The designer's original idea for a garment is usually sketched. After a rough sketch is created, the designer begins to shape the pattern pieces that make the garment. The pieces are drawn to actual size on paper and cut out of a rough material, often muslin. The muslin pieces are sewn together and fitted on a model. The designer makes modifications in the pattern pieces or other features of the rough mock-up to complete the design. From the rough model, sample garments are made in the fabric that the designer intends to use.

Today's designers are greatly assisted by computer software. Computer-aided designing and computer-aided manufacturing allow for thousands of fashion styles and colors to be stored in a computer and accessed at the touch of a button, largely eliminating the long process of gathering fabrics and styling them into samples.

Sample garments are displayed at a "showing," to which *press representatives* and *buyers* are invited and at which designers supervise. Major designers may present large runway shows twice a year to leading retailers and the fashion press for potential publicity and sales. Sample garments may then be mass-produced, displayed by *fashion models,* and shipped to stores where they are available for purchase.

In some companies, designers are involved in every step of the production of a selected line, from the original idea to the completed garments. Many designers prefer to supervise their own workrooms. Others work with supervisors to solve problems that arise in the production of the garments.

Most manufacturers produce new styles four times each year: spring and summer; fall and winter; "cruise," for people on vacations; and "holiday," or special styles, for the winter holiday season. Designers generally are expected to create between 50 and 150 styles for each showing. Their work calendar differs from the actual time of year. They must be working on spring and summer designs during fall and winter and on fall and winter clothing during the summer.

Designers work cooperatively with the head of their manufacturing firm. They design a line that is consistent with the ideas of their employers. They also work cooperatively with those who do the actual production of the garments and must be able to estimate the cost of a garment. Some company designers produce designs and oversee a workroom staff, which may consist of a head designer, an assistant designer, and one or more sample makers. Designers in large firms may plan and direct the work of one or more assistant designers, select fabrics and trims, and help determine the pricing of the products they design.

Designers spend time in exploration and research, visiting textile manufacturing and sales establishments to learn of the latest fabrics and their uses and capabilities. They must know about fabric, weave, draping qualities, and strength of materials. A good understanding of textiles and their potentialities underlies much of designers' work. They browse through stores to see what fashion items the public is buying and which are being ignored. They visit museums and art galleries to get ideas about color and design. They go to places where people congregate—theaters, sports events, business and professional meetings, and resorts—and meet with marketing and production workers, salespeople, and clients to discover what people are wearing and to discuss ideas and styles.

Designers also keep abreast of changing styles. If the styles are too different from public taste, customers will reject the designs. If, however, they cling to styles that have been successful in the past, they may find that the taste of buyers has changed dramatically. In either case, it could be equally disastrous for their employers.

There are many opportunities for specialization in fashion designing. The most common specialties are particular types of garments such as resort wear, bridal wear, or sportswear.

An interesting specialty in fashion designing is theatrical design, a relatively limited field but challenging to those who are interested in combining an interest in theater with a talent for clothing design.

REQUIREMENTS
High School

A high school diploma definitely is needed for fashion designing. Take courses that prepare you for more specialized training after graduation. Art, home economics, mathematics, and chemistry are good choices.

Postsecondary Training

Employers will favor an aspiring designer with a total fashion background that includes marketing and other business skills over a talented person with no knowledge of business procedures. A college degree is recommended, although not required. Graduation from a fashion design school is highly desirable. Employers seek designers who have had courses in mathematics, business, design, sketching, art history, costume history, literature, pattern making, clothing construction, and textiles.

Some colleges offer a four-year degree in fine arts with a major in fashion design. Many reputable schools of fashion design in the United States offer a two- or three-year program that offers a diploma or certificate.

Students interested in fashion should take computer-aided design courses, as these methods increasingly are being used by designers to better visualize a final product, create prototypes, and reduce design production time and cost. Companies are looking for more than design skills: Many require extensive knowledge and experience with software programs used to produce technical drawings.

Other Requirements

Prospective fashion designers must be artistic and imaginative with a flair for color and clothing coordination. They will need a working knowledge of clothing construction and an eye for trends. They must possess technical aptitudes, problem-solving skills, and the ability to conceptualize in two and three dimensions. Personal qualifications include self-motivation, team spirit, and the ability to handle pressure, deadlines, and long hours. This career also demands energy and a good head for business.

EXPLORING

If you enjoy sewing and sew well, you may have taken the first step toward exploring a career in the fashion world. If your skills in garment construction are adequate, the next step may be an attempt at designing and making clothing. Art and design courses will help you assess your talent and ability as a creative artist.

If you are able to obtain summer jobs in a department or specialty store, you can observe retailing practices and gain some practical insights into the merchandising aspects of the fashion world. Working in a fabric store provides the opportunity to learn about fabrics and accessories as well as to observe customers learning to follow patterns to make clothing. You may want to visit a garment manufacturer to see fashion employees at work.

You also can attend style shows, visit art galleries, observe clothing worn by fashion leaders, and browse through a variety of stores in which garments are sold. Many useful books and magazines are published about fashion. The so-called fashion industry bible is *Women's Wear Daily*, a must read for those who want to be knowledgeable and current in this fast-changing business. For headlines and subscription information, visit the website http://www.wwd.com.

EMPLOYERS

Many fashion designers find employment with large fashion houses such as Liz Claiborne or Jones New York. Some large manufacturers produce a secondary line of lower priced designer clothing—Donna Karan's DKNY and Giorgio Armani's Emporio, for example. In the United States, New York City, San Francisco, and Los Angeles are major fashion centers, where positions are available in both large and small companies. Work also may be found in Chicago and other cities, although not as many jobs are available in these locations.

A few fashion designers work for high-fashion firms, but these positions are difficult to come by and competition is very strong. An aspiring designer may have more options in specialized areas of fashion such as sportswear, sleepwear, children's clothing, or accessories.

Other areas for aspiring fashion designers to explore are home fashions such as bed and bath linens, draperies, and rugs or carpeting. Positions also can be found with pattern manufacturers. Some fashion designers work on a freelance basis, contracting with manufacturers or individuals.

An easy way to learn about manufacturers is to visit a department or specialty store and examine labels and tags on merchandise of interest. In addition to major department stores, retailers such as Target carry a variety of manufacturers' lines.

STARTING OUT

Few people begin their careers as fashion designers. College graduates often begin as assistant designers; they must prove their ability and undergo training before being entrusted with the responsible job of the designer. Many young people find that assistant designer jobs are difficult to locate, so they accept beginning jobs in the workroom where they spend time cutting or constructing garments.

Fashion design school graduates may receive placement information from their school or college placement offices. Approaching stores and manufacturers directly is another way to secure a beginning position. This will be easier for those students who are known in the industry through summer or part-time work.

ADVANCEMENT

Advancement in fashion designing varies a great deal. There is much moving from firm to firm, and vacancies occur frequently. Aspiring designers should create, collect, and continuously update their portfolios of designs and look for opportunities to show their work to employers. Beginners may work as cutting assistants or assistant designers. From these entry-level positions, the fashion designer's career path may lead to positions as an assistant technical designer, pattern company designer, designer, and head designer. Those who grow with a company may design less and take on more operational responsibilities.

Designers may choose to move into a business or merchandising position where they direct lines, set prices, supervise production, and work directly with buyers. After years of work, top designers may become partners in the design or apparel firms for which they work. Others may open their own retail clothing stores. A designer may want to work for firms that offer increasing design responsibility and fewer restrictions to become established as a house designer or eventually as an independent-name designer.

EARNINGS

Fashion designers earned an average annual salary of $48,530 in 2000, according to the *Occupational Outlook Handbook.* The lowest paid 10 percent earned less than $24,710; the highest 10 percent earned more than $103,970. A few highly skilled and well-known designers in top firms have annual incomes of over $150,000. Top fashion designers who have successful lines of clothing can earn bonuses that bring their annual incomes into the millions of dollars. As designers become well known, they are usually offered a share of the ownership of the company for which they design. Their ownership percentage increases with their reputation.

Theatrical designers usually work on a contract basis. Although the compensation for the total contract is usually good, there may be long periods of idleness between contracts. The annual incomes for theatrical designers usually are not as great as those of fashion designers, although while they are working they may be making more than $1,000 per week.

WORK ENVIRONMENT

Fashion design is competitive and stressful, but often exciting and glamorous. Many designers work in cluttered and noisy surroundings. Their work environment may consist of a large room with long tables for cutting out patterns or garments. There may be only one or two other people working in the room, or there may be several others. Many designers travel a great deal for showings and conferences. They may spend time in stores or shops looking at clothing that has been manufactured by competitors.

Most designers work a 40-hour week, but they may have to work more during rush periods. Styles previewed in spring and fall require a great amount of work during the weeks and months before a show. The work pace usually is hectic as pressure builds before collection showings.

OUTLOOK

Designers are key people in the garment industry, yet relatively few of them are needed to make employment possible for thousands of people in other apparel occupations. It is estimated that there are approximately 16,000 fashion designers in the United States, which represents less than 1 percent of the garment industry. Some designers work only for the high-priced custom trade, some for the mass market, and some on exclusive designs that will be made for only one person. Many designers are employed by manufacturers of paper patterns.

Good designers will always be needed, although not in great numbers. However, increasing populations and growing personal incomes are expected to spur the demand for fashion designers. According to the *Occupational Outlook Handbook,* employment of designers is expected to grow faster than the average for all occupations through 2010.

Some fashion designers enjoy high pay and prestige. Those at the top of their profession rarely leave their positions. Therefore, opportunities for newcomers are limited. There always will be more people hoping to break into the field than there are available jobs. Experience working with computer-aided design programs is increasingly important to employers and can help to distinguish a qualified job candidate from the rest of his or her competition. Employment prospects may be better in specialized areas, such as children's clothing. Additionally, openings are more readily available for assistant designers.

FOR MORE INFORMATION

Those interested in creating men's fashions should check out the CTDA's website for business and training information.

Custom Tailors and Designers Association of America (CTDA)
PO Box 53052
Washington, DC 20009
Tel: 202-387-7220
http://www.ctda.com

For information about this school, programs, and an application, contact FIT.

Fashion Institute of Technology (FIT)
Admissions Office
Seventh Avenue at 27th Street
New York, NY 10001-5992

Tel: 212-217-7999
Email: FITinfo@fitsuny.edu
http://www.fitnyc.suny.edu

For a list of accredited schools, contact
National Association of Schools of Art and Design
11250 Roger Bacon Drive, Suite 21
Reston, VA 20190
Tel: 703-437-0700
Email: info@arts-accredit.org
http://www.arts-accredit.org/nasad

For information on the fashion industry, check out the following magazine's website:
Women's Wear Daily
http://www.wwd.com

FILM EDITORS

School Subjects Art English	**Certification or Licensing** None available
Personal Skills Artistic Communication/ideas	**Outlook** Faster than the average **DOT** 962
Work Environment Primarily indoors Primarily one location	**GOE** 01.01.01
Minimum Education Level High school diploma	**NOC** 5131
Salary Range $18,970 to $34,160 to $71,280+	**O*NET-SOC** 27-4032.00

OVERVIEW

Film editors perform an essential role in the motion picture and television industries. They take an unedited draft of film or videotape and use specialized equipment to improve the draft until it is ready for viewing. It is the responsibility of the film editor to create the most effective film possible. There are approximately 16,000 film and television editors employed in the United States.

HISTORY

Early film editing was sometimes done by directors, studio technicians, or others for whom this was not their specialty. Now every film, including the most brief television advertisement, has a film editor who is responsible for the continuity and clarity of the film.

The motion picture and television industries have experienced substantial growth in the last few years in the United States. The effect of this is a steady demand for the essential skills that film editors provide. With recent innovations in computer technology, much of the work that film editors perform is accomplished using sophisticated computer programs. All of these factors have enabled many film editors to find steady work as salaried employees of film and television production companies and as independent contractors who provide their services on a per-job basis.

THE JOB

Film editors work closely with producers and directors throughout an entire project. These editors assist in the earliest phase, called preproduction, and during the production phase, when actual filming occurs. Their skills are in the greatest demand during postproduction, the completion of primary filming. During preproduction, in meetings with producers, editors learn about the objectives of the film or video. If the project is a television commercial, for example, the editor must be familiar with the product the commercial will attempt to sell. If the project is a feature-length motion picture, the editor must understand the story line. The producer may explain the larger scope of the project so that the editor knows the best way to approach the work when it is time to edit the film. In consultation with the director, editors may discuss the best way to accurately present the screenplay or script. They may discuss different settings, scenes, or camera angles even before filming or taping begins. With this kind of preparation, film editors are ready to practice their craft as soon as the production phase is complete.

Feature-length films, of course, take much more time to edit than television commercials. Therefore, some editors may spend months on one project, while others may be working on several shorter projects simultaneously.

Steve Swersky owns his own editorial company in Santa Monica, California, and he has done editing for commercials, films, and TV. In addition to editing many Jeep commercials and theatrical trailers for such movies as *Titanic, Fargo,* and *The Usual Suspects,* Swersky has worked on 12 films. Though commercials can be edited quickly, a film project can possibly take six to nine months to edit.

Swersky's work involves taking the film that has been developed in labs and transferring it to videotape for him to watch. He uses "nonlinear" computer editing for his projects, as opposed to traditional "linear" systems involving many video players and screens. "The difference between linear and nonlinear editing," he says, "is like the difference between typing and using a word processor. When you want to change a written page, you have to retype it; with word processing you can just cut and paste."

Swersky uses the Lightworks nonlinear editing system. With this system, he converts the film footage to a digital format. The computer has a database that tracks individual frames and puts all the scenes together in a folder of information. This information is stored on a hard drive and can instantly be brought up on a screen, allowing an editor to access scenes and frames with the click of a mouse.

Film editors are usually the final decision makers when it comes to choosing which segments will stay in as they are, which segments will be cut, or which may need to be redone. Editors look at the quality of the segment, its dramatic value, and its relationship to other segments. They then arrange the segments in an order that creates the most effective finished product. "I assemble the scenes," Swersky says, "choosing what is the best, what conveys the most emotion. I bring the film to life, in a way."

He relies on the script and notes from the director, along with his natural sense of how a scene should progress, in putting together the film, commercial, or show. He looks for the best shots, camera angles, line deliveries, and continuity.

Some editors specialize in certain areas of film. Sound editors work on the soundtracks of television programs or motion pictures. They often keep libraries of sounds that they reuse for various projects. These include natural sounds, such as thunder or raindrops, animal noises, motor sounds, or musical interludes. Some sound editors specialize in music and may have training in music theory or performance. Others work with sound effects. They may use unusual objects, machines, or computer-generated noisemakers to create a desired sound for a film.

REQUIREMENTS
High School

Broadcast journalism and other media and communications courses will provide you with some practical experience in video editing. Because film editing requires a creative perspective along with technical skills, you should take English, speech, theater, and other courses that will allow you to develop writing skills. Art and photography classes will involve you with visual media. Because of the technical nature of film editing, take computer classes to become comfortable and confident using basic computer programs.

Postsecondary Training

Some studios require a bachelor's degree for those seeking positions as film editors, yet actual on-the-job experience is the best guarantee of securing lasting employment. Degrees in liberal arts fields are preferred, but courses in cinematography and audiovisual techniques help film editors get started in their work. You may choose to pursue a degree in such subjects as English, journalism, theater, or film. Community and two-year colleges often offer courses in the study of film as literature. Some of these colleges also teach film editing. Universities with departments of broadcast journalism offer courses in film editing and also may have contacts at local television stations. The American Film Institute hosts an educational website (http://www.afi.edu) that offers listings of high schools with film courses and other resources for teachers and students.

Training as a film or television editor takes from four to 10 years. Many editors learn much of their work on the job as an assistant or apprentice at larger studios that offer these positions. During an apprenticeship, the apprentice has the opportunity to see the work of the editor up close. The editor may eventually assign some of his or her minor duties to the apprentice, while the editor makes the larger decisions. After a few years the apprentice may be promoted to editor or may apply for a position as a film editor at other studios.

Training in film editing is also available in the military, including the Air Force, Marine Corps, Coast Guard, and Navy.

Other Requirements

You should be able to work cooperatively with other creative people when editing a film. You should remain open to suggestions and guidance, while also maintaining your confidence in the presence of other professionals. A successful editor has an understanding of the history of film and television and a feel for the narrative form in general. Computer skills are also important and will help you to learn new technology in the field. You may be required to join a union to do this work, depending on the studio.

"You should have a good visual understanding," Steve Swersky says. "You need to be able to tell a story, and be aware of everything that's going on in a frame."

EXPLORING

Many high schools have film clubs, and some have cable television stations affiliated with the school district. Often school-run televi-

Movies about Artists

- *Lust for Life* (1956): biography on Vincent Van Gogh; describes how his extreme devotion to art eventually leads to his demise

- *The Rebel* (1961): about a starving British artist who becomes an art sensation overnight in Paris

- *Caravaggio* (1986): describes a love triangle between a baroque painter and young couple set in Renaissance Rome

- *I Shot Andy Warhol* (1996): story of the artist and the radical feminist that tried to kill him

- *Pollock* (2000): biography on painter Jackson Pollock; describes his road to fame, which led to deception, infidelity, and a sudden death

- *Frida* (2002): about Frida Kahlo's struggle with her work, life, and sexuality

sion channels give students the opportunity to actually create and edit short programs. Check out what's available at your school.

One of the best ways to prepare for a career as a film editor is to read widely. By reading literature you will get a sense of the different ways in which to present stories. Some high schools even offer film classes.

You should be familiar with all different kinds of films, including documentaries, short films, and feature films. Don't just watch the films you rent from the video store; rather, study them, paying close attention to the decisions the editors made in piecing together the scenes.

Large television stations and film companies occasionally have volunteers or student interns. Most people in the film industry start out doing minor tasks helping with production. These production assistants get the opportunity to see all of the film professionals at work. By working closely with a film editor, a production assistant can learn television or film operations as well as specific film editing techniques.

EMPLOYERS

Some film editors work primarily with news programs, documentaries, or special features. They may develop ongoing working relationships with directors or producers who hire them from one project to another. Many film editors who have worked for a studio or postproduction company for several years often become independent contractors. They offer their services on a per job basis to producers of films and advertisements, negotiating their own fees, and typically have purchased or leased their own editing equipment.

STARTING OUT

With a minimum of a high school diploma or a degree from a two-year college, you can apply for entry-level jobs in many film or television studios. Most studios, however, will not consider people for film editor positions without a bachelor's degree or several years of on-the-job experience. Larger studios may offer apprenticeships for film editors. Apprentices have the opportunity to see the work of the film editor up close. The film editor may eventually assign some of his or her minor duties to the apprentice, while the film editor makes the larger decisions. After a few years, the apprentice may be promoted to film editor or may apply for a position as a film editor at other studios.

Those who have completed bachelor's or master's degrees have typically gained hands-on experience through school projects. Another benefit of going to school is that contacts that you make while in school, both through your school's placement office and alumni, can be a valuable resource when you look for your first job. Your school's placement office may also have listings of job openings. Some studio work is union regulated. Therefore you may also want to contact union locals to find out about job requirements and openings.

ADVANCEMENT

Once film editors have secured employment in their field, their advancement comes with further experience and greater recognition. Some film editors develop good working relationships with directors or producers. These film editors may be willing to leave the security of a studio job for the possibility of working one-on-one with the director or producer on a project. These opportunities often provide film editors with the autonomy they may not get in their regular jobs. Some are willing to take a pay cut to work on a project they feel is important.

Some film editors choose to stay at their studios and advance through seniority to editing positions with higher salaries. They may be able to negotiate better benefits packages or to choose the films they will work on. They may also choose which directors they wish to work with. In larger studios, they may train and supervise staffs of less experienced or apprentice film editors.

"I want to continue doing films," Steve Swersky says. "Every film is a step up the ladder on the long way to the top." He plans to continue to work on commercials, but would also like to work on films with bigger budgets and more prestige. "I'd like to be at the Academy Awards someday," he says, "accepting the Oscar for film editing."

EARNINGS

Film editors are not as highly paid as others working in the film or television industries. They have less clout than directors or producers, but have more authority in the production of a film than many other film technicians. According to the U.S. Department of Labor, the median annual wage for film and television editors was $36,900 in 2001. A small percentage of film editors earn less than $19,430 a year, while some earn over $72,480. The most experienced and sought after film editors can command very high salaries.

WORK ENVIRONMENT

Most film editors' work in film studios or at postproduction companies using editing equipment. The working environment is often a small, cramped studio office. Working hours vary widely depending on the film. During the filming of a commercial, for instance, film editors may be required to work overtime, at night, or on weekends to finish the project by an assigned date. Many feature-length films are kept on tight production schedules that allow for steady work unless filming gets behind.

"As stressful as the work can be," Steve Swersky says, "we joke around that it's not like having a real job. Every day is a fun day."

During filming, film editors may be asked to be on hand at the filming location. Locations may be outdoors or in other cities, and travel is occasionally required. More often, however, the film editor edits in the studio, where the bulk of his or her time is spent.

Disadvantages of the job involve the editor's low rank on the totem pole of film or television industry jobs. However, most film editors feel that this is outweighed by the advantages. Film editors can view the films on which they have worked and be proud of their role in creating them.

OUTLOOK

The outlook for film and television editors is very good. In fact, the U.S. Department of Labor predicts faster than average employment growth for film and television editors over the next decade. The growth of cable television and an increase in the number of independent film studios will translate into greater demand for editors. This will also force the largest studios to offer more competitive salaries in order to attract the best film and television editors.

The digital revolution has greatly affected film editing. Editors now work much more closely with special effects houses in putting together films. When using more effects, film editors have to edit scenes with an eye towards special effects to be added later. Digital editing systems are also available for home computers—users can feed their own digital video into their computers, then edit the material, and add their own special effects and titles. This technology may allow some prospective film editors more direct routes into the industry, but the majority of editors will have to follow traditional routes, obtaining years of hands-on experience.

FOR MORE INFORMATION

The ACE features some career information on its Web page, along with information about internship opportunities and sample articles from Cinemeditor *magazine.*

American Cinema Editors
100 Universal City Plaza, Building 2282, Room 234
Universal City, CA 91608
Tel: 818-777-2900
http://www.ace-filmeditors.org

For information about schools with film and television programs of study and to read interviews with filmmakers, visit the AFI website.

American Film Institute
2021 North Western Avenue
Los Angeles, CA 90027
Tel: 323-856-7600
http://www.afi.com

FURNITURE DESIGNERS

QUICK FACTS

School Subjects
Art
Mathematics
Technical/shop

Personal Skills
Artistic
Communication/ideas

Work Environment
Primarily indoors
Primarily one location

Minimum Education Level
Some postsecondary training

Salary Range
$28,800 to $49,830 to
$100,000

Certification or Licensing
None available

Outlook
Faster than the average

DOT
142

GOE
01.02.03

NOC
2252

O*NET-SOC
27-1021.00

OVERVIEW

Furniture designers develop concepts for building furnishings like chairs, tables, and couches. They work closely with their clients to get a thorough understanding of what kind of product is needed.

Furniture designers may work for a company that specifically builds furniture or for a large design firm that is contracted by furniture manufacturers. Furniture designers spend most of their time in an office working on ideas but also spend time meeting with clients.

HISTORY

During every period in history from early Egyptian times until now, design has ranged from the simple and purely functional to the ornate and intricately crafted. However, civilization has tended to preserve furniture that is more intricate. From a historical point of view, this is fortunate. Ornate craftwork tells more about a period than simple design does because it evolves to reflect artistic concepts and fashions. On the other hand, if you compared a simple farmer's table from 1700 B.C. with a farmer's table from 1700 A.D., you would probably find more similarities than differences.

Evidence of design and construction practices in some cultures is mostly limited to what we can observe in surviving paintings, sculpture, mosaics, and other graphic representations. Not many actual pieces remain from the Mesopotamians, the Minoans (of the Aegean Islands), the ancient Greeks, or from the Byzantine era (the mid- to late centuries of the first millennium A.D.).

In most cultures, artisans have tended to build furniture to mirror elements and styles of architecture. In 15th-century Gothic design, architectural themes such as arches, line tracery, columns, and leaf patterns began to appear in furniture. During the French Renaissance, the architectural style of Jacques du Cerceau, which featured intricate patterns made up of classical elements, was translated into furniture design. From the 1890s until 1910, European architects and artisans inspired by the Art Nouveau movement infused their work with suggestions of shapes in nature and an impression of movement. The Belgian architects Henri van de Velde and Victor Horta created furnishings that echoed the organic curvature prominent in the buildings they designed.

During the 18th and 19th centuries, a wave of revivalism unearthed earlier styles of design. In the mid-1700s, designers in Europe (notably, England and France) began using ancient Greek and Roman ideas, giving rise to Neoclassicism. During this time, artisans used basic geometric shapes in furniture. Surfaces were often variations of the circle or the square, and legs were built with unbroken, tapering lines. Ornament often contained style elements seen in Greco-Roman columns. Later, in the mid-1800s, the Gothic revival saw the return of Gothic architectural themes in furniture design (e.g., pointed arches, columns, and "linenfold," an ornamental carving style mimicking the folds of hanging fabric). In the 1860s, Renaissance revival brought back pieces built with straight lines and decorated with inlaid patterns.

During most of the history of furniture design, each period has been characterized by a single or very few styles and designers (for example, Gustav Stickley was famous in the Arts and Crafts movement of the late 19th and early 20th centuries). Things are very different today. Designers employ hundreds of styles, from the antique to the high tech. Some of the best designers draw from multiple influences in creating their work.

THE JOB

Furniture design encompasses a variety of skills and disciplines, including history, art, mathematics, drafting, ergonomics, interior design, and carpentry. Furniture designers generate ideas for new pieces or lines of furniture. They usually start with a graphic representation (rough sketches) of the piece to be built and then they build an actual model out of wood or foam core to view the piece in three-dimensional space. Once the model is completed, a prototype is built to the correct size using actual materials. After the prototype is approved, it goes into production, which could involve one carpenter for a custom-designed piece, or a huge factory that mass produces a variety of pieces.

Furniture designers sit at a drawing board making technical drawings, usually using computer-aided design/drafting (CAD) software to illustrate their ideas. They must consider the intended function of the piece, its form, its style, and its environment. The furniture may be a reproduction of a period piece or influenced by an earlier style, or it may be a completely original design. Other considerations include materials, cost, manufacturing processes, and the manufacturing time.

Communication is an important part of the design process. Furniture designers must understand the clients' or employers' demands and be able to translate them into a working model. They must then communicate their ideas to builders and manufacturers to explain materials, shapes, patterns, and construction details. Production of furniture is a complex process that usually involves several people. Engineers, carpenters, assemblers, finishers, accountants, salespeople, marketers, and shippers are all part of the team.

Furniture designers who work on their own or for small companies may be involved in the actual construction process in addition to developing designs. They might use such power tools as a table saw, wood lathe, router, joiner/planer, bandsaw, grinders, and sanders, as well as a variety of hand tools. At a larger company, a designer is more likely to be assigned to one function, perhaps technical drawing or building a prototype.

REQUIREMENTS
High School

Art classes are fundamental to your training as a designer. Drawing and sketching classes will help you to get ideas down fast, and sculpture classes will encourage you to think about three-dimensional objects. A drafting course is also essential. Manual drafting will teach you how to make a technical drawing of a three-dimensional object, and, in turn, help you to visualize an object by looking at a two-dimensional drawing. Take shop courses to learn about woodworking and metal fabrication/welding, because wood and metal are among the most common materials used in contemporary furniture building.

Mathematics courses, including algebra, geometry, and trigonometry are necessary. Computer science is beneficial, especially if you have an opportunity to learn CAD software.

Postsecondary Training

Colleges such as the Rhode Island School of Design and the Savannah College of Art and Design have furniture design programs at both the undergraduate and graduate levels. (See contact information at the end of this article.) Also, because it is common now for small furniture manufacturers to contract industrial design firms for their designs, consider schools that have industrial design programs that will allow you to concentrate on furniture design.

In a design program, early classes will focus on the fundamentals of two- and three-dimensional design. Studio classes give you hands-on experience with wood, power and hand tools, welding and metal fabrication, upholstery techniques, and molding plastics. Design history teaches you how craftspeople and artisans have designed furniture in the past and how past styles influence design today.

Most programs help you assemble a portfolio of work and include an internship segment, in which faculty will help you find a working position with a professional for one or more semesters.

Other Requirements

Furniture designers need artistic ability and must be able to visualize and work in three dimensions. Aside from being creative, you should be able to work well both independently and as part of a team. It helps to be persistent and tough-minded to accept criticism of your designs. Good verbal communication skills will help you communicate with clients, builders, and production workers.

EXPLORING

To probe your interest in designing furniture, try to design a chair, bookcase, or table. Make rough sketches. If you haven't had any exposure to technical drawing, find a book that describes drafting techniques and buy or borrow the basic tools (vellum, drafting pencils, architect's scale). Try to make a detailed drawing to scale.

After completing your sketch, try building it. Make arrangements with a shop instructor to use the tools at your school. You may have to find the materials yourself. Find out how well your design builds, holds together, and functions.

Get in the habit of looking at manufactured objects. Anything that is built began with a design. Look at pieces as a whole and at the details, and decide what you like and dislike about the design.

Visit local companies that manufacture and/or design furniture. You may be able to work part time or as a volunteer in exchange for learning about the furniture business.

EMPLOYERS

Some of the largest and most established employers of furniture designers in this country are located in the Midwest. Steelcase is located in Grand Rapids, Michigan; Herman Miller is in Zeeland, Michigan; and Knoll is in East Greenville, Pennsylvania. These companies tend to be selective, so you'll probably need a bachelor's degree in design, a few years of experience, and a professional portfolio to get an interview.

There are many smaller companies in cities throughout the United States that design and manufacture their own lines of furniture. They are more likely to hire designers who can perform other functions as well, such as marketing or production.

Industrial design (ID) firms hire people with backgrounds in furniture design. Furniture manufacturers that are too small to have their own design departments sometimes contract ID firms to create concepts for them. The reverse is true as well; large design firms may create designs and contract builders who have the specific facilities and expertise to create what's needed.

Many furniture designers work on a freelance basis. Some develop their own designs and try to sell them to manufacturers, while others are hired by manufacturers to develop designs according to their needs.

STARTING OUT

Probably the most difficult way to get work in this field is to call a firm or a company cold. If you don't have contacts, check with furniture design associations because they often collect job listings.

If you complete a four-year program in furniture design, your instructors and professors will likely be able to put you in touch with numerous professional contacts. Some internships can lead to full-time positions upon graduation.

Some designers start out as woodworkers or craftworkers. After working in a cabinet or furniture shop for a few years, you may wish to start up your own custom furniture business.

ADVANCEMENT

College graduates can start as *junior designers* for companies that make furniture on a small scale. They may begin by building prototypes in the shop. With some experience, they may begin to work in CAD on company designs. As they gain credibility and experience, designers can advance to a management position, in which they spend most of their time communicating with clients. After several years, they may qualify for a senior designer position with a larger manufacturer.

Another way to advance in this career is to start a business or work as a freelance designer, creating original concepts for furniture, which can be custom built or sold to manufacturers.

EARNINGS

Some furniture designers are employed as industrial designers. According to the U.S. Department of Labor, the median annual salary for commercial and industrial designers was $49,830 in 2001. The lowest paid 10 percent earned less than $28,800 and the highest paid 10 percent earned over $79,690. Designers in managerial or executive positions had higher salaries of up to $100,000.

Benefits for furniture design positions with established firms or manufacturers include health insurance, paid vacation, and sick leave.

WORK ENVIRONMENT

Furniture designers spend a great deal of time in an office working on sketches and technical drawings. They also have to meet with clients on a regular basis. Some work takes place in manufacturing facilities, from a small woodshop to the factory floor of a $2 billion operation. Designers must communicate regularly with builders and production workers to make sure they understand the process, the materials, and the finishes.

Furniture designers working for large companies are more likely to work a regular 40-hour workweek. In smaller companies, they may be required to work extra hours during peak production periods. Design work can be intense and stressful with constant pressure to come up with new ideas.

OUTLOOK

The U.S. Department of Labor predicts faster than average growth for commercial and industrial designers through the next decade. Openings will result from growth in the field as well as the need to replace designers who leave the industry. Demand for furniture designers should remain strong because a growing number of consumers are concerned with purchasing furniture that is not just utilitarian but also fashionable and stylish.

Trade has become more global, and there are more markets available to U.S. manufacturers. Furniture trade in the United States now competes with that of Europe. The big furniture companies are getting bigger, and they will hire new staff designers, or contract them as freelancers. This growth is happening as consumers are able to afford to furnish their homes the way they want and are becoming more design conscious. This trend is evidenced by fans of the Home & Garden Television cable network or readers of design-oriented magazines like *Metropolitan Home* or *Better Homes & Gardens*.

Freelancers who sell designs to companies that manufacture inexpensive furniture on a large scale can collect royalties based on sales of the product. There is a growing trend among collectors in buying "one-off" (that is, unique) pieces of furniture and limited-production furniture. If your interest is in designing unusual work with an emphasis on beauty and artistry, this collecting trend might work to your advantage.

FOR MORE INFORMATION

This not-for-profit group is dedicated to the promotion of furniture design in the Chicago area. Members offer a variety of apprenticeship programs. For information, contact

Chicago Furniture Designers Association
PO Box 3407
Chicago, IL 60654-0407
http://www.cfdainfo.org

For information on the field, educational programs, and other resources, contact

The Furniture Society
Box 18
Free Union, VA 22940

Tel: 434-973-1488
Email: mail@furnituresociety.org
http://www.furnituresociety.org

Visit the education section of the IDSA website to read the career brochure
Getting an Industrial Design Job, *find a listing of undergraduate and graduate ID programs, get information on scholarships and competitions, and more.*

Industrial Designers Society of America (IDSA)
45195 Business Court, Suite 250
Dulles, VA 20166
Tel: 703-707-6000
Email: idsa@idsa.org
http://www.idsa.org

These colleges prepare students for various careers in art and design fields, including furniture design. To read degree requirements typical for the furniture design field, visit the following websites:

Rhode Island School of Design
Two College Street
Providence, RI 02903
Tel: 401-454-6100
http://www.risd.edu

Savannah College of Art and Design
PO Box 3146
Savannah, GA 31402-3146
Tel: 800-869-7223
Email: info@scad.edu
http://www.scad.edu

GRAPHIC DESIGNERS

QUICK FACTS

School Subjects Art Computer science	**Certification or Licensing** None available
Personal Skills Artistic Communication/ideas	**Outlook** Faster than the average
	DOT 141
Work Environment Primarily indoors Primarily one location	**GOE** 01.02.03
Minimum Education Level Some postsecondary training	**NOC** 5241
	O*NET-SOC 27-1024.00
Salary Range $20,000 to $40,000 to $100,000+	

OVERVIEW

Graphic designers are artists whose commercial creations are intended to express ideas, convey information, or draw attention to a product. They design a wide variety of materials including advertisements, displays, packaging, signs, computer graphics and games, book and magazine covers and interiors, animated characters, and company logos to fit the needs and preferences of their various clients. There are approximately 190,000 graphic designers employed in the United States.

HISTORY

The challenge of combining beauty, function, and technology in any form has preoccupied artisans throughout history. Graphic design work has created products and promoted commerce for as long as people have used symbols, pictures, and typography to communicate ideas.

Graphic design has grown along with print media (newspapers, magazines, catalogs, and advertising). The graphic designer would typically sketch several rough drafts of the layout of pictures and words. After one of the drafts was approved, the designer would complete a final layout including detailed type and artwork specifications. The words were sent to a typesetter and the artwork assigned to an illustrator. When the final pieces were returned, the designer or a keyline and paste-up artist would adhere them to an illustration board with rubber cement or wax. Different colored items were placed on acetate overlays. This camera-ready art was then ready to be sent to a printer for photographing and reproduction.

Computer technology has revolutionized the way many graphic designers do their work: Today it is possible to be a successful graphic designer even if you can't draw more than simple stick figures. Graphic designers are now able to draw, color, and revise the many different images they work with daily. They can choose typefaces, size type, and place it without having to align it on the page using a T-square and triangle. Computer graphics enable graphic designers to work more quickly, since details like size, shape, and color are easy to change.

Graphics programs for computers are continually being revised and improved, moving more and more design work from the artist's table to the computer mousepad and graphics tablet. This area of computer technology is booming and will continue to do so in the future, as computer graphics and multimedia move toward virtual reality applications. Many graphic designers with solid computer experience will be needed to work with these systems.

THE JOB

Graphic designers are not primarily fine artists, although they may be highly skilled at drawing or painting. Most designs commissioned to graphic designers involve both artwork and copy (that is, words). Thus, the designer must not only be familiar with the wide range of art media (photography, drawing, painting, collage, etc.) and styles, but he or she must also be familiar with a wide range of typefaces and know how to manipulate them for the right effect. Because design tends to change in a similar way as fashion, designers must keep up to date with the latest trends. At the same time, they must be well grounded in more traditional, classic designs.

Graphic designers can work as *in-house designers* for a particular company, as *staff designers* for a graphic design firm, or as *freelance designers* working for themselves. Some designers specialize in designing advertising materials or packaging. Others focus on corporate identity materials such as company stationery and logos. Some work mainly for publishers, designing book and magazine covers and page layouts. Some work in the area of computer graphics, creating still or animated graphics for computer software, videos, or motion pictures. A highly specialized type of graphic designer, the *environmental graphic designer,* designs large outdoor signs. Some graphic designers design exclusively on the computer, while others may use both the computer and traditional hand drawings or paintings, depending on the project's needs and requirements.

Whatever the specialty and whatever their medium, all graphic designers take a similar approach to a project, whether it is for an entirely new design or for a variation on an existing one. Graphic designers begin by determining as best they can the needs and preferences of the clients and the potential users, buyers, or viewers.

For example, a graphic designer working on a company logo will likely meet with company representatives to discuss how and where the company will use the logo and what size, color, and shape preferences company executives might have. Project budgets must be carefully respected: A design that may be perfect in every way but that it is too costly to reproduce is useless. Graphic designers may need to compare their ideas with similar ones from other companies and analyze the image they project. Thus they must have a good knowledge of how various colors, shapes, and layouts affect the viewer psychologically.

After a plan has been conceived and the details worked out, the graphic designer does some preliminary designs (generally two or three) to present to the client for approval. The client may reject the preliminary design entirely and request a new one, or he or she may ask the designer to make alterations. The designer then goes back to the drawing board to attempt a new design or make the requested changes. This process continues until the client approves the design.

Once a design has been approved, the graphic designer prepares the design for professional reproduction, that is, printing. The printer may require a "mechanical," in which the artwork and copy are arranged on a white board just as it is to be photographed, or the designer may be asked to submit an electronic copy of the design. Either way, designers must have a good understanding of the printing process, including color separation, paper properties, and halftone (i.e., photograph) reproduction.

REQUIREMENTS
High School

While in high school, take any art and design courses that are available. Computer classes are also helpful, particularly those that teach page layout programs or art and photography manipulation programs. Working on the school newspaper or yearbook can provide valuable design experience. You may also volunteer to design flyers or posters for school events.

Postsecondary Training

More graphic designers are recognizing the value of formal training, and at least two out of three people entering the field today have a college degree or some college education. Over 100 colleges and art schools offer graphic design programs that are accredited by the National Association of Schools of Art and Design. At many schools, graphic design students must take a year of basic art and design courses before being accepted into the bachelor's degree program. In addition, applicants to the bachelor's degree programs in graphic arts may be asked to submit samples of their work to prove artistic ability. Many schools and employers depend on samples, or portfolios, to evaluate the applicants' skills in graphic design.

Many programs increasingly emphasize the importance of computers in design work. Computer proficiency among graphic designers will be very important in the years to come. Interested individuals should select an academic program that incorporates computer training into the curriculum, or train themselves on their own.

A bachelor of fine arts program at a four-year college or university may include courses such as principles of design, art and art history, painting, sculpture, mechanical and architectural drawing, architecture, computerized design, basic engineering, fashion designing and sketching, garment construction, and textiles. Such degrees are desirable but not always necessary for obtaining a position as a graphic designer.

Other Requirements

As with all artists, graphic designers need a degree of artistic talent, creativity, and imagination. They must be sensitive to beauty and have an eye for detail and a strong sense of color, balance, and proportion. To a great extent, these qualities are natural, but they can be developed through training, both on the job and in professional schools, colleges, and universities.

It is increasingly important for graphic designers to have solid computer skills and a working knowledge of several of the common drawing, image editing, and page layout programs. Graphic design on the computer is done on both Macintosh systems and on PCs; many designers have both types of computers in their studios.

With or without specialized education, graphic designers seeking employment should have a good portfolio containing samples of their best work. The graphic designer's portfolio is extremely important and can make a difference when an employer must choose between two otherwise equally qualified candidates.

A period of on-the-job training is expected for all beginning designers. The length of time it takes to become fully qualified as a graphic designer may run from one to three years, depending on prior education and experience, as well as innate talent.

EXPLORING

If you are interested in a career in graphic design, there are a number of ways to find out whether you have the talent, ambition, and perseverance to succeed in the field. Take as many art and design courses as possible while still in high school and become proficient at working on computers. To get an insider's view of various design occupations, enlist the help of art teachers or school guidance counselors to arrange a tour of a design company and interviews with designers.

While in school, you can get practical experience by participating in school and community projects that call for design talents. These projects might include building sets for plays, setting up exhibits, planning seasonal and holiday displays, and preparing programs and other printed materials. If you are interested in publication design, work on the school newspaper or yearbook is invaluable.

Part-time and summer jobs are excellent ways to become familiar with the day-to-day requirements of a particular design occupation and gain some basic related experience. Possible places of employment include design studios, design departments in advertising agencies and manufacturing companies, department and furniture stores, flower shops, workshops that produce ornamental items, and museums. Museums also use a number of volunteer workers. Inexperienced people are often employed as sales, clerical, or general helpers; those with a little more education and experience may qualify for jobs in which they have a chance to develop actual design skills and build portfolios of completed design projects.

EMPLOYERS

Graphic designers hold approximately 190,000 jobs. They work in many different industries, including the wholesale and retail trade (department stores, furniture and home furnishings stores, apparel stores, florist shops), manufacturing industries (machinery, motor vehicles, aircraft, metal products, instruments, apparel, textiles, printing, and publishing), service industries (business services, engineering, architecture), construction firms, and government agencies. Public relations and publicity firms, advertising agencies, and mail-order houses all have graphic design departments. The publishing industry is a primary employer of graphic designers, including book publishers, magazines, newspapers, and newsletters.

About one-third of all graphic designers are self-employed, a higher proportion than is found in most other occupations. These freelance designers sell their services to multiple clients.

STARTING OUT

The best way to enter the field of graphic design is to have a strong portfolio. Potential employers rely on portfolios to evaluate talent and how that talent might be used to fit the company's special needs. Beginning graphic designers can assemble a portfolio from work completed at school, in art classes, and in part-time or freelance jobs. The portfolio should continually be updated to reflect the designer's growing skills, so it will always be ready for possible job changes.

Those just starting out can apply directly to companies that employ designers. Many colleges and professional schools have placement services to help graduates find positions, and sometimes it is possible to get a referral from a previous part-time employer or volunteer coordinator.

ADVANCEMENT

As part of their on-the-job training, beginning graphic designers generally are given simple tasks and work under direct supervision. As they gain experience, they move up to more complex work with increasingly less supervision. Experienced graphic designers, especially those with leadership capabilities, may be promoted to chief designer, design department head, or other supervisory positions.

Computer graphic designers can move into other computer-related positions with additional education. Some may pursue graphics programming to further improve their computer design capabilities. Others may become involved with multimedia and interactive graphics. Video games, touch-screen displays in stores, and even laser light shows are all products of multimedia graphic designers.

When designers develop personal styles that are in high demand in the marketplace, they sometimes go into business for themselves. Freelance design work can be erratic, however, so usually only the most experienced designers with an established client base can count on consistent full-time work.

EARNINGS

The range of salaries for graphic designers is quite broad. Many earn as little as $20,000, while others receive more than $100,000. Salaries depend primarily on the nature and scope of the employer, with computer graphic designers earning wages on the high end of the range. The Bureau of Labor Statistics reports that in 2001, graphic designers earned a median salary of $36,020; the highest 10 percent earned $61,050 or more, while the lowest 10 percent earned $21,700 or less.

Self-employed designers can earn a lot one year and substantially more or less the next. Their earnings depend on individual talent and business ability, but, in general, are higher than those of salaried designers, although like any self-employed individual, they must pay their own insurance costs and taxes and are not compensated for vacation or sick days.

The *American Institute of Graphic Arts/Aquent Salary Survey 2002* reports that designers earned a median salary of $40,000 in 2001, while senior designers earned a median of $50,000 annually. Salaried designers who advance to the position of creative/design director earned a median of $80,000 a year. The owner of a consulting firm can make $90,000 or more.

Graphic designers who work for large corporations receive full benefits, including health insurance, paid vacation, and sick leave.

WORK ENVIRONMENT

Most graphic designers work regular hours in clean, comfortable, pleasant offices or studios. Conditions vary depending on the design specialty. Some graphic designers work in small establishments with few employees; others work in large organizations with large design departments. Some deal mostly with their co-workers, while others may have a lot of public contact. Freelance designers are paid by the assignment. To maintain a steady income, they must constantly strive to please their clients and to find new ones. Computer graphic designers may have to work long, irregular hours in order to complete an especially ambitious project.

OUTLOOK

Chances for employment look very good for qualified graphic designers over the next several years, especially for those involved with computer graphics. The design field in general is expected to grow at a faster than average rate. As computer graphic technology continues to advance, there will be a need for well-trained computer graphic designers. Companies that have always used graphic designers will expect their designers to perform work on computers. Companies for which graphic design was once too time-consuming or costly are now sprucing up company newsletters and magazines, among other things, requiring the skills of design professionals.

Because the design field appeals to many talented individuals, competition is expected to be strong in all areas. Beginners and designers with only average talent or without formal education and technical skills may encounter some difficulty in finding a job.

FOR MORE INFORMATION

For more information about careers in graphic design, contact the following organizations:

American Institute of Graphic Arts
National Design Center
164 Fifth Avenue
New York, NY 10010
Tel: 212-807-1990
Email: comments@aiga.org
http://www.aiga.org

National Association of Schools of Art and Design
11250 Roger Bacon Drive, Suite 21
Reston, VA 20190
Tel: 703-437-0700
Email: info@arts-accredit.org
http://www.arts-accredit.org/nasad

Society for Environmental Graphic Design
1000 Vermont Avenue, Suite 400
Washington, DC 20005
Tel: 202-638-5555
Email: segd@segd.org
http://www.segd.org

Society of Publication Designers
60 East 42nd Street, Suite 721
New York, NY 10165
Tel: 212-983-8585
Email: spdnyc@aol.com
http://www.spd.org

ILLUSTRATORS

QUICK FACTS

School Subjects
Art
Computer science

Personal Skills
Artistic
Following instructions

Work Environment
Primarily indoors
Primarily one location

Minimum Education Level
High school diploma

Salary Range
$15,780 to $32,870 to
$64,210+

Certification or Licensing
Voluntary

Outlook
About as fast as the average

DOT
141

GOE
01.02.03

NOC
5241

O*NET-SOC
27-1013.00, 27-1013.01

OVERVIEW

Illustrators prepare drawings for advertisements, magazines, books, newspapers, packaging, websites, computer programs, and other formats. *Medical illustrators,* with special training in biology and the physical sciences, are able draw accurate illustrations of parts of the human body, animals, and plants (see the "Medical Illustrators and Photographers" article in this book for more information). *Fashion illustrators* specialize in distinctive illustrations of the latest women's and men's fashions.

HISTORY

The history of illustration can be traced back to the 8th century. Several famous illuminated manuscripts were created in the Middle Ages, including the *Book of Kells.* In the 15th century, movable type was introduced and came to be used by book illustrators. Other printing methods such as etching, woodcuts, and copper engravings were used as illustration techniques in the 16th century and beyond.

In 1796, lithography was invented in Germany. In the original process of lithography, artists made prints directly from designs drawn on slabs of stone. Metal sheets eventually replaced these stone slabs. By the mid-1800s, illustrators used lithographs and engravings to draw magazine and newspaper pages.

As knowledge of photography developed and advanced reproduction processes were invented, artists increasingly used photographs as illustrations. Many industries today, ranging from advertising to fashion, employ illustrators.

THE JOB

Illustrators create artwork for both commercial and fine art purposes. They use a variety of media: pencil, pen and ink, pastels, paints (oil, acrylic, and watercolor), airbrush, collage, and computer technology. Illustrations are used to decorate, describe, inform, clarify, instruct, and draw attention. They appear everywhere in print and electronic formats, including books, magazines, newspapers, signs and billboards, packaging (for everything from milk cartons to CDs), websites, computer programs, greeting cards, calendars, stationery, and direct mail.

Illustrators often work as part of a creative team, which can include graphic designers, photographers, and *calligraphers*, who draw lettering. Illustrators work in almost every industry. Medical illustration and fashion illustration are two of the fastest growing specialties. (Again, see the "Medical Illustrators and Photographers" article in this book for more information on that subspecialty.)

Fashion illustrators work in a glamorized, intense environment. Their artistic focus is specifically on styles of clothing and personal image. Illustrators can work in a few different categories of the fashion field. They provide artwork to accompany editorial pieces in magazines such as *Glamour, Harper's Bazaar,* and *Vogue,* and in newspapers such as *Women's Wear Daily.* Catalog companies employ fashion illustrators to provide the artwork that sells their merchandise.

Fashion illustrators also work with fashion designers, editors, and models. They make sketches from designers' notes or they may sketch live models during runway shows or other fashion presentations. They may use pencils, pen and ink, charcoal, paint, or a combination of media. Fashion illustrators may work as freelancers, handling all the business aspects that go along with being self-employed.

REQUIREMENTS
High School

Creative talent is more important in this field than education. However, there are academic programs in illustration at most colleges and universities. If you are considering going on to a formal program, be sure to take plenty of art classes while in high school. Elective classes in illustration, ceramics, painting, or photography are common courses offered at many high schools.

Postsecondary Training

To find a salaried position as a general illustrator, you should have at least a high school diploma and preferably an associate or bachelor's degree in commercial art or fine art. Whether you are looking for full-time employment or freelance assignments, you will need an organized collection of samples of your best work, which is called a portfolio. Employers are especially interested in work that has been published or printed. An advantage to pursuing education beyond high school is that it gives you an opportunity to build your portfolio.

Fashion illustrators should study clothing construction, fashion design, and cosmetology in addition to taking art courses. They should also keep up with the latest fashion and illustration trends by reading fashion magazines.

Certification or Licensing

Illustrators need to continue their education and training while pursuing their careers. Licensing and certification are not required in this field. However, illustrators must keep up with the latest innovations in design techniques, computer software, and presentation technology, as well as technological advances in the fields for which they provide illustrations.

Other Requirements

Illustrators must be creative, and, of course, demonstrate artistic talent and skill. They also need to be flexible. Because their art is often commercial in nature, illustrators must be willing to accommodate their employers' desires if they are to build a broad clientele and earn a decent living. They must be able to take suggestions and rejections gracefully.

EXPLORING

You can explore an interest in this career by taking art courses. Artists can always improve their drawing skills by practicing on their own, either producing original artwork, or making sketches from drawings that appear in textbooks and reference manuals that relate to their interests. Participation in art, science, and fashion clubs is also good exposure.

EMPLOYERS

More than half of all visual artists are self-employed. Illustrators who are not self-employed work in advertising agencies, design firms, commercial art and reproduction firms, or printing and publishing firms. They are also employed in the motion picture and television industries, wholesale and retail trade establishments, and public relations firms. Fashion illustrators are employed at magazines, newspapers, and catalog companies.

STARTING OUT

Graduates of illustration programs should develop a portfolio of their work to show to prospective employers or clients. Most schools offer career counseling and job placement assistance to their graduates. Job ads and employment agencies are also potential sources for locating work.

ADVANCEMENT

After an illustrator gains experience, he or she will be given more challenging and unusual work. Those with strong computer skills will have the best chances for advancement. Illustrators can advance by developing skills in a specialized area, or even starting their own business. Illustrators can also go into teaching, in colleges and universities at the undergraduate and graduate levels.

EARNINGS

The pay for illustrations can be as little as a byline, though in the beginning of your career it may be worth it just to get exposure. Some illustrators can earn several thousand dollars for a single work. Freelance work is often insecure because of the fluctuation in pay rates and steadiness of work. The U.S. Bureau of Labor Statistics reports that median earnings for salaried fine artists, including painters, sculptors, and illustrators, were about $32,870 a year in 2001. The middle 50 percent earned between $22,270 and $44,900 a year. The top 10 percent earned more than $64,210 and the bottom 10 percent earned less than $15,780.

Illustrators generally receive good benefits, including health and life insurance, pension plans, vacation, sick, and holiday pay.

WORK ENVIRONMENT

Illustrators generally work in clean, well-lit offices. They spend a great deal of time at their desks, whether in front of a computer or at the drafting table. Fashion illustrators may be required to attend fashion shows and other industry events. Because the fashion world is extremely competitive and fast-paced, fashion illustrators tend to work long hours under the pressure of deadlines and demanding personalities.

OUTLOOK

Employment of visual artists is expected to grow about as fast as the average for all occupations through 2010, according to the *Occupational Outlook Handbook.* The growth of the Internet should provide opportunities for illustrators, although the increased use of computer-aided design systems is a threat because individuals do not necessarily need artistic talent or training to use them.

The outlook for careers in fashion illustration is dependent on the businesses of magazine publishing and advertising. Growth of advertising and public relations agencies will provide new jobs. The popularity of American fashion in other parts of the world will also create a demand for fashion illustrators to provide the artwork needed to sell to a global market.

FOR MORE INFORMATION

For information on educational and career opportunities for medical illustrators, contact
Association of Medical Illustrators
5475 Mark Dabling Boulevard, Suite 108
Colorado Springs, CO 80918
Tel: 719-598-8622
Email: ami@capsys.com
http://medical-illustrators.org

This organization is committed to improving conditions for all creators of graphic art and to raising standards for the entire industry. For information, contact
Graphic Artists Guild
90 John Street, Suite 403
New York, NY 10038-3202

Tel: 212-791-3400
http://www.gag.org

For information on membership, contact
Guild of Natural Science Illustrators
PO Box 652
Ben Franklin Station
Washington, DC 20044-0652
Tel: 301-309-1514
Email: gnsihome@his.com
http://www.gnsi.org

For information on college programs in fashion design, advertising, and design, contact
International Academy of Design and Technology-Chicago
One North State Street, Suite 400
Chicago, IL 60602-3300
Tel: 877-ACADEMY
http://www.iadtchicago.com

International Academy of Design and Technology-Orlando
5959 Lake Ellenor Drive
Orlando, FL 32809
Tel: 877-753-0007
http://www.iadt.edu

This national institution promotes and stimulates interest in the art of illustration by offering exhibits, lectures, educational programs, and social exchange. For information, contact
Society of Illustrators
128 East 63rd Street
New York, NY 10021-7303
Tel: 212-838-2560
http://www.societyillustrators.org

INTERIOR DESIGNERS AND DECORATORS

QUICK FACTS

School Subjects Art Business	**Certification or Licensing** Recommended
Personal Skills Artistic Communication/ideas	**Outlook** Faster than the average
	DOT 141
Work Environment Primarily indoors Primarily multiple locations	**GOE** 01.02.03
Minimum Education Level Associate's degree	**NOC** 5242
Salary Range $19,840 to $36,540 to $66,470+	**O*NET-SOC** 27-1025.00

OVERVIEW

Interior designers and *interior decorators* evaluate, plan, and design the interior areas of residential, commercial, and industrial structures. In addition to helping clients select equipment and fixtures, these professionals supervise the coordination of colors and materials, obtain estimates and costs within the client's budget, and oversee the execution and installation of the project. They also often advise clients on architectural requirements, space planning, and the function and purpose of the environment.

There are currently about 46,000 interior designers working in the United States. These specialists are employed by interior design or architectural firms, department stores, furniture stores, hotel chains, and large corporations.

HISTORY

One way to make such beauty a part of everyday life is through decoration of the interiors of buildings. Individuals throughout history have added personal touches of decoration to their homes. Until recently, however, major design and decorating projects have been the privilege of the wealthy.

Artists such as Michelangelo were employed to design and beautify palaces and other buildings, making use of sculpture, paintings, and other wall coverings. Kings sometimes made names for themselves by the decorating trends initiated in their palaces. Such trends came to include furniture, draperies, and often clothing. Home designs and furniture were either largely functional, as in the early American tradition, or extremely ornate, as in the style of Louis XIV of France.

As society prospered, the field of interior design emerged. Although Elsie de Wolfe was the first person to actually practice interior design as a distinct profession in 1905, it wasn't until the 1950s that the design revolution really began. Today, design professionals plan interiors of homes, restaurants, hotels, hospitals, theaters, stores, offices, and other buildings.

THE JOB

The terms "interior designer" and "interior decorator" are sometimes used interchangeably. However, there is an important distinction between the two. Interior designers plan and create the overall design for interior spaces, while interior decorators focus on the decorative aspects of the design and furnishing of interiors. A further distinction concerns the type of interior space on which the design or decorating professional works. Specifically, *residential designers* focus on individual homes, while *contract* or *commercial designers* specialize in office buildings, industrial complexes, hotels, hospitals, restaurants, schools, factories, and other nonresidential environments.

Interior designers and decorators perform a wide variety of services, depending on the type of project and the clients' requirements. A job may range from designing a single room in a private residence to coordinating interior arrangements for a huge building complex. In addition to planning the interiors of new buildings, interior professionals also redesign existing interiors.

Design and decorating specialists begin by evaluating a project. They first consider how the space will be used. In addition to suiting the project's functional requirements, designs must address the needs, desires, tastes, and budget of the client as well. The designer often works closely with the architect in planning the complete layout of rooms and use of space; the designer's plans must work well with the architect's blueprints and comply with other building requirements. Design work of this kind is usually done in connection with the building or renovation of large structures.

Interior professionals may design the furniture and accessories to be used on a project, or they might work with materials that are already available. They select and plan the arrangement of furniture, draperies, floor coverings, wallpaper, paint, and other decorations. They make their decisions only after considering general style, scale of furnishings, colors, patterns, flow, lighting, safety, communication, and a host of other factors. They must also be familiar with local, state, and federal laws as well as building codes and other related regulations.

Although interior designers may consult with clients throughout the conceptual phase of the design project, they usually make a formal presentation once the design has been formulated. Such presentations may include sketches, scaled floorplans, drawings, models, color charts, photographs of furnishings, and samples of materials for upholstery, draperies, and wall coverings. Designers also usually provide a cost estimate of furnishings, materials, labor, transportation, and incidentals required to complete the project.

Once plans have been approved by the client, the interior designer assembles materials—drapery fabrics, upholstery fabrics, new furniture, paint, and wallpaper—and supervises the work, often acting as agent for the client in contracting the services of craftworkers and specifying custom-made merchandise. Designers must be familiar with many materials used in interior furnishing. They must know when certain materials are suitable, how they will blend with other materials, and how they will wear over time. They must also be familiar with historical periods influencing design and have a knack for using and combining the best contributions of these designs of the past. Since designers supervise the work done from their plans, they should know something about painting, carpet installation, carpentry, cabinet making, and other craft areas. They must also be able to buy materials and services at reasonable prices while producing quality work.

Some designers specialize in a particular aspect of interior design, such as furniture, carpeting, or artwork. Others concentrate on particular environments, such as offices, hospitals, restaurants, or transportation, including ships, aircraft, and trains. Still others specialize in the renovation of old buildings. In addition to researching the styles in which rooms were originally decorated and furnished, these designers often supervise the manufacture of furniture and accessories to be used.

Considerable paperwork is involved in interior design, much of it related to budgets and costs. The designer must determine quantities and make and obtain cost estimates. In addition, designers write up and administer contracts, obtain permits, place orders, and check deliveries carefully. All of this work requires an ability to attend to detail in the business aspect of interior design.

REQUIREMENTS
High School

Although formal training is not always necessary in the field of interior design, it is becoming increasingly important and is usually essential for advancement. Most architectural firms, department stores, and design firms accept only professionally trained people, even for beginning positions.

If you're considering a career as an interior designer or decorator, classes in home economics, art history, design, fine arts, and drafting will prove to be valuable. Since interior design is both an art and a business, such courses as marketing, advertising, accounting, management, and general business are important as well.

Postsecondary Training

Professional schools offer two- or three-year certificates or diplomas in interior design. Colleges and universities award undergraduate degrees in four-year programs, and graduate study is also available. College students interested in entering the interior design field should take courses in art history, architectural drawing and drafting, fine arts, furniture design, codes and standards of design, and computer-aided design, as well as classes that focus on the types of materials primarily used, such as fibers, wood, metals, and plastics. Knowledge of lighting and electrical equipment as well as furnishings, art pieces, and antiques, is important.

In addition to art and industry-specific areas of study, courses in business and management are vital to aspiring interior designers and decorators. Learning research methods will help you stay abreast of government regulations and safety standards. You should also have knowledge of zoning laws, building codes, and other restrictions. Finally, keeping up with product performance and new developments in materials and manufacture is an important part of the ongoing education of the interior designer.

Art historians, people with architecture or environmental planning experience, and others with qualifications in commercial or industrial design may also qualify for employment in interior design.

Certification or Licensing

Currently, 19 states and the District of Columbia require licensing for interior designers. Each of these states has its own requirements for licensing and regulations for practice, so it's important to contact the specific state in order to find out how one can apply. You must apply using a written application and submit evidence that you have met the required educational, examination, and experience minimums. Applications are sent to your state department of professional regulation. To learn about the specific requirements, call the local licensing board in your area.

When licensing is not required, accreditation programs are often recommended. These programs provide interior designers with valuable information and promote the achievement of high academic standards in the field of interior design. The Foundation for Interior Design Education Research's accreditation programs are recognized in the industry as providing the education needed for entry into the profession. Although the time required for the entire accreditation process is about 12–18 months, successful completion of the program can give you a competitive edge in the job market. There are more than 120 accredited interior design programs offered through art, architecture, and home economics schools in the United States and Canada.

In addition to licensing, accreditation, formal education, and on-the-job experience, membership in a professional association is important. Membership in the American Society of Interior Designers, for example, generally requires a combination of formal education and experience in the field. To be eligible for membership, designers must also pass the two-day National Council for Interior Design Qualification examination.

Other Requirements

First and foremost, interior designers and decorators need to have artistic talent, including an eye for color, proportion, balance, and detail as well as the ability to visualize. Designers must be able to render an image clearly and carry it out consistently. At the same time, artistic taste and knowledge of current and enduring fashion trends are essential.

In addition, interior designers need to be able to supervise craftworkers and work well with a variety of other people, including clients and suppliers. Designers should be creative, analytical, and ethical. They also need to be able to focus on the needs of clients, develop a global view, and have an appreciation of diversity. Finally, precision, patience, perseverance, enthusiasm, and attention to detail are vital.

EXPLORING

If you're thinking about becoming an interior designer or decorator, there are several ways to learn about the field. Courses in home economics or any of the fine arts, offered either at school or through a local organization, can give you a taste of some of the areas of knowledge needed by interior designers.

To get a sense of the work that design specialists do, you may be able to find a part-time or summer job in a department or furniture store. Such experience will enable you to learn more about the materials used in interior design and decorating and to see the store's interior design service in action. Since the business aspects of interior design are just as important as the creative side, any kind of general selling or business experience will be valuable. As a salesperson at any type of store, for example, you'll learn how to talk to customers, write up orders, close sales, and much more.

In addition to learning about interior design itself, knowledge of auxiliary and support industries will be useful as well. To get a firsthand look at associated fields, you may want to arrange a visit to a construction site, examine an architect's blueprints, talk to someone who specializes in lighting, or tour a furniture manufacturing plant.

Ultimately, the best way to learn about interior design or decorating is to talk to a design professional. While interviewing an interior designer will be interesting and enlightening, finding a mentor who is doing the type of work that you may want to do in the future is ideal. Such a person can suggest other activities that may be of interest to you as you investigate the interior design field, provide you with the names of trade magazines and/or books that can shed some light on the industry, and serve as a resource for questions you might have.

EMPLOYERS

Interior designers and decorators can be found wherever there is a need to style or beautify the interior environment of a building. The principal professional areas in which they work are residential, government, commercial, retail, hospitality, education and research, health care, and facilities management. Approximately 60 percent of all interior designers and decorators are self-employed, 12 percent work for interior design firms, 10 percent for retail stores, and 7 percent for architectural firms. The remainder are employed by large corporations.

In addition to "traditional" interior design and decorating opportunities, some professionals design theater, film, and television settings. A few designers become teachers, lecturers, or consultants, while others work in advertising and journalism.

About 80 percent of interior designers work either for themselves or for companies employing fewer than five people. Since the industry is not dominated by giant conglomerates or even mid-sized firms, employment opportunities are available all across the United States, as well as abroad, in cities both large and small.

STARTING OUT

Most large department stores and design firms with established reputations hire only trained interior designers. More often than not, these employers look for prospective employees with a good portfolio and a bachelor of fine arts degree. Many schools, however, offer apprenticeship or internship programs in cooperation with professional studios or offices of interior design. These programs make it possible for students to apply their academic training in an actual work environment prior to graduation.

After graduating from a two- or three-year training program (or a four-year university), the beginning designer must be prepared to spend one to three years as an assistant to an experienced interior designer before achieving full professional status. This is the usual method of entering the field of interior design and gaining membership in a professional organization.

Finding work as an assistant can often be difficult, so be prepared to take any related job. Becoming a sales clerk for interior furnishings, a shopper for accessories or fabrics, or even a receptionist or stockroom assistant can help you get a foot in the door and provide valuable experience as well.

ADVANCEMENT

While advancement possibilities are available, competition for jobs is intense and interior designers and decorators must possess a combination of talent, personality, and business sense to reach the top. Long years of training and experience are necessary before you can expect to make any real advancement, and income is often only moderate—even for many experienced interior designers. A beginning designer must take a long-range career view, accept jobs that offer practical experience, and put up with long hours and occasionally difficult clients. It usually takes three to six years of practical, on-the-job experience in order to become a fully qualified interior designer.

As interior professionals gain experience, they can move into positions of greater responsibility and may eventually be promoted to such jobs as design department head or interior furnishings coordinator. Professionals who work with furnishings in architectural firms often become more involved in product design and sales. Designers and decorators can also establish their own businesses. Consulting is another common area of work for the established designer.

EARNINGS

Interior designers earned median annual salaries of $36,540 in 2000, according to the *Occupational Outlook Handbook.* The highest 10 percent earned more than $66,470, while the lowest 10 percent earned less than $19,840 annually. In general, interior designers working in large urban areas make significantly more than those working in smaller cities.

Designers and decorators at interior design firms can earn a straight salary, a salary plus a bonus or commission, or a straight commission. Such firms sometimes pay their employees a percentage of the profits as well. Self-employed professionals may charge an hourly fee, a flat fee, or a combination of the two depending on the project. Some designers charge a percentage on the cost of materials bought for each project.

The benefits enjoyed by interior designers and decorators, like salaries and bonuses, depend on the particular employer. Benefits may include paid vacations, health and life insurance, paid sick or personal days, employee-sponsored retirement plans, and an employer-sponsored 401-K program.

WORK ENVIRONMENT

Working conditions for interior designers vary, depending on where they are employed. While professionals usually have an office or a studio, they may spend the day at a department store, architecture firm, or construction site working with the decorating materials sold by the firm and the clients who have purchased them. In addition, designers often go on-site to consult with and supervise the projects being completed by various craftworkers.

Whether designers are employed by a firm or operate their own businesses, much of their time is spent in clients' homes and businesses. While more and more offices are using the services of interior designers, the larger part of the business still lies in the area of home design. Residential designers work intimately with customers, planning, selecting materials, receiving instructions, and sometimes subtly guiding the customers' tastes and choices in order to achieve an atmosphere that is both aesthetic and functional.

While beginning designers and those employed by department stores, furniture stores, or design firms often work regular 40-hour weeks, self-employed professionals usually work irregular hours—including evenings and weekends—in order to accommodate their clients' schedules. Deadlines must be met, and if there have been problems and delays on the job, the designer must work hard to complete the project on schedule. In general, the more successful a designer becomes, the longer and more irregular their hours are.

The interior designer's main objective is ultimately to please the customer and thus establish a good reputation. Customers may be difficult at times. They may often change their minds, forcing the designer to revise plans. Despite difficult clients, the work is interesting and provides the interior professional with a variety of activities.

OUTLOOK

Employment opportunities are expected to be very good for interior designers and decorators through 2010, according to the U.S. Department of Labor. However, since the services of design professionals are in many ways a luxury, the job outlook is heavily dependent on the economy. In times of prosperity, there is a steady increase in jobs. When the economy slows down, however, opportunities in the field decrease markedly.

Marketing futurist Faith Popcorn predicts that people will be staying home more (cocooning) and that there will be an increase in what she calls "fantasy adventure." This trend is based on people's desire to stay at home but, at the same time, feel like they are in exotic, remote places. In the future, Popcorn sees homes containing rooms designed like Las Vegas-style resorts, African plains, and other interesting destinations. Both cocooning and fantasy adventure, if these trends do occur, will further add to the many opportunities that will be available to interior designers.

According to the International Interior Designers Association's Industry Advisory Council (IAC), a number of trends specific to the industry will also positively influence the employment outlook for interior designers and decorators. Clients in all market areas, for example, will develop an appreciation for the value of interior design work as well as increased respect for the designer's expertise. In addition, businesses, ever mindful of their employees' safety, health, and general welfare, will rely more heavily on designers to create interior atmospheres that will positively impact workplace performance.

The IAC also notes the importance of technology in the field of interior design. In addition to affecting the design of homes, technology will impact the production of design materials as well as create the need for multidisciplinary design. Professionals both familiar and comfortable with technology will definitely have an edge in an ever-competitive job market. Finally, the IAC points to the continued importance of education and research in the field of interior design. According to Allison Carll-White, director of the International Interior Designers Association's Research and Education Forum, design organizations will have to offer programs focusing on basic interior design in order to attract talented students to the profession.

While competition for good designing positions is expected to be fierce, especially for those lacking experience, there is currently a great need for industrial interior designers in housing developments, hospital complexes, hotels, and other large building projects. In addition, as construction of houses increases, there will be many projects available for residential designers.

FOR MORE INFORMATION
For industry trends, career guidance, and other resources, contact
American Society of Interior Designers
608 Massachusetts Avenue, NE
Washington, DC 20002-6006
Tel: 202-546-3480
Email: asid@asid.org
http://www.asid.org

FIDER promotes excellence in interior design education through research and the accreditation of academic programs. For information, contact
Foundation for Interior Design Education Research (FIDER)
146 Monroe Center, NW, Suite 1318
Grand Rapids, MI 49503-2822

Tel: 616-458-0400
Email: fider@fider.org
http://www.fider.org

For information on continuing education and publications, contact
Interior Design Educators Council
9202 North Meridan Street, Suite 200
Indianapolis, IN 46260-1810
Tel: 317-816-6261
Email: info@idec.org
http://www.idec.org

For information on the industry, contact
International Interior Design Association
13-122 Merchandise Mart
Chicago, IL 60654-1104
Tel: 888-799-4432
Email: iidahq@iida.org
http://www.iida.com

NCIDQ is an independent organization created to establish minimum standards and to develop and administer a minimum competency examination for the qualification of professional interior designers. For information on the examinations, contact
National Council for Interior Design Qualification (NCIDQ)
1200 18th Street, NW, Suite 1001
Washington, DC 20036-2506
Tel: 202-721-0220
Email: ncidq@ncidq.org
http://www.ncidq.org

INTERNET DEVELOPERS

QUICK FACTS

School Subjects	Certification or Licensing
Computer science	Voluntary
Mathematics	**Outlook**
Personal Skills	Faster than the average
Artistic	**DOT**
Communication/ideas	N/A
Technical/scientific	**GOE**
Work Environment	N/A
Primarily indoors	**NOC**
Primarily one location	2175
Minimum Education Level	**O*NET-SOC**
Bachelor's degree	N/A
Salary Range	
$30,000 to $56,250 to $76,750	

OVERVIEW

An *Internet developer,* otherwise known as a *Web developer* or *Web designer,* is responsible for the creation of an Internet site. Most of the time, this is a public website, but it can also be a private Internet network. Web developers are employed by a wide range of employers from small entrepreneurs to large corporate businesses to Internet consulting firms.

HISTORY

With the explosive growth of the World Wide Web, companies have flocked to use Internet technology to communicate worldwide—with employees, customers, clients, buyers, future stockholders, and so on. As a result, these companies need people who can create sites to fit their needs and the needs of their target audience.

In the early years of the Internet, most information presented was text only with no pictures. Today, a few sites still use a text-only format, but the vast majority have evolved to use the latest technologies, using graphics, video, audio, and interactive forms and applications. For most companies, the first Internet sites were created and maintained by a sole individual who was a jack-of-all-trades. Today, these sites are often designed, implemented, and managed by entire departments composed of numerous individuals who specialize in specific areas of website work. The Web developer is the individual with the technical knowledge of programming to implement the ideas and goals of the organization into a smoothly flowing, informative, interesting website. Because of evolving technology, the future will require more specialized skills and technological expertise of Web developers.

THE JOB

After determining the overall goals, layout, and performance limitations of a client's website with input from marketing, sales, advertising, and other departments, an Internet or Web developer designs the site and writes the code necessary to run and navigate it. To make the site, a working knowledge of the latest Internet programming languages such as Perl, Visual Basic, Java, C++, HTML, and XML is a must. The developer must also be up to date on the latest in graphic file formats and other Web production tools.

The concept of the site must be translated to a general layout. It is here that the Internet developer's creative talents must come into play, as the layout of the site must accomplish the client's goals, but also be unique, engaging, and easy to follow. The layout must be turned into a set of pages, which are designed, written, and edited. Those pages are then converted into the proper code so that they can be placed on the server. There are software packages that exist to help the developer create the sites. However, software packages often use templates to create sites that have the same general look to them—which is not a good thing if the site is to stand out and look original. Also, no one software package does it all. Additional scripts or special features, such as banners with the latest advertising slogan, spinning logos, forms that provide data input from users, and easy online ordering, are often needed to add punch to a site.

Perhaps the trickiest part of the job is effectively integrating the needs of the organization with the needs of the customer. For example, the organization might want the content to be visually cutting-edge and entertaining, however, the targeted customer might not have the modem speed needed to view those highly graphical pages and might prefer to get "just the facts" quickly. The developer must be creative and able to improvise to find a happy medium and deliver the information in a practical yet interesting manner.

REQUIREMENTS

High School

In high school, take as many courses as possible in computer science, science, and mathematics. These classes will provide you with a good foundation in computer basics and analytical-thinking skills. You should also take English and speech classes in order to hone your written and verbal communication skills. Art classes will help you develop and expand your creative sensibilities.

Postsecondary Training

There currently is no established educational track for Internet developers. They typically hold bachelor's degrees in computer science or computer programming—although some have degrees in noncomputer areas, such as marketing, graphic design, library and information science, or information systems. Regardless of educational background, you need to have an understanding of computers and computer networks and a knowledge of Internet programming languages. Formal college training in these languages may be hard to come by because of the rapid evolution of the Internet. What's hot today might be obsolete tomorrow. Because of this volatility, most of the postsecondary training comes from hands-on experience. This is best achieved through internships or entry-level positions. One year of experience working on a site is invaluable toward landing a job in the field.

Certification or Licensing

Because there is no central governing organization or association for this field, certification is not required. Certifications are available, however, from various vendors of development software applications. These designations are helpful in proving your abilities to an employer. The more certifications you have, the more you have to offer.

Other Requirements

A good Internet developer balances technological know-how with creativity. You must be able to make a site stand out from the sea of other sites on the Web. For example, if your company is selling a product on the Web, your site needs to "scream" the unique qualities and benefits of the product.

Working with Internet technologies, you must be able to adapt quickly to change. It is not uncommon to learn a new programming language and get comfortable using it, only to have to learn another new language and scrap the old one. If you're a quick study, then you should have an advantage.

EXPLORING

You can read national news magazines, newspapers, and trade magazines or surf the Web for information about Internet careers. You can also visit a variety of websites to study what makes them either interesting or not so appealing. Does your high school have a Web site? If so, get involved in the planning and creation of new content for it. If not, talk to your computer teachers about creating one, or create your own site at home.

EMPLOYERS

Everyone is getting online these days, from the Fortune 500 companies to the smallest of mom-and-pop shops. The smaller companies might have one person in charge of everything Web related: the server, the site, the security, and so on. Larger companies employ a department of many workers, each one taking on specific responsibilities.

An obvious place of employment is Internet consulting firms. Some firms specialize in Web development or website management; other firms offer services relating to all aspects of website design, creation, management, and maintenance.

The Internet is worldwide; thus, Internet jobs are available worldwide. Wherever there is a business connected to the Internet, people with the right skills can find Web-related jobs.

STARTING OUT

If you are looking for a job as an Internet developer, remember that experience is key. College courses are important, but if you graduate and have lots of book knowledge and no experience, you're going to get a slow start. If at all possible, seek out internships while in school.

Use the Internet to find a job. The search engines of popular websites aimed at job seekers, such as http://www.hotjobs.com or http://www.monster.com, can be useful. While you're online, check out some of the Internet trade magazines for a job bank or classifieds section.

ADVANCEMENT

The next step up the career ladder for Internet developers might be a move to a larger company where the website presence consists of more pages. Some websites have hundreds and even thousands of pages. Another option is to become a *Webmaster*. Webmasters generally have the responsibility of overseeing all aspects (technical, management, maintenance, marketing, and organization) of a website.

EARNINGS

An entry-level position in Web development at a small company pays around $30,000. According to Robert Half International, salaries for Internet developers ranged from $56,250 to $76,750 in 2001.

Differences in pay tend to follow the differences found in other careers: the Northeast pays more than the Midwest or South, and men are generally paid more than women (although this may change as the number of women rivals the number of men employed in these jobs).

Benefits include paid vacation, paid holidays, paid sick days, health insurance, dental insurance, life insurance, personal days, and bonuses.

WORK ENVIRONMENT

Web developers work at computers in comfortable offices. Most of their work is done alone; however, developers consult frequently with the webmaster and others who work to write or edit the content of a site.

OUTLOOK

The career of Internet developer, like the Internet itself, is growing faster than the average. As more and more companies look to expand their business worldwide, they need technically skilled employees to create the sites to bring their products, services, and corporate images to the Internet. In a survey of information architects by the Argus Center for Information Architecture, respondents predicted that certification and graduate degrees will become increasingly important in this career. Postsecondary training in Internet technology is growing, including graduate degrees in information design, informatics, interactive arts, human-computer interaction, and communication design. Universities that now offer strong programs in computer science, writing, and design will be developing liberal arts programs in information architecture. Jobs will be plentiful in the next decade for anyone with this specialized training.

FOR MORE INFORMATION

The Association of Internet Professionals represents the worldwide community of people employed in Internet-related fields.

Association of Internet Professionals
4790 Irvine Boulevard, Suite 105-283
Irvine, CA 92620
Tel: 866-247-9700
Email: info@association.org
http://www.association.org

For information on scholarships, student membership, and the student newsletter, looking.forward, *contact*

IEEE Computer Society
1730 Massachusetts Avenue, NW
Washington, DC 20036-1992
Tel: 202-371-0101
http://www.computer.org

JEWELERS AND JEWELRY REPAIRERS

QUICK FACTS

School Subjects
Art
Technical/shop

Personal Skills
Artistic
Mechanical/manipulative

Work Environment
Primarily indoors
Primarily one location

Minimum Education Level
Apprenticeship

Salary Range
$14,550 to $26,330 to $44,120+

Certification or Licensing
Voluntary

Outlook
Little change or more slowly than the average

DOT
700

GOE
01.06.02

NOC
7344

O*NET-SOC
51-9071.00, 51-9071.01, 51-9071.03, 51-9071.04, 51-9071.05, 51-9071.06

OVERVIEW

Jewelers fabricate rings, necklaces, bracelets, and other jewelry out of gold, silver, or platinum, either from their own design or one by a design specialist. *Jewelry repairers* alter ring sizes, reset stones, and refashion old jewelry. Restringing beads and stones, resetting clasps and hinges, and mending breaks in ceramic and metal pieces also are aspects of jewelry repair. A few jewelers are also *gemologists*, who examine, grade, and evaluate gems, or *gem cutters*, who cut, shape, and polish gemstones. Many jewelers also repair watches and clocks. There are about 43,000 jewelers employed in the United States.

HISTORY

Many of the metals jewelers use today, such as gold, silver, copper, brass, and iron, were first discovered or used by ancient jewelers.

During the Heshamite Empire, a court jeweler discovered iron while seeking a stronger metal to use in battles. During the Renaissance period in Europe, jewelers became increasingly skillful. Artists such as Botticelli and Cellini used gold and silver with precious stones of every sort to create masterpieces of the gold and silversmiths' trades. Jewelers perfected the art of enameling during this time.

Many skilled artisans brought their trades to Colonial America. The first jewelers were watchmakers, silversmiths, and coppersmiths. In early America, a versatile craft worker might create a ring or repair the copper handle on a cooking pot. By the 1890s, New York City had emerged as a center of the precious metal jewelry industry. It became a center for the diamond trade as well as for other precious stones. The first jewelry store, as we know it today, opened at the turn of the 19th century.

By the early 20th century, machines were used to create jewelry, and manufacturing plants began mass production of costume jewelry. These more affordable items quickly became popular and made jewelry available to large numbers of people.

New York City continues today as a leading center of the precious metals industry and jewelry manufacturing in the United States. Along with Paris and London, it is a prime location for many fine jewelry designers.

During the 1980s, a small niche of jewelers began creating their own designs and either making them themselves or having other jewelers fabricate them. Also called *jewelry artists,* they differ from more traditional designers both in the designs they create and the methods and materials they use. They sell their designer lines of jewelry in small boutiques, galleries, or at crafts shows or market them to larger retail stores. Many of these jewelers open their own stores. The American Jewelry Design Council was founded in 1990 to help promote designer jewelry as an art form.

THE JOB

Jewelers may design, make, sell, or repair jewelry. Many jewelers combine two or more of these skills. Designers conceive and sketch ideas for jewelry that they may make themselves or have made by another craftsperson. The materials of the jeweler and the jewelry repairer usually are precious and semiprecious or synthetic stones and gold, silver, and platinum. The jeweler begins by forming an article in wax or metal with carving tools; the jeweler then places the wax model in a casting ring and pours plaster into the ring to form a mold.

The mold is inserted into a furnace to melt the wax and a metal model is cast from the plaster mold. The jeweler pours the precious molten metal into the mold or uses a centrifugal casting machine to cast the article. Cutting, filing, and polishing are final touches to the item.

Jewelers do most of their work sitting down. They use small hand and machine tools, such as drills, files, saws, soldering irons, and jewelers' lathes. They often wear an eye *loupe,* or magnifying glass. They constantly use their hands and eyes and need good finger-hand dexterity.

Most jewelers specialize in creating or making certain kinds of jewelry or in a particular operation, such as making, polishing, or stone-setting models and tools. Specialists include gem cutters; stone setters; fancy-wire drawers; locket, ring, and hand chain makers; and sample makers.

Silversmiths design, assemble, decorate, or repair silver articles. They may specialize in one or more areas of the jewelry field such as repairing, selling, or appraising. *Jewelry engravers* carve printing, identification, or decoration on jewelry. *Watchmakers* repair, clean, and adjust mechanisms of watches and clocks.

Gem and diamond workers select, split, saw, cut, shape, polish, or drill gems and diamonds used in jewelry or for tools and industrial purposes, using measuring instruments, machines, or hand tools. Some work as *diamond die polishers,* while others are gem cutters. Fewer than 600 of these specialists are employed in jewelry making today. Others in the industry may perform such operations as precision casting and modeling of molds, or setting precious and semiprecious stones for jewelry. They may make gold or silver chains and cut designs or lines in jewelry using hand tools or cutting machines. Still others work as pearl restorers or jewelry bench hands.

Experienced jewelers may become qualified to make and repair any kind of jewelry. Assembly line methods are used to produce costume jewelry and some types of precious jewelry, but the models and tools needed for factory production must be made by highly skilled jewelers. Some molds and models for manufacturing are designed and created using computer-aided design/manufacturing systems. Costume jewelry often is made by a die stamping process. In general, the more precious the metals, the less automated the manufacturing process.

Some jewelers and jewelry repairers are self-employed; others work for manufacturing and retail establishments. Workers in a manufacturing plant include skilled, semiskilled, and unskilled positions. Skilled positions include jewelers, ring makers, engravers, toolmakers, electroplaters, and stone cutters and setters. Semiskilled positions include polishers, repairers, toolsetters, and solderers. Unskilled workers are press operators, carders, and linkers.

Although some jewelers operate their own retail stores, an increasing number of jewelry stores are owned or managed by business persons who are not jewelers. In such instances, a jeweler or jewelry repairer may be employed by the owner, or the store may send its repairs to a trade shop operated by a jeweler who specializes in repair work. Jewelers who operate their own stores sell jewelry, watches, and often merchandise such as silverware, china, and glassware. Many retail jewelry stores are located in or near large cities, with the eastern section of the country providing most of the employment in jewelry manufacturing.

Other jobs in the jewelry business include *appraisers,* who examine jewelry and determine its value and quality; *sales staff,* who set up and care for jewelry displays, take inventory, and help customers; and *buyers,* who purchase jewelry, gems, and watches from wholesalers so they can resell the items to the public in retail stores.

REQUIREMENTS
High School
A high school education usually is necessary for persons desiring to enter the jewelry trade. While you are in high school, take courses in chemistry, physics, mechanical drawing, and art. Computer-aided design classes will be especially beneficial to you if you are planning to design jewelry. Sculpture and metalworking classes will prepare you for design and repair work.

Postsecondary Training
A large number and variety of educational and training programs are available in jewelry and jewelry repair. Trade schools and community colleges offer a variety of programs, including classes in basic jewelry-making skills, techniques, use and care of tools and machines, stone setting, casting, polishing, and gem identification. Programs usually run from six to 36 months, although individual classes are shorter and can be taken without enrolling in an entire program.

Some colleges and universities offer programs in jewelry store management, metalwork, and jewelry design. You can also find classes at fashion institutes, art schools, and art museums. In addition, you can take correspondence courses and continuing education classes. For sales and managerial positions in a retail store, college experience is usually helpful. Recommended classes are sales techniques, gemology, advertising, accounting, business administration, and computers.

The work of the jeweler and jewelry repairer may also be learned through an apprenticeship or by informal on-the-job training. The latter often includes instruction in design, quality of precious stones, and chemistry of metals. The apprentice becomes a jeweler upon the successful completion of a two-year apprenticeship and passing written and oral tests covering the trade. The apprenticeship generally focuses on casting, stone setting, and engraving.

Most jobs in manufacturing require on-the-job training, although many employers prefer to hire individuals who have completed a technical education program.

Certification or Licensing

Certification is available in several areas through the trade organization Jewelers of America. Those who do bench work (the hands-on work creating and repairing jewelry) can be certified at one of four levels: Certified Bench Jeweler Technician, Certified Bench Jeweler, Certified Senior Bench Jeweler, and Certified Master Bench Jeweler. Each certification involves passing a written test and a bench test. Jewelers of America also offers certification for management and sales workers. Although voluntary, these certifications show that a professional has met certain standards for the field and is committed to this work.

Other Requirements

Jewelers and jewelry repairers need to have extreme patience and skill to handle the expensive materials of the trade. Although the physically disabled may find employment in this field, superior eye-hand coordination is essential. Basic mechanical skills such as filing, sawing, and drilling are vital to the jewelry repairer. Jewelers who work from their own designs need creative and artistic ability. They also should have a strong understanding of metals and their properties. Retail jewelers and those who operate or own trade shops and manufacturing establishments must work well with people and be knowledgeable about merchandising and business management and practices. Sales staff should be knowledgeable and friendly, and buyers must have good judgment, self-confidence, and leadership abilities. Because of the expensive nature of jewelry, some people working in the retail industry are bonded, which means they must pass the requirements for an insurance company to underwrite them.

EXPLORING

If you are interested in becoming a jeweler or jewelry repairer, you can become involved in arts and crafts activities and take classes in crafts and jewelry making. Many community education programs are available through high schools, park districts, or local art stores and museums. Hobbies such as metalworking and sculpture are useful in becoming familiar with metals and the tools jewelers use. Visits to museums and fine jewelry stores to see collections of jewelry can be helpful.

If you are interested in the retail aspect of this field, you should try to find work in a retail jewelry store on a part-time basis or during the summer. A job in sales, or even as a clerk, can provide a firsthand introduction to the business. You will become familiar with a jewelry store's operations, its customers, and the jewelry sold. In addition, you will learn the terminology unique to the jewelry field. Working in a retail store with an in-house jeweler or jewelry repairer provides many opportunities to observe and speak with a professional engaged in this trade. In a summer or part-time job as a bench worker or assembly line worker in a factory, you may perform only a few of the operations involved in making jewelry, but you will be exposed to many of the skills used within a manufacturing plant.

You also may want to visit retail stores and shops where jewelry is made and repaired or visit a jewelry factory. Some boutiques and galleries are owned and operated by jewelers who enjoy the opportunity to talk to people about their trade. Art fairs and craft shows where jewelers exhibit and sell their products provide a more relaxed environment where jewelers are likely to have time to discuss their work.

EMPLOYERS

Jewelers work in a variety of settings, from production work in multinational corporations or smaller firms to jewelry stores and repair shops. Some jewelers specialize in gem and diamond work, watch making, jewelry appraisal, repair, or engraving, where they may work in manufacturing or at the retail level. Other jewelers work as appraisers and some stores employ an appraiser to do only that work. In most cases, though, appraisals are done by store owners or jewelers who have years of experience. About one-third of all jewelers are self-employed. The majority of the self-employed jewelers own their own stores or repair shops or specialize in designing and creating custom jewelry.

STARTING OUT

A summer or part-time job in a jewelry store or the jewelry department of a department store will help you learn about the business. Another method of entering this line of work is to obtain employment in jewelry manufacturing establishments in major production centers. A trainee can acquire the many skills needed in the jewelry trade. The number of trainees accepted in this manner, however, is relatively small. Students who have completed a training program improve their chances of finding work as an apprentice or trainee. Students may learn about available jobs and apprenticeships through the placement offices of training schools they attend, from local jewelers, or from the personnel offices of manufacturing plants.

Those desiring to establish their own retail businesses find it helpful to first obtain employment with an established jeweler or a manufacturing plant. Considerable financial investment is required to open a retail jewelry store, and jewelers in such establishments find it to their advantage to be able to do repair work on watches as well as the usual jeweler's work. Less financial investment is needed to open a trade shop. These shops generally tend to be more successful in or near areas with large populations where they can take advantage of the large volume of jewelry business. Both retail jewelry stores and trade shops are required to meet local and state business laws and regulations.

ADVANCEMENT

There are many opportunities for advancement in the jewelry field. Jewelers and jewelry repairers can go into business for themselves once they have mastered the skills of their trade. They may create their own designer lines of jewelry that they market and sell, or they can open a trade shop or retail store. Many self-employed jewelers gain immense satisfaction from the opportunity to specialize in one aspect of jewelry or to experiment with new methods and materials.

Workers in jewelry manufacturing have fewer opportunities for advancement than in other areas of jewelry because of the declining number of workers needed. Plant workers in semiskilled and unskilled positions can advance based on the speed and quality of their work and by perseverance. On-the-job training can provide opportunities for higher-skilled positions. Workers in manufacturing who show proficiency can advance to supervisory and management positions, or they may leave manufacturing and go to work in a retail shop or trade shop.

The usual avenue of advancement is from employee in a factory, shop, or store to owner or manager of a trade shop or retail store. Sales is an excellent starting place for people who want to own their own store. Sales staff receive firsthand training in customer relations as well as knowledge of the different aspects of jewelry store merchandising. Sales staff may become gem experts who are qualified to manage a store, and *managers* may expand their territory from one store to managing several stores in a district or region. Top management in retail offers many interesting and rewarding positions to people who are knowledgeable, responsible, and ambitious. Buyers may advance by dealing exclusively with fine gems that are more expensive, and some buyers become *diamond merchants,* buying diamonds on the international market.

Jewelry designers' success depends not only on the skill with which they make jewelry but also on the ability to create new designs and to keep in touch with current trends in the consumer market. Jewelry designers attend craft shows, trade shows, and jewelry exhibitions to see what others are making and to get ideas for new lines of jewelry.

EARNINGS

Median annual earnings for jewelers and precious stone and metal workers were $26,330 in 2000, according to the U.S. Department of Labor. Salaries ranged from less than $14,550 to more than $44,120. Those who worked in retail stores earned a median of $32,290 and those who worked in the jewelry, silverware, and plated ware industry earned a median of $22,920. Retail store owners and jewelry artists and designers can earn anywhere from $25,000 to $50,000 or more yearly, based on their volume of business. Most jewelers start out with a base salary, but with experience they might begin charging by the number of pieces completed. Jewelers who work in retail stores may earn a commission for each piece of jewelry sold, in addition to their base salary.

Most employers offer benefit packages that include paid holidays and vacations and health insurance. Retail stores may offer discounts on store purchases.

WORK ENVIRONMENT

Jewelers work in a variety of environments. Some self-employed jewelers design and create jewelry in their homes; others work in small studios or trade shops. Some use computer-aided designing software to create their sketches. Jewelers who create their own designer lines of jewelry may travel to retail stores and other sites to promote their merchandise. Many designers also attend trade shows and exhibitions to learn more about current trends. Some sell their jewelry at both indoor and outdoor art shows and craft fairs. These shows are held on weekends, evenings, or during the week. Many jewelry artists live and work near tourist areas or in art communities.

Workers in jewelry manufacturing plants usually work in clean, air-conditioned, and relatively quiet environments. Workers in departments such as polishing, electroplating, and lacquer spraying may be exposed to fumes from chemicals and solvents. Workers may do bench work where they sit at a workstation or on an assembly line where they may be standing or sitting. Assembly line workers may operate machinery. Many workers in a manufacturing plant perform only one or two types of operations so the work can become repetitive. Most employees in a manufacturing plant work 35-hour workweeks, with an occasional need for overtime.

Retail store owners, managers, jewelers, and sales staff work a variety of hours and shifts that include weekends, especially during the Christmas season, the busiest time of year. Buyers may work more than 40 hours a week because they must travel to see wholesalers. Work settings vary from small shops and boutiques to large department stores. Most jewelry stores are clean, quiet, pleasant, and attractive. However, most jewelry store employees spend many hours on their feet dealing with customers, and buyers travel a great deal.

OUTLOOK

Employment of jewelers is expected to experience little or no change through 2010, according to the *Occupational Outlook Handbook.* Consumers now are purchasing jewelry from mass marketers, discount stores, catalogs, television shopping shows, and the Internet as well as from traditional retail stores. This may result in some stores closing or in limited opportunities within them for employment. However, jewelers and jewelry repairers will continue to be needed to replace those workers who leave the workforce or move to new positions within it. Since jewelry sales are increasing at rates that exceed the number of new jewelers entering the profession, employers are finding it difficult to find employees with master-level skills.

The number of workers in manufacturing plants is declining because of increased automation, but opportunities in retail should remain steady or improve slightly. Demand in retail is growing for people who are skilled in personnel, management, sales and promotion, advertising, floor and window display, and buying.

FOR MORE INFORMATION

For a list of accredited technical schools with jewelry design programs, contact

Accrediting Commission of Career Schools and Colleges of Technology
2101 Wilson Boulevard, Suite 302
Arlington, VA 22201
Tel: 703-247-4212
Email: info@accsct.org
http://www.accsct.org

For an information packet with tuition prices, application procedures, and course descriptions, contact

Gemological Institute of America
The Robert Mouawad Campus
5345 Armada Drive
Carlsbad, CA 92008-9525
Tel: 800-421-7250, ext. 4001
Email: eduinfo@gia.edu
http://www.gia.org

For certification information, a school directory, and a copy of Careers in Retail Jewelry: A Jewelers of America Guide, *contact*

Jewelers of America
52 Vanderbilt Avenue, 19th Floor
New York, NY 10017
Tel: 646-658-0246
Email: contactus@jewelers.org
http://www.jewelers.org

For career and school information, contact

Manufacturing Jewelers and Silversmiths of America
45 Royal Little Drive
Providence, RI 02904
Tel: 800-444-6572
Email: mjsa@mjsainc.com
http://mjsa.polygon.net

LANDSCAPE ARCHITECTS

QUICK FACTS

School Subjects
Agriculture
Art
Earth science

Personal Skills
Artistic
Technical/scientific

Work Environment
Indoors and outdoors
Primarily multiple locations

Minimum Education Level
Bachelor's degree

Salary Range
$28,640 to $46,710 to
$79,580+

Certification or Licensing
Required by certain states

Outlook
Faster than the average

DOT
001

GOE
05.01.07

NOC
2151

O*NET-SOC
17-1012.00

OVERVIEW

Landscape architects plan and design areas such as highways, housing communities, college campuses, commercial centers, recreation facilities, and nature conservation areas. They work to balance beauty and function in developed outdoor areas. There are approximately 22,000 landscape architects employed in the United States.

HISTORY

In the United States, landscape architecture has been practiced as a profession for the last 100 years. During the early part of the 20th century, landscape architects were employed mainly by the wealthy or by the government on public-works projects. In 1918, the practice of dividing large plots of land into individual lots for sale was born. In addition, there was a new public interest in the development of outdoor recreational facilities. These two factors provided many new opportunities for landscape architects.

The most dramatic growth occurred following the environmental movement of the 1960s, when public respect for protection of valuable natural resources reached an all-time high. Landscape architects have played a key role in encouraging the protection of natural resources while providing for the increasing housing and recreation needs of the American public.

In the last 30 years, the development of recreational areas has become more important, as has the development of streets, bypasses, and massive highways. Landscape architects are needed in most projects of this nature. Both developers and community planners draw upon the services of landscape architects now more than ever.

THE JOB

Landscape architects plan and design outdoor spaces that make the best use of the land; in doing this, landscape architects also respect the needs of the natural environment. They may be involved in a number of different types of projects, including the design of parks or gardens, scenic roads, housing projects, college or high school campuses, country clubs, cemeteries, or golf courses. Their employers are in both the public and private sectors.

Landscape architects begin a project by carefully reviewing their client's desires, including the purpose, structures needed, and funds available. They study the work site itself, observing and mapping such features as the slope of the land, existing structures, plants, and trees. They also consider different views of the location, taking note of shady and sunny areas, the structure of the soil, and existing utilities.

Landscape architects consult with a number of different people, such as engineers, architects, city officials, zoning experts, real estate agents and brokers, and landscape nursery workers to develop a complete understanding of the job. Then they develop detailed plans and drawings of the site to present to the client for approval. Some projects take many months before the proposed plans are ready to be presented to the client.

After developing final plans and drawing up a materials list, landscape architects invite construction companies to submit bids for the job. Depending upon the nature of the project and the contractual agreement, landscape architects may remain on the job to supervise construction, or they may leave the project once work has begun. Those who remain on the job serve as the client's representative until the job is completed and approved.

REQUIREMENTS
High School

To prepare for a college program in landscape architecture, you should take courses in English composition and literature; social sciences, including history, government, and sociology; natural sciences, including biology, chemistry, and physics; and mathematics. If available, take drafting and mechanical drawing courses to begin building the technical skills needed for the career.

Postsecondary Training

A bachelor's or master's degree in landscape architecture is usually the minimum requirement for entry into this field. Undergraduate and graduate programs in landscape architecture are offered in various colleges and universities; 75 programs are accredited by the Landscape Architecture Accreditation Board of the American Society of Landscape Architects. Courses of study usually focus on six basic areas of the profession: landscape design, landscape construction, plants, architecture, graphic expression (mechanical and freehand drawings), and verbal expression.

Hands-on work is a crucial element to the curriculum. Whenever possible, students work on real projects to gain experience with computer-aided design (CAD) programs and video simulation.

Certification or Licensing

Almost all states require landscape architects to be licensed. To obtain licensure, applicants must pass the Landscape Architect Registration Examination, sponsored by the Council of Landscape Architectural Registration Boards. Though standards vary by state, most require applicants to have a degree from an accredited program and to be working towards one to four years of experience in the field. In addition, 16 states require prospective landscape architects to pass another exam that tests knowledge of local environmental regulations, vegetation, and other characteristics unique to the particular state. Because these standards vary, landscape architects may have to reapply for licensure if they plan to work in a different state. However, in many cases, workers who meet the national standards and have passed the exam may be granted the right to work elsewhere.

Landscape architects working for the federal government need a bachelor's or master's degree, but they do not need to be licensed.

Other Requirements

You should be interested in art and nature and have good business sense, especially if you hope to work independently. Interest in environmental protection, community improvement, and landscape design is also crucial for the profession. You should also be flexible and be able to think creatively to solve unexpected problems that may develop during the course of a project. Finally, you need to be in good physical shape to endure long days of hard work.

EXPLORING

If you are interested in learning more about the field, you can gather information and experience in a number of ways. Apply for a summer internship with a landscape architectural firm or at least arrange to talk with someone in the job. Ask them questions about their daily duties, the job's advantages and disadvantages, and if they recommend any landscape architecture programs.

EMPLOYERS

There are roughly 22,000 landscape architects employed in the United States, according to the U.S. Department of Labor. Landscape architects are found in every state in the United States, in small towns and cities as well as heavily populated areas. Some work in rural areas, such as those who plan and design national parks and recreational areas. However, the majority of positions are found in suburban and urban areas.

Landscape architects work for a variety of different employers in both the public and private sectors. They may work with a school board planning a new elementary or high school, with manufacturers developing a new factory, with homeowners improving the land surrounding their home, or with a city council planning a new suburban development.

In the private sector, most landscape architects do some residential work, though few limit themselves entirely to projects with individual homeowners. Larger commercial or community projects are usually more profitable. Workers in the public sector plan and design government buildings, parks, and public lands. They also may conduct studies on environmental issues and restore lands such as mines or landfills.

STARTING OUT

After graduating from a landscape architecture program, you can usually receive job assistance from the school's career placement service. Although these services do not guarantee a job, they can be of great help in making initial contacts. Many positions are posted by the American Society of Landscape Architects and published in their two journals, *Landscape Architectural News Digest Online* (http://www.asla.org/members/land) and *Landscape Architecture* (http://www.asla.org/nonmembers/lam.cfm). Government positions are normally filled through civil service examinations. Information regarding vacancies may be obtained through the local, state, or federal civil service commissions.

Most new hires are often referred to as interns or apprentices until they have gained initial experience in the field and have passed the necessary examinations. Apprentices' duties vary by employer: Some handle background project research, others are directly involved in planning and design. Whatever their involvement, all new hires work under the direct supervision of a licensed landscape architect. All drawings and plans must be signed and sealed by the licensed supervisor for legal purposes.

ADVANCEMENT

After obtaining licensure and gaining work experience in all phases of a project's development, landscape architects can become project managers, responsible for overseeing the entire project and meeting schedule deadlines and budgets. They can also advance to the level of associate, increasing their earning opportunities by gaining a profitable stake in a firm.

The ultimate objective of many landscape architects is to gain the experience necessary to organize and open their own firm. According to the U.S. Department of Labor, over 25 percent of all landscape architects are self-employed—four times the average of workers in other professions. After the initial investment in CAD software, few start-up costs are involved in breaking into the business independently.

EARNINGS

Salaries for landscape architects vary depending on the employer, work experience, location, and whether they are paid a straight salary or earn a percentage of a firm's profits.

According to 2001 data from the U.S. Department of Labor, the median annual salary for landscape architects was $46,710. The lowest paid 10 percent earned less than $28,640 and the highest paid 10 percent earned over $79,580. The average salary for those working with the federal government was generally higher than average, at $62,824 a year.

Benefits also vary depending on the employer but usually include health insurance coverage, paid vacation time, and sick leave. Many landscape architects work for small landscaping firms or are self-employed. These workers generally receive fewer benefits than those who work for large organizations.

WORK ENVIRONMENT

Landscape architects spend much of their time in the field gathering information at the work site. They also spend time in the office, drafting plans and designs. Those working for larger organizations may have to travel further away to worksites.

Work hours are generally regular, except during periods of increased business or when nearing a project deadline. Hours vary for self-employed workers because they determine their own schedules.

OUTLOOK

According to the *Occupational Outlook Handbook*, the employment of landscape architects is expected to increase faster than the average for all occupations over the next decade. The increase in demand for landscape architects is a result of several factors: a boom in the construction industry, the need to refurbish existing sites, and the increase in city and environmental planning and historic preservation. In addition, many job openings are expected to result from the need to replace experienced workers who leave the field.

The need for landscape architecture depends to a great extent on the construction industry. In the event of an economic downturn, when real estate transactions and the construction business is expected to drop off, opportunities for landscape architects will also dwindle.

Opportunities will be the greatest for workers who develop strong technical skills. The growing use of technology such as CAD will not diminish the demand for landscape architects. New and improved techniques will be used to create better designs more efficiently rather than reduce the number of workers needed to do the job.

FOR MORE INFORMATION

For information on the career, accredited education programs, licensure requirements, and available publications, contact

American Society of Landscape Architects
636 Eye Street, NW
Washington, DC 20001-3736
Tel: 202-898-2444
http://www.asla.org

For information on student resources, license examinations, and continuing education, contact

Council of Landscape Architectural Registration Boards
144 Church Street, NW, Suite 201
Vienna, VA 22180
Tel: 703-319-8380
http://www.clarb.org

For career and educational information, visit the following website sponsored by the Landscape Architecture Foundation:

LAprofession.org
http://www.laprofession.org

MEDICAL ILLUSTRATORS AND PHOTOGRAPHERS

QUICK FACTS

School Subjects
Art
Computer science

Personal Skills
Artistic
Technical/scientific

Work Environment
Primarily indoors
Primarily one location

Minimum Education Level
Some postsecondary training

Salary Range
$35,000 to $75,000 to $200,000

Certification or Licensing
None available

Outlook
Faster than the average

DOT
141

GOE
01.02.03

NOC
5241

O*NET-SOC
27-4021.02

OVERVIEW

Medical illustrators and *photographers* open the visual world of the medical field through graphics, drawings, and photographs that make things easier to understand. Medical illustrators provide illustrations of anatomical and biological structures and processes, as well as surgical and medical techniques and procedures. Medical photographers take photos that communicate complex medical or scientific information for use in textbooks, professional journals, and other teaching materials.

HISTORY

Illustration featured prominently in the ancient civilizations of Mesopotamia, Egypt, and later Greek and Roman civilizations. Drawings depicting biological, zoological, and medical knowledge have also been found among ancient Assyrian, Babylonian, Egyptian, and Chinese societies. Modern illustration began during the Renaissance of the 15th and 16th centuries, with the work of Leonardo da Vinci, Andreas Vesalius, and Michelangelo Buonarotti.

In 1625, Francesco Stelluti used the newly invented microscope to create a series of drawings of a honeybee that were magnified 10 times. The microscope became an important tool for illustrators seeking to represent details of biological and medical processes.

Over time, tools have been developed to aid illustrators and photographers in their work. Illustrators have made use of parallel bars, compasses, French curves, and T squares, but the development of computer technology has largely replaced these mechanical tools with software such as computer-aided design. And the growing sophistication of cameras makes it possible to capture medical processes with complete clarity and accuracy.

THE JOB

Medical illustrators work in a specialized area of technical illustration. These illustrators are concerned with representing human anatomy and processes, as well as other biological information. Their work is found in medical textbooks, magazines and journals, advertisements for medical products, instructional films and videotapes, television programs, exhibits, lectures and presentations, and computer-assisted learning programs. Some medical illustrators create three-dimensional physical models, such as anatomical teaching models, models used for teaching medical procedures, and prosthetics.

The role of the medical illustrator is to aid in making medical and biological information, procedures, and techniques more understandable. They combine a knowledge of biology and anatomy with strong artistic and graphic skills.

Medical illustrators generally work with physicians, surgeons, biologists, and other scientists. When detailing a surgical procedure, they may observe the surgeon during surgery and take instruction and advice from the surgeon about which parts of an operation to illustrate. They may illustrate parts of the body such as the eyes, the skeletal structure, the muscular structure, the structure of a cell, etc. for textbooks, encyclopedias, medical product brochures, and related literature. They may work with researchers to identify new organisms, develop new drugs, and examine cell structures, illustrating aspects of the researchers' work. They may also assist in developing sophisticated computer simulations that allow physicians in training to "perform" a surgical procedure entirely on a computer before they are skilled enough to operate on actual patients. Medical illustrators also animate physical, biological, and anatomical processes for films and videotapes. Some medical illustrators sculpt or build three-dimensional models as well.

A medical illustrator may work in a wide range of medical and biological areas or specialize in a particular area, such as cell structure, blood, disease, or the eye. Much of their work is done with computers; however, they must still have strong skills in traditional drawing and drafting techniques.

Like illustrators, photographers can vary their style depending on the purpose of a photograph. They often take photos to document patients' conditions before and after surgery, for example. This task requires technical proficiency in photography but does not call for innovative use of space or lighting in a shot. Photos taken for brochures or advertising materials, however, can be stylized and dramatic. In this case, medical photographers use lighting, camera angles, and design principles to create different effects in their photos.

REQUIREMENTS
High School

While in high school, make sure to develop your skills in the two areas you'll need the most: science and art. Classes in anatomy, chemistry, biology, and nutrition are all helpful science topics. Aside from taking illustration and/or photography, check out classes in visual design, if available. Most medical illustrators use computers in their art work, so gain familiarity with digital cameras and computer art, design, and layout programs.

Postsecondary Training

Medical illustrators are required to complete an advanced degree program in medical illustration. You may enter graduate school with a bachelor's degree in either art or biology. Medical illustration programs usually include training in traditional illustration and design techniques, computer illustration, two-dimensional and three-dimensional animation, prosthetics, medical computer graphics, instructional design and technology, photography, motion media production, and pharmaceutical advertising. Course work will also include pharmacology, basic sciences including anatomy and physiology, pathology, histology, embryology, neuroanatomy, and surgical observation and/or participation.

After college, you must attend one of the five accredited graduate programs in medical illustration. These programs last from two to three years and are offered at five U.S. institutions and one in Canada. These programs are accredited by the Commission on Accreditation of Allied Health Education Programs (CAAHEP).

Most medical illustrators are members of the Association of Medical Illustrators (AMI). The AMI works with the CAAHEP to establish accreditation and curriculum standards, offer certification in medical illustration, and provide other educational and support services to members and prospective members of this profession.

Medical photographers must finish a bachelor's or associate's degree that emphasizes art and photography. Very few schools offer graduate programs in medical photography. Completing a postsecondary degree in a photography-related field and taking additional course work in science will prepare you for this career.

Certification or Licensing

Medical photographers can become certified as registered biological photographers upon successfully passing written, oral, and practical examinations. You must assemble an extensive portfolio of medical photography to complete the practical portion of the certification process.

A certified medical illustrator (CMI) designation is offered by the Association of Medical Illustrators and requires graduation from an accredited program or at least five years' experience and completion of a course.

Medical illustrators and photographers need to continue their education and training while pursuing their careers. Licensing is not required in either field. While certification is not mandatory for either profession, you must keep up with the latest innovations in design techniques, computer software, photography equipment, and presentation technology, as well as technological advances in the fields for which you provide illustrations and photos.

EXPLORING

You can explore an interest in this career by taking art courses and photography courses. Participation in science clubs and fairs is good exposure. Artists can always improve their drawing skills by practicing on their own, either producing original artwork, or making sketches from scientific drawings that appear in textbooks and reference manuals, such as *Gray's Anatomy*. Visit the AMI website for a gallery of award-winning images.

EMPLOYERS

Both medical illustrators and photographers are employed at hospitals, medical centers and schools, and academic institutions. Laboratories, pharmaceutical companies, publishers of medical and scientific textbooks, and advertising agencies also employ illustrators and photographers.

STARTING OUT

Graduates of medical illustration programs should develop a portfolio of their work to show to prospective employers or clients. Most schools offer career counseling and job placement assistance to their graduates. Job ads and employment agencies are also potential sources for locating work. Likewise, aspiring medical photographers should assemble a professional portfolio of their best photos to show potential employers.

Medical illustrators can also find job placement assistance with the AMI. Joining the AMI is helpful for beginning illustrators, and many employers prefer to hire illustrators who have also been certified by the AMI. BioCommunications Association, Inc. can assist medical photographers just starting out by sharing information and posting job openings.

ADVANCEMENT

After an illustrator gains experience, he or she will be given more challenging and unusual work. Those with strong computer skills will have the best chances for advancement. Illustrators and photographers can advance by developing skills in a specialized area, or even starting their own business.

Those medical illustrators and photographers who work for large hospitals or teaching institutions can become managers of media and communications departments. Illustrators can also go into teaching, in colleges and universities at the undergraduate and graduate levels.

EARNINGS

Medical illustrators start at around $35,000 per year. The average pay for an experienced medical illustrator ranges from $40,000 to

A Great City for Artists

According to *Money* magazine, Providence, Rhode Island is one of the best cities for artists. Not only is the city the home of the Rhode Island School of Design (named one of the top schools for art majors), but it also is the first city to offer artists tax breaks just for living and working there. In 1996, Mayor Vincent "Buddy" Cianci established the Arts and Entertainment District in the downtown center to encourage growth of the arts and clean up a previously rundown section of the city. Developers were rewarded for converting abandoned and neglected buildings into residential space. Cianci also helped convert some of the area's unused buildings into art centers, galleries, and theaters. Though Cianci is no longer mayor, the Arts and Entertainment District is still alive and thriving. Many artists have flocked to live in the affordable lofts and studios and still receive tax incentives to sell their work.

$75,000 per year, depending on location and level of experience. At the high end, medical illustrators can earn $100,000–$200,000 per year, particularly if they combine freelance work with a full-time position.

Medical photographers generally earn salaries similar to medical illustrators at the entry level. The field's competitiveness, though, sometimes leads to lower salaries for experienced photographers—around $35,000–$40,000—than for experienced illustrators.

Medical illustrators and photographers employed by hospitals and other large institutions generally receive good benefits, including health and life insurance, pension plans, and vacation, sick, and holiday pay.

WORK ENVIRONMENT

Medical illustrators generally work in clean, well-lit offices. They spend a great deal of time at their desks, whether in front of a computer or at the drafting table. They are sometimes required to visit operating rooms. Photographers may have to run around if employed at a hospital to take photos in surgery, then at an official hospital event. They also may spend time in a darkroom or in front of a computer, looking for and preparing photos for publishing.

OUTLOOK

The outlook for employment as a medical illustrator is good. Because there are only a few graduate programs in medical illustration, and small graduation classes, medical illustrators will find great demand for their skills. The field of medicine and science in general is always growing, and medical illustrators will be needed to depict new techniques, procedures, and discoveries.

The demand for medical photographers has declined somewhat in recent years. Cost-cutting measures at institutions have led to increased purchases of stock photography rather than hiring photographers to take original photos. Some physicians also take their own photos, or rely on media members to take them. At the same time, the growing field of scientific information ensures a continued need for medical photographers.

FOR MORE INFORMATION

For information on educational and career opportunities for medical illustrators, contact

Association of Medical Illustrators
5475 Mark Dabling Boulevard, Suite 108
Colorado Springs, CO 80918
Tel: 719-598-8622
Email: ami@capsys.com
http://medical-illustrators.org

For industry information, contact

BioCommunications Association, Inc.
220 Southwind Lane
Hillsborough, NC 27278
Tel: 919-967-8246
Email: BCAoffice@aol.com
http://www.bca.org

For information on membership, contact

Guild of Natural Science Illustrators
PO Box 652
Ben Franklin Station
Washington, DC 20044-0652
Tel: 301-309-1514
Email: gnsihome@his.com
http://www.gnsi.org

The following national institution promotes and stimulates interest in the art of illustration by offering exhibits, lectures, educational programs, and social exchange.

Society of Illustrators
128 East 63rd Street
New York, NY 10021-7303
Tel: 212-838-2560
http://www.societyillustrators.org

MERCHANDISE DISPLAYERS

QUICK FACTS

School Subjects	Certification or Licensing
Art	None available
Technical/shop	
Theater/dance	**Outlook**
	About as fast as the average
Personal Skills	
Artistic	**DOT**
Mechanical/manipulative	298
Work Environment	**GOE**
Primarily indoors	01.02.03
Primarily one location	
	NOC
Minimum Education Level	N/A
High school diploma	
	O*NET-SOC
Salary Range	27-1026.00
$14,630 to $21,870 to	
$37,920+	

OVERVIEW

Merchandise displayers design and install displays of clothing, accessories, furniture, and other products to attract customers. They set up these displays in windows and showcases and on the sales floors of retail stores. Display workers who specialize in dressing mannequins are known as *model dressers*. These workers use their artistic flair and imagination to create excitement and customer interest in the store. They also work with other types of merchandising to develop exciting images, product campaigns, and shopping concepts. There are approximately 76,000 merchandise displayers and window trimmers employed in the United States.

HISTORY

Eye-catching displays of merchandise attract customers and encourage them to buy. This form of advertising has been used throughout history. Farmers in the past who displayed their produce at markets were careful to place their largest, most tempting fruits and vegetables at the top of the baskets. Peddlers opened their bags and cases and arranged their wares in attractive patterns. Store owners decorated their windows with collections of articles they hoped to sell. Their business success often was a matter of chance, however, and depended heavily on their own persuasiveness and sales ability.

As glass windows became less expensive, storefronts were able to accommodate larger window frames. This exposed more of the store to passersby, and stores soon found that decorative window displays were effective in attracting customers. Today, a customer may see nearly the entire store and the displays of the products it sells just by looking in the front window.

The advent of self-service stores has minimized the importance of the salesperson's personal touch. The merchandise now has to sell itself. Displays have become an important inducement for customers to buy. Advertising will bring people into stores, but an appealing product display can make the difference between a customer who merely browses and one who buys.

Merchandise displayers are needed year-round, but during the Christmas season they often execute their most elaborate work. Small retail stores generally depend on the owner or manager to create the merchandise displays, or they may hire a freelance window dresser on a part-time basis. Large retail operations, such as department stores, retain a permanent staff of display and visual merchandising specialists. Competition among these stores is intense, and their success depends on capturing a significant portion of the market. Therefore, they allocate a large share of their publicity budget to creating unique, captivating displays.

THE JOB

Using their imagination and creative ability, as well as their knowledge of color harmony, composition, and other fundamentals of art and interior design, merchandise displayers in retail establishments create an idea for a setting designed to show off merchandise and attract customers' attention. Often the display is planned around a theme or concept. After the display manager approves the design or idea, the display workers create the display. They install background settings, such as carpeting, wallpaper, and lighting, gather props and other accessories, arrange mannequins and merchandise, and place price tags and descriptive signs where they are needed.

Displayers may be assisted in some of these tasks by carpenters, painters, or store maintenance workers. Displayers may use merchandise from various departments of the store or props from previous displays. Sometimes they borrow special items that their business doesn't carry from other stores; for example, toys or sports equipment. The displays are dismantled and new ones installed every few weeks. In very large stores that employ many display workers, displayers may specialize in carpentry, painting, making signs, or setting up interior or window displays. A *display director* usually supervises and coordinates the display workers' activities and confers with other managers to select merchandise to be featured.

Ambitious and talented display workers have many possible career avenues. The importance of visual merchandising is on the rise as retail establishments compete for consumer dollars. Some display workers can advance to display director or even a position in store planning.

In addition to traditional stores, the skills of *visual marketing workers* are now in demand in many other types of establishments. Restaurants often try to present a distinct image to enhance the dining experience. Outlet stores, discount malls, and entertainment centers also use visual marketing to establish their identities with the public. Chain stores often need to make changes in or redesign all their stores and turn to display professionals for their expertise. Consumer product manufacturers also are heavily involved in visual marketing. They hire display and design workers to come up with exciting concepts, such as in-store shops, that present a unified image of the manufacturer's products and are sold as complete units to retail stores.

There are also opportunities for employment with store fixture manufacturers. Many companies build and sell specialized props, banners, signs, displays, and mannequins and hire display workers as sales representatives to promote their products. The display workers' understanding of retail needs and their insight into the visual merchandising industry make them valuable consultants.

Commercial decorators prepare and install displays and decorations for trade and industrial shows, exhibitions, festivals, and other special events. Working from blueprints, drawings, and floor plans, they use woodworking power tools to construct installations (usually referred to as booths) at exhibition halls and convention centers. They install carpeting, drapes, and other decorations, such as flags, banners, and lights. They arrange furniture and accessories to attract the people attending the exhibition. Special event producers, coordinators, and party planners may also seek out the skills of display professionals.

This occupation appeals to imaginative, artistic individuals who find it rewarding to use their creative abilities to visualize a design concept and transform it into reality. Original, creative displays grow out of an awareness of current design trends and popular themes. Although display workers use inanimate objects such as props and materials, an understanding of human motivations helps them create displays with strong customer appeal.

REQUIREMENTS
High School

To work as a display worker, you must have at least a high school diploma. Important high school subjects include art, woodworking, mechanical drawing, and merchandising.

Postsecondary Training

Some employers require college courses in art, interior decorating, fashion design, advertising, or related subjects. Community and junior colleges that offer advertising and marketing courses may include display work in the curriculum. Fashion merchandising schools and fine arts institutes also offer courses useful to display workers.

Much of the training for display workers is gained on the job. They generally start as helpers for routine tasks, such as carrying props and dismantling sets. Gradually they are permitted to build simple props and work up to constructing more difficult displays. As they become more experienced, display workers who show artistic talent may be assigned to plan simple designs. The total training time varies depending on the beginner's ability and the variety and complexity of the displays.

Other Requirements

Besides education and experience, you will also need creative ability, manual dexterity, and mechanical aptitude to do this work. You should possess the strength and physical ability needed to be able to carry equipment and climb ladders. You also need agility to work in close quarters without upsetting the props.

EXPLORING

To explore the work of merchandise displayers, try to get a part-time or summer job with a department or retail store or at a convention center. This will give you an overview of the display operations in these establishments. Photographers and theater groups need helpers to work with props and sets, although some may require previous experience or knowledge related to their work. You school's drama and photo clubs may offer opportunities to learn basic design concepts. You also should read about this line of work; *Display & Design Ideas* (http://www.ddimagazine.com) publishes articles on the field and related subjects.

EMPLOYERS

Most merchandise displayers work in department and clothing stores, but many are employed in other types of retail stores, such as variety, drug, and shoe stores. Some have their own design businesses, and some are employed by design firms that handle interior and professional window dressing for small stores. Employment of display workers is distributed throughout the country, with most of the jobs concentrated in large towns and cities.

STARTING OUT

School placement offices may have job listings for display workers or related positions. Individuals wishing to become display workers can apply directly to retail stores, decorating firms, or exhibition centers. Openings also may be listed in the classified ads of newspapers.

A number of experienced merchandise displayers choose to work as freelance designers. Competition in this area, however, is intense, and it takes time to establish a reputation, build a list of clients, and earn an adequate income. Freelancing part-time while holding down another job provides a more secure income for many display workers. Freelancing also provides beginners with opportunities to develop a portfolio of photographs of their best designs, which they can then use to sell their services to other stores.

ADVANCEMENT

Display workers with supervisory ability can become regional managers. Further advancement may lead to a position as a display director or head of store planning.

Another way to advance is by starting a freelance design business. This can be done with very little financial investment, although freelance design workers must spend many long hours generating new business and establishing their names in the field.

Experienced display workers also may be able to transfer their skills to jobs in other art-related fields, such as interior design or photography. This move, however, requires additional training.

EARNINGS

According to the Bureau of Labor Statistics, the median annual earnings of merchandise displayers were $21,870 in 2001. The lowest 10 percent earned less than $14,630 and the highest 10 percent earned more than $37,920. The *Occupational Outlook Handbook* reports that displayers working with groceries and related goods earned a median salary of $22,210 in 2000, while those working in department stores earned a median salary of $18,820.

Freelance displayers may earn as much as $30,000 a year, but their income depends entirely on their talent, reputation, number of clients, and amount of time they work.

WORK ENVIRONMENT

Display workers usually work 35–40 hours a week, except during busy seasons, such as Christmas. Selling promotions and increased sales drives during targeted seasons can require the display staff to work extra hours in the evening and on weekends.

The work of constructing and installing displays requires prolonged standing, bending, stooping, and working in awkward positions. There is some risk of falling off ladders or being injured from handling sharp materials or tools, but serious injuries are uncommon.

OUTLOOK

Employment for display workers is expected to grow as fast as the average for all occupations over the next decade, according to the U.S. Department of Labor. Growth in this profession is expected due to an expanding retail sector and the increasing popularity of visual merchandising. Most openings will occur as older, experienced workers retire or leave the occupation.

Fluctuations of the economy affect the volume of retail sales because people are less likely to spend money during recessionary times. For display workers this can result in layoffs or hiring freezes.

FOR MORE INFORMATION

For information on student membership, scholarship opportunities, schools with student chapters, and additional career materials, contact

American Society of Interior Designers
608 Massachusetts Avenue, NE
Washington, DC 20002-6006
Tel: 202-546-3480
Email: asid@asid.org
http://www.asid.org

To read about industry events and news, check out the following magazine's website:

Display & Design Ideas
http://www.ddimagazine.com

MUSEUM DIRECTORS AND CURATORS

QUICK FACTS

School Subjects Art Business	**Certification or Licensing** None available
Personal Skills Communication/ideas Leadership/management	**Outlook** About as fast as the average **DOT** 102
Work Environment Primarily indoors One location with some travel	**GOE** N/A **NOC** 0511
Minimum Education Level Bachelor's degree	**O*NET-SOC** 25-4012.00
Salary Range $18,910 to $60,000 to $500,000+	

OVERVIEW

A *museum director* is equivalent to the chief executive officer of a corporation. The museum director is responsible for the daily operations of the museum, for long-term planning, policies, any research conducted within the museum, and for the museum's fiscal health. Directors must also represent the museum at meetings with other museums, business and civic communities, and the museum's governing body. Finally, directors ensure that museums adhere to state and federal guidelines for safety in the workplace and hiring practices, as well as industry recommendations concerning the acquisitions and care of objects within the museum.

Museum curators care for objects in a museum's collection. The primary curatorial activities are maintenance, preservation, archiving, cataloguing, study, and display of collection components. Curators must fund-raise to support staff in the physical care and study of collections. They also add to or alter a museum's collection by trading objects with other museums or purchasing new pieces. They educate others through scholarly articles and public programs that showcase the items.

HISTORY

More than any other museum workers, curators and directors are closely identified with the image and purposes of a museum, and the history of these positions has followed the fortunes of museums themselves.

Early precolonial and colonial museums were privately owned "cabinets of curios," but occasionally they were attached to a library or philosophical society, which allowed restricted viewing to members only. As the cabinet evolved into the museum through organized collecting and increased public access, there simultaneously arose some confusion over the mission of a museum and how that mission might best be achieved. Over time, the goals of museums alternated between a professional concentration on acquiring and studying collections, with some indifference to the interests of the public, and a contrary focus on visitor education and entertainment that occasionally turned into spectacles and sideshows for profit. According to Joel Orosz, museum historian and author of *Curators and Culture*, the alternating between museum professionalism and public education marked the first long span of U.S. museum history, from about 1740 to 1870. By 1870, however, the two trends had blended together, which Orosz refers to as the American compromise: *both* popular education *and* scholarly research would be held as equal, coexisting goals. This achievement, the author asserts, arose out of uniquely American conditions, prior to several decades of efforts by British and European museums to instate a similar mixture of goals, and permanently shaped the rest of U.S. museum history.

At different times during the first century of U.S. museum history, new scientific inventions and technologies shifted the professional focus of museums, as many museums of this era were devoted to natural history. In addition, popular education benefited from improved mass transportation. Robert Fulton's design of the steamboat, the opening of the Erie Canal in 1825, and the rise of the railroads gave travelers an alternative to tiring and dusty journeys by horse-drawn coach; thus, people from states as far away as Ohio and Kentucky could include museums on the eastern seaboard in their travel plans. As distant travelers sought out museums, curators were gratified and responded with programs of more general, less scholarly interest. The concept of a national museum, free to all and representative of the nation as a whole, took root in the popular imagination and was finally achieved in 1846 with the opening of the Smithsonian Institution.

Following a period of national economic prosperity and intense museum-building activities in the years 1950–1980, the American compromise has again reached center stage, this time in a controversial light. In a weakened economy, some museum directors believe it is no longer economically viable to maintain to two separate enterprises under one roof. Because public service is at the forefront of a modern museum's mission, museums are focusing on exhibits and programs for the public at the expense of support for research. Few taxpayers are repeat visitors to museums in a given year, and even fewer have any notion of what it is that museum directors and curators do. The coming decade will likely see increased revenue-generating activities for museums, a temporary freeze on museum allocations for research areas, or both. The financial stress is not uniquely felt by museums, for other civic institutions, notably symphony orchestras, have folded or sharply curtailed programs in the past few years. The American compromise faces some restructuring, introducing a period of uncertainty for many museum employees.

THE JOB

A museum director's most important duties are administrative, including staff leadership, promoting fund-raising campaigns, and ensuring that the museum's mission is carried out. Directors of large museums may have the assistance of several divisional directors with the authority for specific areas of museum management, such as a director of finance, director of development, director of public programs, director of research, director of education, director of operations, and director of marketing and public relations. In recognition of the museum director's role as "director of directors," the museum director sometimes has the title of *executive director.*

One unusual but not uncommon activity for a museum director is the design of new facilities. A director may spend a year or more working with architects and planners to reconfigure existing areas of the museum, add a wing, or build a museum from the ground up. Construction can draw resources away from other museum operations and may be accompanied by a massive capital campaign.

Every museum is unique in its mission, the community it serves, its resources, and the way it operates. Therefore, the responsibilities of museum directors vary widely. Directors of children's museums typically have a background in education and apply educational philosophies to the design of exhibits and programs suitable for children. Interactive displays, live interpretation, and participatory theater are frequent components of children's museums, and community outreach programs help ensure that children of all backgrounds benefit from the museum's programs.

A director of a natural history museum may have a background in science and manage a staff of scientists. Concern for the disturbance of regional habitats and species extinction has prompted some museums to replace traditional galleries exhibiting birds, mammals, or fish with conceptual exhibits emphasizing ecology and evolution. In museums with a strong anthropological component, returning religious objects or ancestral remains to the country or people of origin is an important and controversial area. Museum directors must have considerable intercultural understanding and knowledge of the state laws governing the disposition of materials in state-tax-funded museums.

Directors of art museums typically have academic credentials in a specific area of art history and have good financial and fund-raising skills to manage costly collections. The director may be personally involved in making acquisitions for the museum. Directors of museums reflecting a specific culture, such as Mexican, Asian, or Native American culture, need knowledge of that culture and diplomatic skills to arrange the exchange of exhibit material. An issue facing art museums today is the opinion that such institutions are for well-to-do patrons. Art museums are countering that impression by developing programs of interest to people from less advantaged backgrounds.

At science and technology museums, exhibits demonstrate basic physical or biological laws, such as those governing the workings of the human heart, or they may present historical or futuristic exhibits, displaying the actual spacecraft used in early flight or the technology of the future. Directors of science and technology museums place a high priority on instructing the young, and hands-on exhibits are a featured attraction.

Directors of folk museums and historical reconstructions are historians of culture during a particular period. Authenticity, preservation, and providing an historical perspective on modes of living, past and present, are concerns of the director.

A curator's chief responsibilities include study and preservation of the museum's collections. Depending on the museum's size, resources, and deployment of staff, those responsibilities can vary. In museums with a large curatorial staff, senior curators may function primarily as administrators, overseeing departmental budgets and hiring new curators. In a different employment environment, curators may focus closely on the study and shape of the collections, exchanging materials with other museums or acquiring new specimens and artifacts to create a representative study collection of importance to scholarly work. In a third type of environment, curators may be primarily educators who describe and present collections to the visiting public. At any time, museum administrators may ask curators to redirect efforts toward a different goal of priority to the museum. Thus, a curator develops or brings to the position substantial knowledge of the materials in the collection, and that knowledge is used by the museum for a changing mix of purposes over time.

Curators may also spend time in the field or as visiting scholars at other museums as a means of continuing research related to the home institution's collections. Fieldwork is usually supported by grants from external sources. As specialists in their disciplines, curators may teach classes in local schools and universities, sometimes serving as academic advisors to doctoral degree candidates whose research is based on museum holdings. Almost all curators supervise a staff ranging from volunteers, interns, and students to research associates, collections managers, technicians, junior curators, and secretarial staff. Some sort of written work, whether it is labeling exhibits, preparing brochures for museum visitors, or publishing in scholarly journals, is typically part of the position.

In related positions, *collections managers* and *curatorial assistants* perform many of the same functions as curators, with more emphasis on study and cataloguing of the collections and less involvement with administration and staff supervision. The educational requirements for these positions may be the same as for a curatorial position. A curatorial candidate may accept a position as collections manager while awaiting a vacancy on the curatorial staff, since the opportunity to study, publish research, and conduct fieldwork is usually equally available in both positions. In art, historical, and anthropological museums, *registrars* and *archivists* may act as collections managers by cataloguing and preserving documents and objects and making information on these items available for scholarly use.

Once hired, curators embark on what is essentially a lifelong program of continuing self-education in museum practices. Curators of large collections must remain current with preservation techniques, including climate control and pest control methods. The human working environment can affect collections in unpredictable ways. As an example, common fungi that afflict houseplants may degrade the preservation environment of a collection of amphibians and reptiles, which may mean that all staff in the area are prohibited from introducing house plants into their workstations.

An important development in collections management is computerized cataloguing of holdings for registry in national electronic databases. A number of larger museums and universities are working together to standardize data entry fields for these electronic registries, after which data on every item in a collection must be entered by hand and cross-checked for accuracy. Concurrently, there is a trend toward publishing through nonprint media, such as academic networks administered by the National Sciences Foundation. Continuing self-education in electronic technologies and participation in national conferences addressing these issues will be expected of curators throughout the upcoming decade and beyond, for electronic storage and retrieval systems have radically changed the face of collections management.

REQUIREMENTS
High School
Museum directors and curators need diverse educational backgrounds to perform well in their jobs. At the high school level, you should take courses in English, literature, creative writing, history, art, the sciences, speech, business, and foreign languages. These courses will give you the general background knowledge needed to understand both the educational and administrative functions of museums. Math and computer skills are also essential. Museum directors and curators are responsible for preparing budgets and seeking funds from corporations and federal agencies.

Postsecondary Training
Museum directors and curators must have a bachelor's degree. Some colleges and universities offer undergraduate degrees in museology, or the study of museums. Most museums require their directorial staff and chief curators to hold doctoral degrees. Directors and curators usually work in museums that specialize in art, history,

or science. These individuals often have degrees in fields related to the museum's specialty. Directors often have advanced degrees in business management, public relations, or marketing. All curators must have a good working knowledge of the art, objects, and cultures represented in their collections.

Other Requirements

Excellent written and oral communication skills are essential. Directors have a primary responsibility to supervise museum staff members, relay information to museum board members, and acquire funding for all museum programming. Museum directors must have extraordinary people skills and feel at ease when soliciting funds. Curators must have excellent research skills. They must be able to meet deadlines, write scholarly articles, and give presentations while managing their traditional museum duties. Museum directors and curators should be well organized and flexible.

Occasionally museums have specific requirements, such as foreign language fluency for an art or anthropology museum or practical computer skills for a science or natural history museum. A student usually acquires these skills as part of the background study within his or her area of concentration.

EXPLORING

Because of the diversity of U.S. museums and the academic background required for directorship and curatorial positions, high school students should simply concentrate on doing well in academic studies as preparation for either field. Museum directorships and curatorial positions are highly competitive and reward high academic achievement. Outside of school, participation in clubs that involve fund-raising activities can serve as a strong introduction to one important aspect of a museum director's job. Becoming the president of one of these clubs can provide you with supervisory skills and experience with delegating authority.

Museums offer public programs for people of all ages. Field trips or tours introduce students to activities conducted by local museums. You may consider participating in an archaeological dig. College-age students may work at museums as volunteers or perhaps as interns for course credit. Depending on the museum's needs, volunteers and interns may be placed anywhere in the museum, including administration, archives, and other areas where a student may observe staff functions firsthand.

EMPLOYERS

Museums as well as historical societies and state and federal agencies with public archives and libraries hire directors and curators. These institutions are located throughout the world, in both small and large cities, and are responsible for providing public access to their collections. Museums and similar institutions employ directors and curators to fulfill their educational goals through continued research, care of collections, and public programs.

STARTING OUT

As mentioned earlier, some U.S. colleges offer undergraduate programs in museology, but most museum workers at all levels enter museum work because they possess specific skills and a body of knowledge useful to a particular museum. For a museum director, as for a well-qualified curator, this translates into content knowledge, managerial and administrative skills, fund-raising ability, leadership ability, and excellent communication skills for effective interaction with the media and the board of trustees. While the role of a curator is focused primarily on collections and the role of director is often more administrative and interpersonal, the two positions both require a great degree of knowledge across the board regarding the museum's mission statement, acquisitions, and community involvement.

Museum directors typically move into their positions in one of three ways: laterally, from a previous directorship of another museum; vertically, from an administrative or curatorial position within the same museum; or laterally from a different sphere of employment, such as a university presidency, business management, government agency, or law practice.

A position as curator usually is not anticipated and prepared for in advance, but becomes available as an employment option following a long period of training in a discipline. College and advanced degree students who have identified a curatorial position as a career goal may be able to apply for curatorial internships of varying terms, usually a year or less. Interns typically work on a project identified by the museum, which may involve only one task or several different tasks. Additionally, museums thrive on a large base of volunteer labor, and this method of gaining museum experience should not be overlooked. Curators may ask volunteers to assist in a variety of tasks, ranging from clerical duties to conservation and computerized cataloguing. When funds are available, volunteer work may be converted to hourly paid work.

ADVANCEMENT

Museum directors typically succeed one another, moving from smaller museums to larger museums or from a general to a specialty museum. A museum directorship is a lifetime career goal and may be held for decades by the same person. A museum director who retires from the position is well prepared to sit on state or national advisory councils to the arts and sciences. Some return to academic life through teaching, research, or curricula development. Others provide oversight and guidance to large institutions, sit on corporate boards, or become involved in the start-up of new museums.

Curatorial positions follow the assistant, associate, and full (or senior) track of academic employment, with advancement depending on research and publishing, education, and service to the institution. A curator with a taste for and skill in administration may serve as departmental chair or may seek a higher administrative post.

In the course of their museum duties, curators may act as advisers to or principals in external nonprofit endeavors, such as setting up international ecological preserves or providing technical assistance and labor to aid a developing country in the study of its archaeological past. Many teach in local schools or universities. Curators who leave museum work may devote themselves full time to these or similar pursuits, although a university professorship as a second choice is difficult to achieve, for curators and professors are essentially competing for the same market position and have similar credentials. Occasionally curators find fieldwork so compelling that they leave not only the museum, but all formal employment, relying on grants and personal contributions from supporters to support their work. To maintain an independent life as a researcher without formal affiliation requires a high profile in the discipline, continuing demonstration of productivity in the form of new research and publications, and some skill in self-promotion.

EARNINGS

The salaries of museum directors and curators cover a broad range, reflecting the diversity, size, and budget of U.S. museums, along with the director or curator's academic and professional achievements. In general, museum workers' salaries are low compared to salaries for similar positions in the business world or in academia. This is due in part to the large number of people competing for the relatively small number of positions available. At the high end of the scale, museum directors at museums like the Whitney and the

Metropolitan Museum of Art in New York City, or the Art Institute of Chicago earn more than $500,000 a year.

A survey of its members conducted by the Association of Art Museum Directors reported that the average salary of an art museum director is roughly $110,000. The average salary of a deputy director ranges from $65,000 to $123,000, while the average salary of an assistant to the director is roughly $31,000. The same study reported entry-level curatorial positions, often titled curatorial assistant or curatorial intern, as averaging $24,000, while assistant curator salaries average from $26,000 to $37,000 per year. Both the position of associate curator, a title with supervisory duties, and the position of curator of exhibitions average $34,000 to $53,000. Chief curator salaries average $57,000, but, as with many museum titles, may be considerably higher or lower depending on the demands of the job and the museum's overall budget. Curators directing an ongoing program of conservation and acquisitions in a large, national or international urban museum command the highest salaries and may earn as much as $152,000.

According to the Bureau of Labor Statistics, the median annual earnings of archivists, curators, museum technicians, and conservators were $34,190 in 2001. Salaries ranged from less than $18,910 to more than $63,870.

Fringe benefits, including paid vacations and sick leave, medical and dental insurance, and retirement plans, vary between museum directors and curators and according to each employing institution's policies.

WORK ENVIRONMENT

The directorship of a museum is an all-consuming occupation. Considerable travel, program development, fund-raising, and staff management may be involved. Evenings and weekends are often taken up by social activities involving museum donors or affiliates. A museum director must be willing to accept the pressure of answering to the museum's board of trustees while also overseeing museum staff and handling public relations.

As new issues affecting museums arise in the national consciousness and draw media attention, a director must be able to respond appropriately. The director must maintain the delicate balance in observing the museum's role as both public institution and research facility. Museum directors must juggle competing interests and requests for the museum's resources.

The office of a director is typically housed within the museum. Many directors have considerable staff support, to which they can delegate specific areas of responsibility, and thus must have strong interpersonal and diplomatic skills.

Curators typically have an office in a private area of the museum, but may have to share office space. Employment conditions and benefits are more like those of industry than academia, although the employment contract may stipulate that the curator is free to pursue a personal schedule of fieldwork for several weeks during the year.

A curatorial post and a directorship are typically nine-to-five jobs, but that does not take into account the long hours of study necessary to sustain scholarly research, weekend time spent on public programs, or evening meetings with donors, trustees, and museum affiliates. The actual hours spent on curatorial-related and directorship activities may be double those of the employment contract. Directors and curators must enjoy their work, be interested in museum operations and a museum's profile in the community, and willingly put in the necessary time. Becoming a museum director only occurs after years of dedication to the field and a great deal of tenacity. Likewise, curatorial positions are won by highly educated, versatile people, who in turn accept long hours and relatively (in comparison to industry) low pay in exchange for doing work they love.

OUTLOOK

There are few openings for directors and curators and competition for them is high. New graduates may have to start as interns, volunteers, assistants, or research associates before finding full-time curator or director positions. Turnover is very low in museum work, so museum workers may have to stay in a lower level position for some years before advancing to a director or curator position. The employment outlook for museum directors and curators is expected to increase about as fast as the average over the next several years, according to the *Occupational Outlook Handbook*. The best opportunities are in art, history, and technology museums.

Curators must be able to develop revenue-generating public programs based on the study collections and integrate themselves firmly into programs of joint research with area institutions (other museums or universities) or national institutions, ideally programs of some duration and supported by external funding. Museums are affected by economic conditions and the availability of grants and other charitable funding.

FOR MORE INFORMATION

For information on careers, education and training, and internships, contact

American Association of Museums
1575 Eye Street, NW, Suite 400
Washington, DC 20005
Tel: 202-289-1818
http://www.aam-us.org

This organization represents directors of the major art museums in North America. It sells a publication on professional practices, a salary survey, and a sample employment contract.

Association of Art Museum Directors
41 East 65th Street
New York, NY 10021
Tel: 212-249-4423
http://www.aamd.org

PACKAGING DESIGNERS

QUICK FACTS

School Subjects Art Computer science	**Certification or Licensing** None available
Personal Skills Artistic Mechanical/manipulative	**Outlook** Faster than the average **DOT** 141
Work Environment Primarily indoors Primarily one location	**GOE** 01.02.03
Minimum Education Level Some postsecondary training	**NOC** N/A **O*NET-SOC** 27-1024.00
Salary Range $21,700 to $36,020 to $61,050+	

OVERVIEW

Packaging designers, sometimes more generally referred to as *graphic designers* or *graphic artists,* design product packaging and related materials. They often work with packaging engineers, product managers, and marketing and sales personnel to design packages that not only protect the product but also present the product in a manner that is visually pleasing and adds to its marketability.

HISTORY

Throughout history, people have always needed to express themselves creatively through the use of pictures, graphics, and words. This means of expression remains a vital part of today's manufacturing and marketing.

All product packaging has been influenced by the elements of design. From the labels on soup cans to the cans holding the soup, packaging designers work to create "the look" that they hope will entice consumers and bring in sales. Designers are responsible for the placement of corporate logos on all items that we recognize at a glance. Their graphic work builds brand-name recognition and consumer loyalty.

Old packaging designs can illustrate the evolution of this field. Soda that was once packaged in curvy glass bottles is now sold in similarly curvy plastic bottles and smaller aluminum cans. Older product labeling generally uses less color and graphics. Today's packaging designers use endless amounts of images and colors to advertise and promote their products. Although computers now aid many of today's artists and designers, creativity, imagination, and ingenuity must still drive the artistic process.

THE JOB

Packaging designers usually work in plants of various industries or for a company that contracts for package design services. They usually work with a team of employees to design and implement the packaging for products.

Typically, the designer meets with the product manager, the packaging engineer, the copywriter, and the marketing manager to determine the type of package to be produced, safety and storage issues, and the intended market. The designer must consider all of these factors to determine the final product weight and size, packaging production methods, design elements (such as logo, product pictures, instructions), labeling requirements (such as ingredients or warnings), and the method of shipment and storage. The designer then designs the packaging and graphics by using traditional design methods and computer software. Packaging ideas are usually presented to the product manager or before a committee for feedback. Prototypes may be developed and analyzed.

When a packaging design is agreed upon, the package designer develops the final layout and works with the production workers and product manager to produce the package.

REQUIREMENTS
High School

In high school, you should take classes in art and computers, including computer-aided design (CAD) and graphics. Technical classes such as electrical shop, machine shop, and mechanical drawing will also be helpful when working in the manufacturing industry. In addition to developing artistic abilities, you should also develop communication skills through English and writing classes. Foreign language skills are also beneficial.

Postsecondary Training

Educational requirements vary, but because competition in this field can be fierce, postsecondary education is highly recommended. Some design occupations require a bachelor's degree or a degree from a design school. There are two- and three-year design schools that award certificates or associate's degrees upon completion. Another option is to attend an appropriate college or university to earn a bachelor's or master's degree in fine arts. Programs usually cover core subjects such as English, history, and the sciences, and include various art classes such as design, studio art, and art history. Other beneficial classes include CAD, business administration, basic engineering, computerized design, mechanical drawing, psychology, sales, and marketing.

Other Requirements

If you are interested in packaging design, you should be highly creative, imaginative, have mechanical aptitude and manual dexterity, and verbal and visual communication skills. In addition, you will need analytical and problem-solving skills and should enjoy working with others because packaging designers often work in teams. You should be familiar with the use of computers in design and manufacturing and be able to work well under pressure.

EXPLORING

To get a taste of what the job of packaging designer is like, talk to your high school guidance counselor about arranging an interview with someone in the field. Think of some questions you might like to ask, such as how they prepared for the field, what got them interested in the work, and what they like best about their job. Chances are, their answers will be very enlightening to your own search.

While in high school, take as many art classes as you can and get involved in outside projects to further develop your skills. See if you can get some design experience through the theater department, designing costumes, stage sets, or even playbills. Getting involved in the arts is not only fun, but can help you gain a sense of whether or not you enjoy design work.

EMPLOYERS

Various packaging and manufacturing industries employ packaging designers. Employment opportunities are also available with companies who contract out package design services. Package designers usually work with a team of employees and managers involved with the product to be packaged.

Packaging is one of the largest industries in the United States, so jobs are plentiful. However, the field of graphic design is highly competitive because there are many talented people attracted to this career. Fortunately, there are many areas of employment for designers. In addition, many prefer to be self-employed as freelance designers.

Opportunities in the packaging field can be found in almost any company that produces and packages a product. Practically all products, such as food, chemicals, cosmetics, electronics, pharmaceuticals, automotive parts, hardware, and plastics, need to be packaged before reaching the consumer market. Because of this diverse industry, jobs are not restricted to any geographic location or plant size.

STARTING OUT

Students in a graphic arts program may be able to get job leads through their schools' job placement services. Many jobs in packaging are unadvertised and are discovered through contacts with professionals in the industry. Students may learn about openings from teachers, school administrators, and industry contacts they have acquired during training.

Applicants can also apply directly to machinery manufacturing companies or companies with packaging departments. Employment opportunities may also be available with design studios that specialize in packaging designs.

ADVANCEMENT

Packaging designers who work with a design firm usually begin in entry-level positions and work their way up as they gain design experience and build their portfolio. Packaging designers who work for a manufacturing company may advance within the department to become product manager, or may choose to move into corporate communications and marketing areas.

Some packaging designers pursue additional education to qualify as design engineers. Others may pursue business, economics, and finance degrees and use these additional skills in other areas of the manufacturing or design industries.

EARNINGS

Earnings for packaging designers vary with the skill level of the employee, the size of the company and the type of industry. The U.S. Department of Labor reports that the median salary for graphic artists, which includes packaging designers, was approximately $36,020 a year in 2001. The lowest paid 10 percent earned $21,700, while the highest paid 10 percent earned $61,050 or more. A designer who has established an excellent reputation can earn considerably more.

Benefits vary and depend upon the company, but generally include paid holidays, vacations, sick days, and medical and dental insurance. Some companies also offer tuition assistance programs, pension plans, profit sharing, and 401-K plans. Designers who are freelancers usually have to provide their own insurance and savings plans.

WORK ENVIRONMENT

Packaging designers who work in a manufacturing setting usually work in a studio or office that is well lit and ventilated. However, they may be subjected to odors from glues, paint, and ink when paste-up procedures are used. Also, as computers are used more and more, designers are often sitting in front of a computer for a considerable amount of time.

Occasionally, they may have to be in the noisy factory floor environment when observing product packaging and production. Most plants are clean and well ventilated although actual conditions vary based on the type of product manufactured and packaged. Certain types of industries and manufacturing methods can pose special problems. For example, plants involved in paperboard and paper manufacturing may be very dusty from the use of paper fibers. Workers in food plants may be exposed to strong smells from processing. Pharmaceutical and electronic component plants may require special conditions to ensure that the environment is free from dirt, contamination, and static. Though these conditions may require some adjustment, in general, most plants have no unusual hazards.

Most designers work 40 hours a week, although overtime may be required for the introduction of a new product line or during other busy manufacturing periods.

OUTLOOK

According to the *Occupational Outlook Handbook,* employment of all designers is predicted to grow faster than the average for all occupations over the next decade. Opportunities will be great for packaging designers as businesses will always need talented workers to develop appealing packaging design concepts. However, there is tough competition for the jobs available. Individuals with little or no formal education and limited experience may find it difficult to find a job.

Because packaging is one of the largest industries in the United States, jobs can be found across the country, in small towns and large cities, in small companies or multi-plant international corporations. In addition, jobs are not restricted to any one industry or geographical location.

FOR MORE INFORMATION

For information on graphic design careers, contact the following organizations:

American Institute of Graphic Arts
164 Fifth Avenue
New York, NY 10010
Tel: 212-807-1990
http://www.aiga.org

Industrial Designers Society of America
45195 Business Court, Suite 250
Dulles, VA 20166
Tel: 703-707-6000
Email: idsa@idsa.org
http://www.idsa.org

PAINTERS AND SCULPTORS

QUICK FACTS

School Subjects
Art
History

Personal Skills
Artistic
Communication/ideas

Work Environment
Indoors and outdoors
One location with some
travel

Minimum Education Level
High school diploma

Salary Range
$15,780 to $32,870 to
$64,210+

Certification or Licensing
None available

Outlook
About as fast as the average

DOT
144

GOE
01.02.02

NOC
5136

O*NET-SOC
27-1013.01, 27-1013.04

OVERVIEW

Painters use watercolors, oils, acrylics, and other substances to paint pictures or designs onto flat surfaces. *Sculptors* design and construct three-dimensional artwork from various materials, such as stone, concrete, plaster, and wood.

HISTORY

At their essence, painting and sculpture are attempts to bring order and focus to life and society. The earliest known artworks were probably created for functional purposes rather than for artistic or aesthetic reasons. For example, the cave paintings of France and Spain, which date from 15,000 B.C., were probably ceremonial in nature, meant to bring good luck to the hunt. From an earlier period, around 21,000 to 25,000 B.C., the Venus of Willendorf is a figure carved from limestone, which along with other figures from the same time might have formed a part of fertility rites and rituals and prehistoric relief sculptures, that is, sculptures carved into the walls of caves in France.

Painting and sculpture have ranged from purely decorative to narrative (art that tells a story), from symbolic to realistic. Much of early visual art was religious in nature, reflecting the beliefs and myths with which people tried to understand their place in the world and in life. Art was also used to glorify society or the leaders of society. The immense sculptures of Ramses II of ancient Egypt, and much of Roman art, served to glorify their rulers and reinforce their stature in society. Often, the main subject of a painting or sculpture would appear out of proportion to the other figures in the work, symbolizing his or her importance or dominance. While this use of artists and their art continues today, the independence we typically associate with modern artists also has its roots in ancient times, as ancient artists sought to create art based on more immediately personal concerns.

The art of Greece and Rome exerted a profound influence on much of the history of Western art. The sculptural ideals developed by the ancient Greeks, particularly with their perfection of anatomical forms, continued to dominate Western sculpture until well into the 19th century. In painting, artists sought methods to depict or suggest a greater realism, experimenting with techniques of lighting, shading, and others to create an illusion of depth.

The rise of the Christian era brought a return to symbolism over realism. Illuminated manuscripts, which were written texts, usually religious in content, and decorated with designs and motifs meant to provide further understanding of the text, became the primary form of artistic expression for nearly a millennium. The artwork for these manuscripts often featured highly elaborate and detailed abstract designs. The human figure was absent in much of this work, reflecting religious prohibition of the creation of idols.

Artists returned to more naturalistic techniques during the 14th century with the rise of Gothic art forms. The human figure returned to art; artists began creating art not only for rulers and religious institutions, but also for a growing wealthy class. Portrait painting became an increasingly important source of work and income for artists. New materials, particularly oil glazes and paints, allowed artists to achieve more exact detailing and more subtle light, color, and shading effects.

During the Renaissance, artists rediscovered the art of ancient Greece and Rome. This brought new developments not only in artists' techniques but also in their stature in society. The development of perspective techniques in the 14th and 15th centuries revolutionized painting. Through perspective artists created the illusion of three dimensions, so that a spectator felt that he or she looked not merely at a painting but into it. Advances in the study of anatomy enabled artists to create more dramatic and realistic figures, whether in painting or sculpture, providing the illusion of action and fluidity and heightening the naturalism of their work. The role of the artist changed from simple artisan or craftsworker to creative force. They were sought out by the wealthy, the church, and rulers for their talent and skill, receiving commissions for new work or being supported by patrons as they worked.

The work of Giotto, Michelangelo, Raphael, Leonardo da Vinci, Titian, and other Renaissance artists continue to fascinate people today. Artists developed new concerns for the use of line, color, contour, shading, setting, and composition, presenting work of greater realism and at the same time of deeper emotional content. The style of an artist became more highly individualized, more a personal reflection of the artist's thoughts, beliefs, ideas, and feelings. The fantastic, nightmare-like paintings of Hieronymus Bosch opened new areas of thematic and subjective exploration. In the late Renaissance, new styles began to emerge, such as the mannerist style of El Greco of Spain and the northern styles of Albrecht Durer and Pieter Bruegel the Elder, and the subject matter of painting was extended to depict common scenes of ordinary life.

Artists continued to influence one another, but national and cultural differences began to appear in art as the Catholic church lost its dominance and new religious movements took hold. Art academies, such as the Academie Royale de Peinture et de Sculture in Paris, were established and sought to codify artistic ideals. The works of the Flemish painter Peter Paul Rubens, the Dutch painters Vermeer and Rembrandt, and the French painter Nicolas Poussin highlight the different techniques, styles, and concerns rising during the baroque period of the 17th century.

The next two centuries would see profound changes in the nature of art, leading to the revolutionary work of the impressionists of the late 19th century and the dawn of the modern era in art. Sculpture, which had remained largely confined to the Greek and Roman ideals, found new directions beginning with the work of Rodin. The individual sensibility of the artist himself took on a greater importance and led to a greater freedom of painting techniques, such as in the work of John Constable and J. M. W. Turner of England. In France, Gustave Courbet challenged many of the ideals of the French academy, leading to the avant-garde work of the early French impressionists. Artists began to take on a new role by challenging society with new concepts, ideas, visions, and radical departures in style. Artists no longer simply reflected prevailing culture, but adopted leadership positions in creating culture, often rejecting entirely the artistic principles of the past. The revolutionary works of Edouard Manet, Edgar Degas, Claude Monet, Georges Seurat, Paul Cezanne, and others would in turn be rejected by succeeding generations of artists intent on developing new ideas and techniques. The image of the artist as cultural outsider, societal misfit, or even tormented soul took hold, with painters such as Paul Gauguin, Edvard Munch, and Vincent van Gogh. Artists working in the avant garde achieved notoriety, if not financial reward, and the "misunderstood" or "starving" artist became a popular 20th-century image.

The 20th century witnessed an explosion of artistic styles and techniques. Art, both in painting and sculpture, became increasingly abstracted from reality, and purely formal concerns developed. Impressionism and postimpressionism gave way to futurism, expressionism, Henri Matisse's fauvism, the cubism developed by Pablo Picasso and Georges Braque, the nonobjective paintings of Wassily Kandinsky, Piet Mondrian and Salvadore Dali's surrealism, and others.

American art, which had largely followed the examples set by European artists, came into its own during the 1940s and 1950s, with the rise of abstract expressionism lead by Willem de Kooning and Jackson Pollock. During the 1950s, a new art form, pop art, reintroduced recognizable images. The work of Richard Hamilton, Andy Warhol, Roy Lichtenstein, and others used often mundane objects, such as Warhol's Campbell soup cans, to satirize and otherwise comment on cultural and societal life.

More recent trends in art have given the world the graffiti-inspired works of Keith Haring and the "non-art" sculpture of Jeff Koons, as well as the massive installations of Christo. Artists today work in a great variety of styles, forms, and media. Many artists combine elements of painting, sculpture, and other art forms, such as photography, music, and dance, into their work. The rise of video recording techniques, and especially of three-dimensional computer animations has recently begun to challenge many traditional ideas of art.

THE JOB

Painters and sculptors use their creative abilities to produce original works of art. They are generally classified as fine artists rather than commercial artists because they are responsible for selecting the theme, subject matter, and medium of their artwork.

Painters use a variety of media to paint portraits, landscapes, still lifes, abstracts, and other subjects. They use brushes, palette knives, and other artist's tools to apply color to canvas or other surfaces. They work in a variety of media, including oil paint, acrylic paint, tempera, watercolors, pen and ink, pencil, charcoal, crayon, pastels, but may also use such nontraditional media as earth, clay, cement, paper, cloth, and any other material that allows them to express their artistic ideas. Painters develop line, space, color, and other visual elements to produce the desired effect. They may prefer a particular style of art, such as realism or abstract, and they may be identified with a certain technique or subject matter. Many artists develop a particular style and apply that style across a broad range of techniques, from painting to etching to sculpture.

Sculptors use a combination of media and methods to create three-dimensional works of art. They may carve objects from stone, plaster, concrete, or wood. They may use their fingers to model clay or wax into objects. Some sculptors create forms from metal or stone, using various masonry tools and equipment. Others create works from found objects, such as car parts or tree branches. Like painters, sculptors may be identified with a particular technique or style. Their work can take monumental forms, or they may work on a very small scale.

There is no single way to become or to be an artist. As with other areas of the arts, painting and sculpting usually are intensely personal endeavors. If it is possible to generalize, most painters and sculptors are people with a desire and need to explore visual representations of the world around them or the world within them, or both. Throughout their careers, they seek to develop their vision and the methods and techniques that allow them to best express themselves. Many artists work from or within a tradition or style of art. They may develop formal theories of art or advance new theories of visual presentation. Painters and sculptors are usually aware of the art that has come before them as well as the work of their contemporaries.

Every painter and sculptor has his or her own way of working. Many work in studios, often separate from their homes, where they can produce their work in privacy and quiet. Many artists, however, work outdoors. Most artists probably combine both indoor and outdoor work during their careers. Some artists may choose complete solitude in order to work; others thrive on interaction with other artists and people. Artists engaged in monumental work, particularly sculptors, often have helpers who assist in the creation of a piece of art, working under the artist's direction. They may contract with a foundry in order to cast the finished sculpture in bronze, iron, or another metal. As film, video, and computer technology has developed, the work of painters and sculptors has expanded into new forms of expression. The recently developed three-dimensional computer animation techniques in particular often blur the boundaries between painting, sculpture, photography, and cinema.

Checklist for Hopeful Artists

You've decided to become an art major, and you want to work for yourself. What do you need to do before you are able to set up shop as a working artist? Use this list as a guide before working on your own.

- Apply for a business tax registration certificate and sales tax permit. This will allow you to buy art supplies at wholesale prices and deduct some of your working expenses at tax time.
- Document your work using photographs, slides, computer files, or whatever is appropriate for your art form.
- Research potential buyers and art galleries.
- Send out at least one letter per week with art samples to gallery owners, museum curators, and collectors.
- Read art publications such as *Artweek* (http://www.artweek.com) and *ArtNews* (http://www.artnewsonline.com) to keep up with the latest developments in the industry.
- Commit a certain amount of time per week tending to the business aspects of your career. This is separate time from the time you spend on your artwork.
- Set price ranges for your work based on the amount of hours spent on each piece.
- Create business cards to hand out to perspective buyers.
- Update your resume to reflect any new art exhibitions, awards, and education.

REQUIREMENTS
High School

There are no specific educational requirements for becoming a painter or sculptor. However, several high school classes can help you prepare for a career in this field, including art and history. Take many kinds of art classes to learn different techniques and styles, and determine which you excel at. Business and finance classes may also be beneficial, since you will likely have to manage your own financial transactions as a painter or sculptor.

Postsecondary Training

Although there isn't a clear path to success in this field, most artists benefit from training, and many attend art schools or programs in colleges and universities. There are also many workshops and other ways for artists to gain instruction, practice, and exposure to art and the works and ideas of other artists. You should learn a variety of techniques, be exposed to as many media and styles as possible, and gain an understanding of the history of art and art theory. By learning as much as possible, you'll be better able to choose the appropriate means for your own artistic expression.

Certification or Licensing

Artists who sell their works to the public may need special permits from the local or state tax office. In addition, artists should check with the Internal Revenue Service for laws on selling and tax information related to income received from the sale of artwork. Many artists join professional organizations, such as The Sculptors Guild, that provide informative advice and tips as well as opportunities to meet with other artists.

Other Requirements

An important requirement for a career as a painter or sculptor is artistic ability. Of course, this is entirely subjective, and it is perhaps more important that you believe in your own ability and in your own potential. Apart from being creative and imaginative, you should exhibit such traits as patience, persistence, determination, independence, and sensitivity. You will also need to be good at business and sales if you intend to support yourself through your art. As a small businessperson, you must be able to market and sell your products to wholesalers, retailers, and the general public.

EXPLORING

Experience in drawing, painting, and even sculpting can be had at a very early age, even before formal schooling begins. Most elementary, middle, and high schools offer classes in art. Aspiring painters and sculptors can undertake a variety of artistic projects at school or at home. Many arts associations and schools also offer beginning classes in various types of art for the general public.

If art seems like an interesting career option, visits museums and galleries to view the work of other artists. In addition, you can learn about the history of art and artistic techniques and methods through books, videotapes, and other sources. The New York Foundation for the Arts sponsors a toll-free hotline (800-232-2789) that offers information on programs and services and answers to specific questions on visual artists.

EMPLOYERS

Because earning a living as a fine artist is very difficult, especially when one is just starting out, many painters and sculptors work at another job. With the proper training and educational background, many painters and sculptors are able to work in art-related positions as art teachers, art directors, or graphic designers while pursuing their own art activities independently. For example, many art teachers hold classes in their own studios.

Sculptors creating large works, especially those that will be placed outdoors and in public areas, usually work under contract or commission. Most artists, however, create works that express their personal artistic vision and then hope to find someone to purchase them.

STARTING OUT

Artists interested in exhibiting or selling their products should investigate potential markets. Reference books, such as the *Artist's & Graphic Designer's Market* (published annually by Writers Digest Books), may be helpful, as well as library books that offer information on business law, taxes, and related issues. Local fairs and art shows often provide opportunities for new artists to display their work. Art councils are a good source of information on upcoming fairs in the area.

Some artists sell their work on consignment. When a painter or sculptor sells work this way, a store or gallery displays an item; when the item is sold, the artist gets the price of that item minus a commission that goes to the store or gallery. Artists who sell on consignment should read contracts very carefully.

ADVANCEMENT

Because most painters and sculptors are self-employed, the channels for advancement are not as well defined as they are at a company or firm. An artist may become increasingly well known, both nationally and internationally, and as an artist's reputation increases, he or she can command higher prices for his or her work. The success of the fine artist depends on a variety of factors, including talent, drive, and determination. However, luck often seems to play a role in many artists' success, and some artists do not achieve recognition until late in life, if at all. Artists with business skills may open their own galleries to display their own and others' work. Those with the appropriate educational backgrounds may become art teachers, agents, or critics.

EARNINGS

The amount of money earned by visual artists varies greatly. About 60 percent are self-employed—a figure six times greater compared to other occupations. As freelancers, artists can set their hours and prices. Those employed by businesses usually work for the motion picture and television industries, wholesale or retail trades, or public relations firms. According to the U.S. Department of Labor's *2001 National Occupational Employment and Wage Estimates,* the median annual salary for fine artists, including painters, sculptors, and illustrators, was $32,870. The lowest paid 10 percent earned $15,780 per year, while the highest-paid 10 percent made $64,210 or more annually. Some internationally known artists may command millions of dollars for their work.

Artists often work long hours and earn little, especially when they are first starting out. The price they charge is up to them, but much depends on the value the public places on their work. A particular item may sell for a few dollars or tens of thousands of dollars, or at any price in between. Often, the value of an artwork may increase considerably after it has been sold. An artwork that may have earned an artist only a few hundred dollars may earn many thousands of dollars the next time it is sold.

Some artists obtain grants that allow them to pursue their art; others win prizes and awards in competitions. Most artists, however, have to work on their projects part time while holding down a regular, full-time job. Many artists teach in art schools, high schools, or out of their studios. Artists who sell their products must pay Social Security and other taxes on any money they receive.

WORK ENVIRONMENT

Most painters and sculptors work out of their homes or in studios. Some work in small areas in their apartments; others work in large, well-ventilated lofts. Occasionally, painters and sculptors work outside. In addition, artists often exhibit their work at fairs, shops, museums, and other locations.

Artists often work long hours, and those who are self-employed do not receive paid vacations, insurance coverage, or any of the other benefits usually offered by a company or firm. However, artists are able to work at their own pace, set their own prices, and make their own decisions. The energy and creativity that go into an artist's work brings feelings of pride and satisfaction. Most artists genuinely love what they do.

OUTLOOK

Employment for visual artists is expected to grow about as fast as the average for all occupations. Because they are usually self-employed, much of artists' success depends on the amount and type of work created, the drive and determination involved in selling their artwork, and the interest or readiness of the public to appreciate and purchase their work. Population growth, higher incomes, and increased appreciation for fine art will create a demand for visual artists, but competition for positions in this field will be keen.

Success for an artist is difficult to quantify. Individual artists may consider themselves successful as their talent matures and they are better able to present their vision in their work. This type of success goes beyond financial considerations. Few artists enter this field for the money. Financial success depends on a great deal of factors, many of which have nothing to do with the artist or his or her work. Artists with good marketing skills will likely be the most successful in selling their work. Although artists should not let their style be dictated by market trends, those interested in financial success can attempt to determine what types of artwork are wanted by the public.

It often takes several years for an artist's work and reputation to be established. Many artists have to support themselves through other employment. There are numerous employment opportunities for commercial artists in such fields as publishing, advertising, fashion and design, and teaching. Painters and sculptors should consider employment in these and other fields. However, they should be prepared to face strong competition from others who are attracted to these fields.

FOR MORE INFORMATION

The following organization helps artists market and sell their art. It offers marketing tools, a newsletter, a directory of artists, and reference resources. To learn more and to receive a free 24-page brochure, contact

ArtNetwork
PO Box 1360
Nevada City, CA 95959
Tel: 800-383-0677
Email: info@artmarketing.com
http://www.artmarketing.com

For general information on ceramic arts study, contact

National Art Education Association
1916 Association Drive
Reston, VA 20191-1590
Tel: 703-860-8000
Email: naea@dgs.dgsys.com
http://www.naea-reston.org

The following organization provides an information exchange and sharing of professional opportunities.

Sculptors Guild
110 Greene Street, Suite 601
New York, NY 10012
Tel: 212-431-5669
http://www.sculptorsguild.org

PHOTO STYLISTS

QUICK FACTS

School Subjects
Art
Business

Personal Skills
Artistic
Communication/ideas

Work Environment
Indoors and outdoors
Primarily multiple locations

Minimum Education Level
Some postsecondary
training

Salary Range
$40 to $350 to $500+ per
day

Certification or Licensing
None available

Outlook
About as fast as the average

DOT
N/A

GOE
N/A

NOC
5243

O*NET-SOC
N/A

OVERVIEW

Photo styling is actually an all-encompassing term for the many and varied contributions that a *photo stylist* brings to the job. Primarily, the photo stylist works with a photographer to create a particular image, using props, backgrounds, accessories, clothing, costumes, food, linens, and other set elements. Much of the work exists within the print advertising industry, although stylists are also called to do film and commercial shoots. There are many specialties that can be included on a photo stylist's resume, from fashion to food, bridal to bathrooms, hair and makeup styling to prop shopping and location searches. Some stylists may focus on one specialty; others may seek to maintain a wide repertoire of skills. While photo styling may seem like a vague and nebulous profession, it is an increasingly vital part of the photography and advertising industries.

HISTORY

Photo styling has existed since the first photographs were taken. Someone, maybe the photographer, an assistant, a studio worker, a designer, or an editor, had to make sure all the elements within the frame were arranged in a certain way. Hair and makeup stylists in the film and publishing industries were probably the first to gain recognition (and credit lines). In fact, most people still associate "styling" exclusively with hair and makeup work, without fully appreciating the contribution of other stylists to the finished photo or film. To this day, photo styling credits are only occasionally listed in fashion and advertising spreads, but that trend is changing. Society is becoming more visually oriented, and the contributions made by stylists are becoming more important. Stylists are gaining the respect of people within the industry. Some photographer/stylist teams are as well known for their collaborative work as are actors and directors. After toiling in relative obscurity for many years, photo stylists are emerging as powerful voices in industry and in society.

THE JOB

The photo stylist is a creative collaborator, working with photographers, art directors, models, design houses, and clients to produce a visual image, usually for commercial purposes. It is both a technical and artistic occupation. The kind of work a photo stylist performs depends upon, among other things, the nature of the photography; the needs of the photographer, studio, and art director; and the requests of the client. Because these vary from one situation to another, it is impossible to list all the aspects of a photo stylist's job. In simple terms, what a stylist does is help to create a "look." The specifics of how it is done are far more complicated. These depend on the stylist's skill, resourcefulness, ingenuity, artistic sense, and collaborative relationship with the rest of the crew. Moreover, "photo styling" itself is a very general term—there are many kinds of styling, almost as many as there are reasons for taking a photograph.

Prop gathering and set decoration are the most common assignments in photo styling, but there are many subspecialties within the field, each requiring different skills and experience. For example, fashion, wardrobe, and portrait shoots often require a number of professional stylists on hand to scout locations, prepare the set, acquire clothes and accessories, dress the models, and style hair and makeup.

Food stylists employ a variety of techniques, from painting to glazing, to make everything from a bowl of cereal to a crawfish etouffee appear especially appetizing.

Home furnishings and domestic items specialists often introduce various props to give a natural look to the photographic set.

On-figure stylists fit clothes to a model, and *off-figure stylists* arrange clothes in attractive stacks or against an interesting background.

Soft-goods stylists introduce appropriate fabric, linens, and clothing into a shoot. The *tabletop stylist* may use anything from glue to Vaseline to give an added allure to a set of socket wrenches. *Hair and makeup stylists* are almost invariably cosmetic specialists, and are usually present on any set that employs live models.

Casting stylists locate modeling talent. Others specialize in set design, child photography, bedding, bridal, and catalogs. Many stylists are adept in more than one area, making them difficult to categorize.

Stylists may also bring special talents to the set, like floral design, gift wrapping, model building, or antiquing. They usually have a "bag of tricks" that will solve problems or create certain effects (a stylist's work kit might include everything from duct tape and cotton wadding to C-clamps and salt shakers). Sometimes a photo stylist is called upon to design and build props, perform on-set, last-minute tailoring, even coordinate the entire production from the location search to crew accommodations. The most successful stylists will adapt to the needs of the job, and if they can't produce something themselves, they will know in an instant how and where to find someone who can. Versatility and flexibility are key attributes no matter what the stylist's specialty.

Being prepared for every possible situation is simply part of the photo stylist's job. For example, knowledge of photographic techniques, especially lighting, lenses, and filters, can help a stylist communicate better with the photographer. An understanding of the advertising industry and familiarity with specific product lines and designers are also good tools for working with clients.

Organization is another vital aspect of the photo stylist's job. Before the shoot, the stylist must be sure that everything needed has been found and will arrive on time at the studio or location. During the shoot, even while working on a model or set, the stylist must be sure that all borrowed materials are being treated with care and that preparations for the next shot are underway. Afterwards, he or she must return items and maintain receipts and records, so as to keep the project within budget. The freelance stylist does all this while also rounding up new assignments and maintaining a current portfolio.

Only part of the stylist's time is spent in photo studios or on location. Much of the work is done on the phone and on the street, preparing for the job by gathering props and materials, procuring clothes, contacting models, or renting furniture. For the freelancer, lining up future employment can be a job in itself. A senior stylist working in-house at a magazine may have additional editorial duties, including working with art directors to introduce concepts and compose advertising narratives.

Even during downtime, the stylist must keep an eye out for ways to enhance his or her marketability. The chance discovery of a new boutique or specialty shop on the way to the grocery store can provide the stylist with a valuable new resource for later assignments. Maintaining a personal directory of resources is as essential as keeping a portfolio. Staying abreast of current trends and tastes through the media is also important, especially in the areas of fashion and lifestyle.

What a stylist does on the job depends largely upon his or her unique talents and abilities. Photo stylists with the most experience and creative resources will make the greatest contribution to a project. As a premier stylist, that contribution extends beyond the set to the society as a whole: shaping its tastes, making its images, and creating art that defines the era.

REQUIREMENTS
High School

There are a number of classes you can take to help prepare you for this career while you are still in high school. For example, take classes in the visual arts to learn about design and composition. Develop your hand-eye coordination in sculpture or pottery classes where you will be producing three-dimensional objects. Painting classes will teach you about colors, and photography classes will give you a familiarity using this medium. Skill with fabric is a must, so take family and consumer science classes that concentrate on fabric work. You will be able to cultivate your skills pressing and steaming clothes, doing minor alterations, and completing needlework. Because your work as a photo stylist may require you to work as a freelancer (running your own business) take mathematics classes or business and accounting classes that will prepare you to keep your own financial records. Of course, English classes are important. English classes will give you the communication skills that you will need to work well with a variety of people, to promote your own work, and to drum up new business. The specialties employed for certain shoots require a familiarity with, for instance, food preparation, home decorating, children, formal attire, bedding, and any number of other potential subjects. A photo stylist, like any artist, draws from his or her own experience for inspiration, so exposure to a wide variety of experiences will benefit anyone entering the field.

Postsecondary Training

There is no specific postsecondary educational or training route you must take to enter this field. Some photo stylists have attended art schools, receiving degrees in photography. Others have entered the field by going into retail, working for large department stores, for example, to gain experience with advertising, marketing, and even product display. The Association of Stylists and Coordinators (ASC) recommends entering the field by working as an assistant for an established stylist. According to ASC, such an informal apprenticeship usually lasts about two years. By then, the assistant typically has enough skills and connections to begin working on his or her own.

If you are interested in a specialized type of styling, you may want to consider gaining experience in that area. For example, if hair and makeup styling interests you, consider taking classes at a local cosmetology school that will teach you how to work with different kinds of hair. If food styling interests you, consider taking cooking or baking classes at a culinary school. Again, this will give you experience working with the materials to be photographed. It is essential to have a knowledge of photography for this work, so continue to take photography classes to build your skills. Advertising courses may also be useful.

Other Requirements

The personal qualities most sought in a photo stylist are creativity, taste, resourcefulness, and good instincts. Stylists work with a variety of people, such as clients, models, and prop suppliers, and therefore they need to have a calm and supportive personality. Schedules can be hectic and work is not always done during normal business hours, so stylists need flexibility, the ability to work under pressure, and patience. Stylists who are easy to work with often find that they have a large number of clients. Finally, an eye for detail is a must. Stylists are responsible for making sure that everything appearing in

a photo—from a model's hairstyle to the size and color of a lamp—
is exactly right.

EXPLORING

There are a number of fun ways to explore your interest in this
career. Try teaming up with a friend to conduct your own photo
shoot. Arm yourself with a camera, decide on a location (inside or
outside), and gather some props or costumes, then take a series of
photographs. At a professional level, these are known as *test shots*
and are used to build up the portfolios of photographers, models,
and stylists. But a backyard photo shoot can be a good way to appreciate the elements involved with this career. Obviously, any opportunity to visit a real photographer's set can be an invaluable learning
experience; ask a guidance counselor to help you arrange for such a
field trip. Join a photography or art club. Besides giving you the
opportunity to work with the medium, such clubs may also sponsor
talks or meetings with professionals in the field. Look for part-time
or summer work in the retail field where you may have the opportunity to set up displays and learn about advertising. Even if you
can't find such work, watch someone prepare a display in a department store window. Many stylists start out as window dressers or
doing in-store display work.

EMPLOYERS

There are relatively few positions available for full-time, salaried
photo stylists. Some ad agencies, magazines, and companies that sell
their merchandise through catalogs have stylists on staff. Most photo
stylists, however, work as freelancers. They are hired for individual
assignments by photographers, ad agencies, design firms, catalog
houses, and any other enterprise that uses photographic services.

STARTING OUT

A person can enter the field of photo styling at any point in life, but
there is no clear-cut way to go about it. Some people, if they have the
resources, hire photographers to shoot a portfolio with them, then
shop it around to production houses and other photographers.
However, most prospective employers prefer that a stylist has previous on-set experience.

As the ASC recommends, one of the best ways to break into this
field is to find work as a stylist's assistant. Production houses and
photo studios that employ full-time stylists usually keep a directory

of assistants. Most cities have a creative directory of established stylists who may need assistants. It is important to always leave a name and number; they may have no work available immediately, but might be desperate for help next month. Assisting provides you with important on-set experience as well as showing you the nuts and bolts of the job, including the drudgery along with the rewards. Building a reputation is the most important thing to do at any stage of this career, since most photographers find stylists by word of mouth and recommendations, in addition to reviewing portfolios. Assistants will also be introduced to the people who may hire them down the road as full-fledged stylists, giving them an opportunity to make a good impression. Eventually, you can seek out a photographer who needs a stylist and work together on test shots. Once you have enough examples of your work for a portfolio, you can show it to agents, editors, and photographers.

Agency representation can be of enormous help to the freelancer. An agent finds work for the stylist and pays him or her on a regular basis (after extracting an average commission of 20 percent). The benefit of representation is that while a stylist is working one job, the agent is lining up the next. Some agencies represent stylists exclusively; others also handle models, photographers, and actors.

ADVANCEMENT

Advancement in this field can be measured by the amount of bookings a stylist obtains, the steadiness of work, and a regularly increasing pay rate. It can also be determined by the quality of a stylist's clients, the reputation of the photographer, and the nature of the assignments. Some stylists start out with lower end catalogs and work their way up. If the goal is to do high fashion, then the steps along the way will be readily apparent in the quality of the merchandise and the size of the client. The opportunity to work with highly regarded photographers is also a step up, even if the stylist's pay rate remains the same. In a career built on reputation, experience with the industry's major players is priceless. Senior stylists at magazines often help in ad design and planning. Some stylists advance to become art directors and fashion editors. Ultimately, each stylist has his or her own goals in sight. The "rare-air" of high fashion and celebrity photography may not be the end-all for all stylists; a good steady income and the chance to work regularly with friendly, creative people may, in fact, be of more importance to a stylist.

EARNINGS

Like almost everything else in this field, earning potential varies from one stylist to the next. Salaries at production houses can start as low as $8 an hour, but usually include fringe benefits like health insurance, not to mention a regular paycheck. The freelancer, on the other hand, has enormous earning potential. An experienced fashion or food stylist can demand as much as $800 or more a day, depending on his or her reputation and the budget of the production. Regular bookings at this level, along with travel and accommodation costs (almost always paid for), translate into a substantial income.

Most photo stylists, however, earn less and average approximately $350–$500 per day. According to the ASC, assistant stylists, who are hired by the day, can expect to make approximately $150–$200 per day. Neither assistants nor stylists who are freelancers receive any kind of benefits. For example, they must provide for their own health insurance and retirement, and they receive no pay for sick days or vacation days. And while a stylist may have a job that pays $500 a day for several days, the stylist may also have unpaid periods when he or she is looking for the next assignment.

WORK ENVIRONMENT

Work conditions for a photo stylist are as varied as the job itself. Preparation for a shoot may involve hours on the telephone, calling from the home or office, and more hours shopping for props and materials to use on the set. Much of the work is done inside comfortable photo studios or at other indoor locations, but sometimes, especially in fashion and catalog photography, outdoor locations are also used. If the merchandise is of a seasonal nature, this could mean long days working in a cold field photographing winter parkas against a snowy background, or it could mean flying down to Key West in January for a week shooting next summer's line of swimwear. Travel, both local and long distance, is part of the job. Workdays can be long, from dawn to dusk, or a stylist may be on the set for only a few hours. Hours vary, but a stylist must always be flexible, especially the freelancer who may be called in on a day's notice.

There are numerous financial outlays to contend with, whether one keeps a personal inventory of props or rents the materials. Most clients and studios budget for these expenses and reimburse the stylist, but the initial funds must sometimes come from the stylist's own pocket. Maintaining a portfolio, purchasing equipment, and paying agents' fees may also add to the cost of doing business.

Photo styling can be an extremely lucrative career, but there is no assurance that a stylist will find steady employment. It is wise to establish an emergency fund in the event that work disappears for a time. Busy periods often correspond to seasonal advertising campaigns and film work, and between them there can be slow periods. A stylist might have a great year followed by a disappointing one. Freelancers must file their own quarterly tax returns and purchase their own health insurance.

Stress levels vary from one assignment to the next. Some shoots may go smoothly, others may have a crisis occur every minute. Stylists must be able to remain calm and resilient in the face of enormous pressure. Personality clashes may also occur despite every effort to avoid them, adding to the stress of the job. For the freelancer, the pressure to find new work and maintain proper business records are still further sources of stress. Photo stylists will also spend considerable time on their feet, stooping and kneeling in uncomfortable positions, trying to get something aligned just right. They also may need to transport heavy material and merchandise to and from the studio or location, or move these elements around the set during the shoot. Reliable transportation is essential.

The irregular hours of a photo stylist can be an attraction for people who have other commitments and enjoy variety in their lives. Work conditions are not always that strenuous. The work can also be pleasant and fun, as the crew trades jokes and experiences, solves problems together, and shares the excitement of a sudden inspiration. The rewards of working with a team of professionals on an interesting, creative project is a condition of the job that most stylists treasure.

OUTLOOK

The value of a good photo stylist is becoming more and more apparent to photographers and advertising clients. However, the outlook for employment for stylists depends a great deal on their perseverance and reputation. Large cities offer the most work, but there are photo studios in nearly every community. The fortunes of the stylist are related to the health of the advertising, film, video, and commercial photography industries. However, stylists should try to maintain a wide client base so they can be assured of regular work in case one source dries up.

Technological advances, especially in the areas of digital photography and photo enhancement, may transform, but not eliminate, the role of the photo stylist in the future. Someday there may be educational avenues for the stylist to enter into the field, and this may increase the amount of competition for styling assignments. Ultimately, though, maintaining the quality of work is the best insurance for continued employment.

FOR MORE INFORMATION

For information on the career of photo stylist, contact

Association of Stylists and Coordinators
24 Fifth Avenue
New York, NY 10011-8818
Tel: 212-780-3483
http://www.stylistsASC.com

To see examples of professional photography and read about news in the field, check out the following publication and website:

Photo District News
770 Broadway
New York, NY 10003
Tel: 646-654-5800
http://www.pdn-pix.com

PHOTOGRAPHERS

QUICK FACTS

School Subjects Art Chemistry	**Certification or Licensing** None available
Personal Skills Artistic Communication/ideas	**Outlook** About as fast as the average
Work Environment Indoors and outdoors Primarily multiple locations	**DOT** 143
Minimum Education Level Some postsecondary training	**GOE** 01.02.03
	NOC 5221
Salary Range $14,260 to $23,040 to $48,050+	**O*NET-SOC** 27-4021.00, 27-4021.01, 27-4021.02

OVERVIEW

Photographers take and sometimes develop and print pictures of people, places, objects, and events by using a variety of cameras and photographic equipment. They work in the publishing, advertising, public relations, science, and business industries, as well as provide personal photographic services. They may also work as fine artists. There are approximately 131,000 photographers employed in the United States.

HISTORY

The word *photograph* means, literally, "to write with light." Although the art of photography goes back only about 150 years, the two Greek words that were chosen and combined to refer to this skill quite accurately describe what it does.

The discoveries that led eventually to photography began early in the 18th century when a German scientist, Dr. Johann H. Schultze, experimented with the action of light on certain chemicals. He found that when these chemicals were covered by dark paper they did not change color, but when they were exposed to sunlight, they darkened. A French painter named Louis Daguerre became the first photographer in 1839, when he perfected the process of using silver-iodide-coated plates inside a small box. He then developed the plates by means of mercury vapor. The daguerreotype, as these early photographs came to be known, took minutes to expose and the developing process was directly to the plate. There were no prints made.

Although the daguerreotype was the sensation of its day, it was not until George Eastman invented a simple camera and flexible roll film that photography began to come into widespread use in the late 1800s. After exposing this film to light and developing it with chemicals, the film revealed a color-reversed image, which is called a negative. To make the negative positive (i.e., to print a picture), light must be shone though the negative on to light-sensitive paper. This process can be repeated to make multiple copies of an image.

THE JOB

Photography is both an artistic and technical occupation. There are many variables in the process that a knowledgeable photographer can manipulate to produce a precise documentation or a work of fine art. First, photographers know how to use cameras and can adjust focus, shutter speeds, aperture, lenses, and filters. They know about the types and speeds of films. Photographers know about light and shadow, how to use available light and how to set up artificial lighting to achieve desired effects.

Some photographers send their film to laboratories, but some develop their own negatives and make their own prints. These processes require knowledge about chemicals such as developers and fixers and how to use enlarging equipment. Photographers must also be familiar with the large variety of papers available for printing photographs, all of which deliver a different effect. Most photographers continually experiment with photographic processes to improve their technical proficiency or to create special effects.

Digital photography is a relatively new development. With this new technology, film is replaced by microchips that record pictures in digital format. Pictures can then be downloaded onto a computer's hard drive. Photographer uses special software to manipulate the images on screen. Digital photography is used primarily for electronic publishing and advertising.

Photographers usually specialize in one of several areas: portraiture, commercial and advertising photography, photojournalism, fine art, educational photography, or scientific photography. There are subspecialties within each of these categories. A *scientific photographer*, for example, may specialize in aerial or underwater photography. A *commercial photographer* may specialize in food or fashion photography.

Some photographers write for trade and technical journals, teach photography in schools and colleges, act as representatives of photographic equipment manufacturers, sell photographic equipment and supplies, produce documentary films, or do freelance work.

REQUIREMENTS
High School
While in high school, take as many art classes and photography classes as you can. Chemistry is useful for understanding developing and printing processes. You can learn about photo manipulation software and digital photography in computer classes, and business classes will help if you are considering a freelance career.

Postsecondary Training
Formal educational requirements depend upon the nature of the photographer's specialty. For instance, photographic work in scientific and engineering research generally requires an engineering background with a degree from a recognized college or institute.

A college education is not required to become a photographer, although college training probably offers the most promising assurance of success in fields such as industrial, news, or scientific photography. There are degree programs at the associate's, bachelor's, and master's levels. Many schools offer courses in cinematography, although very few have programs leading to a degree in this specialty. Many men and women, however, become photographers without pursuing formal education beyond high school.

To become a photographer, you should have a broad technical understanding of photography plus as much practical experience with cameras as possible. Take many different kinds of photographs with a variety of cameras and subjects. Learn how to develop photographs and, if possible, build your own darkroom or rent one. Experience in picture composition, cropping prints (cutting images to a desired size), enlarging, and retouching are all valuable skills.

Other Requirements

You should possess manual dexterity, good eyesight and color vision, and artistic ability to succeed in this line of work. You need an eye for form and line, an appreciation of light and shadow, and the ability to use imaginative and creative approaches to photographs or film, especially in commercial work. In addition, you should be patient and accurate and enjoy working with detail.

Self-employed (or freelance) photographers need good business skills. They must be able to manage their own studios, including hiring and managing photographic assistants and other employees, keeping records, and maintaining photographic and business files. Marketing and sales skills are also important to a successful freelance photography business.

EXPLORING

Photography is a field that anyone with a camera can explore. To learn more about this career, you can join high school camera clubs, yearbook or newspaper staffs, photography contests, and community hobby groups. You can also seek a part-time or summer job in a camera shop or work as a developer in a laboratory or processing center.

EMPLOYERS

About 131,000 photographers work in the United States, more than half of whom are self-employed. Most jobs for photographers are provided by photographic or commercial art studios; other employers include newspapers and magazines, radio and TV broadcasting, government agencies, and manufacturing firms. Colleges, universities, and other educational institutions employ photographers to prepare promotional and educational materials.

STARTING OUT

Some photographers enter the field as apprentices, trainees, or assistants. Trainees may work in a darkroom, camera shop, or developing laboratory. They may move lights and arrange backgrounds for a commercial or portrait photographer or motion picture photographer. Assistants spend many months learning this kind of work before they move into a job behind a camera.

Many large cities offer schools of photography, which may be a good way to start in the field. Beginning press photographers may work for one of the many newspapers and magazines published in their area. Other photographers choose to go into business for themselves as soon as they have finished their formal education. Setting up a studio may not require a large capital outlay, but beginners may find that success does not come easily.

ADVANCEMENT
Because photography is such a diversified field, there is no usual way in which to get ahead. Those who begin by working for someone else may advance to owning their own businesses. Commercial photographers may gain prestige as more of their pictures are placed in well-known trade journals or popular magazines. Press photographers may advance in salary and the kinds of important news stories assigned to them. A few photographers may become celebrities in their own right by making contributions to medical science, engineering science, or natural or physical science.

EARNINGS
The U.S. Bureau of Labor Statistics reports that salaried photographers earned median annual salaries of $23,040 in 2001. Salaries ranged from less than $14,260 to more than $48,050.

Self-employed photographers often earn more than salaried photographers, but their earnings depend on general business conditions. In addition, self-employed photographers do not have the benefits that a company provides its employees.

Photographers who combine scientific training and photographic expertise, as do scientific photographers, usually start at higher salaries than other photographers. They also usually receive consistently larger advances in salary than do others, so that their income, both as beginners and as experienced photographers, place them well above the average in their field. Photographers in salaried jobs usually receive benefits such as paid holidays, vacations, and sick leave and medical insurance.

WORK ENVIRONMENT
Work conditions vary based on the job and employer. Many photographers work a 35- to 40-hour workweek, but freelancers and news photographers often put in long, irregular hours. Commercial and portrait photographers work in comfortable surroundings. Photojournalists seldom are assured physical comfort in their work and may in fact face danger when covering stories on natural disasters or military conflicts. Some photographers work in research lab-

oratory settings; others work on aircraft; and still others work under-water. For some photographers, conditions change from day to day. One day, they may be photographing a hot and dusty rodeo; the next they may be taking pictures of a dog sled race in Alaska.

In general, photographers work under pressure to meet deadlines and satisfy customers. Freelance photographers have the added pressure of continually seeking new clients and uncertain incomes.

For specialists in fields such as fashion photography, breaking into the field may take years. Working as another photographer's assistant is physically demanding when carrying equipment is required.

For freelance photographers, the cost of equipment can be quite expensive, with no assurance that the money spent will be repaid through income from future assignments. Freelancers in travel-related photography, such as travel and tourism photographers and photojournalists, have the added cost of transportation and accommodations. For all photographers, flexibility is a major asset.

OUTLOOK

Employment of photographers will increase about as fast as the average for all occupations through 2010, according to the *Occupational Outlook Handbook*. The demand for new images should remain strong in education, communication, entertainment, marketing, and research. As the Internet grows and more newspapers and magazines turn to electronic publishing, demand will increase for photographers to produce digital images. Additionally, as the population grows, demand should increase for photographers who specialize in portraiture.

Photography is a highly competitive field. There are far more photographers than positions available. Only those who are extremely talented and highly skilled can support themselves as self-employed photographers. Many photographers take pictures as a sideline while working another job.

FOR MORE INFORMATION

The ASMP promotes the rights of photographers, educates its members in business practices, and promotes high standards of ethics.

American Society of Media Photographers (ASMP)
150 North Second Street
Philadelphia, PA 19106
Tel: 215-451-2767
http://www.asmp.org

The NPPA maintains a job bank, provides educational information, and makes insurance available to its members. It also publishes News Photographer *magazine.*

National Press Photographers Association (NPPA)
3200 Croasdaile Drive, Suite 306
Durham, NC 27705-2588
Tel: 919-383-7246
http://www.nppa.org

This organization provides training, publishes its own magazine, and offers various services for its members.

Professional Photographers of America, Inc.
229 Peachtree Street, NE, Suite 2200
Atlanta, GA 30303
Tel: 800-786-6277
Email: csc@ppa.com
http://www.ppa.com

SECONDARY SCHOOL TEACHERS

QUICK FACTS

School Subjects
English
Psychology

Personal Skills
Communication/ideas
Helping/teaching

Work Environment
Primarily indoors
Primarily one location

Minimum Education Level
Bachelor's degree

Salary Range
$27,980 to $43,280 to
$67,940+

Certification or Licensing
Required by all states

Outlook
About as fast as the average

DOT
091

GOE
11.02.01

NOC
4141

O*NET-SOC
25-2022.00, 25-2023.00,
25-2031.00, 25-2032.00

OVERVIEW

Secondary school teachers teach students in grades 7–12. Specializing in one subject area, such as art or math, these teachers work with five or more groups of students during the day. They lecture, direct discussions, and test students' knowledge with exams, essays, and homework assignments. There are close to 1 million secondary school teachers employed in the United States.

HISTORY

Early secondary education was typically based upon training students to enter the clergy. Benjamin Franklin pioneered the idea of a broader secondary education with the creation of the academy, which offered a flexible curriculum and a wide variety of academic subjects.

It was not until the 19th century, however, that children of different social classes commonly attended school into the secondary grades. The first English Classical School, which was to become the model for public high schools throughout the country, was established in 1821 in Boston. An adjunct to the high school, the junior high school was conceived by Dr. Charles W. Eliot, president of Harvard University. In a speech before the National Education Association in 1888, he recommended that secondary studies be started two years earlier than was the custom. The first such school opened in 1908, in Columbus, Ohio. Another opened a year later in Berkeley, California. By the early 20th century, secondary school attendance was made mandatory in the United States.

THE JOB

Many successful people credit secondary school teachers with helping guide them into college, careers, and other endeavors. The teachers' primary responsibility is to educate students in a specific subject. But secondary teachers also inform students about colleges, occupations, and such varied subjects as the arts, health, and relationships.

Secondary school teachers may teach in a traditional area, such as science, English, history, and math, or they may teach more specialized classes, such as information technology, business, and theater. Many secondary schools are expanding their course offerings to better serve the individual interests of their students. "School-to-work" programs, which are vocational education programs designed for high school students and recent graduates, involve lab work and demonstrations to prepare students for highly technical jobs. Though secondary teachers are likely be assigned to one specific grade level, they may be required to teach students in surrounding grades. For example, a secondary school mathematics teacher may teach algebra to a class of ninth-graders one period and trigonometry to high school seniors the next.

In the classroom, secondary school teachers rely on a variety of teaching methods. They spend a great deal of time lecturing, but they also facilitate student discussion and develop projects and activities to interest the students in the subject. They show films and videos, use computers and the Internet, and bring in guest speakers. They assign essays, presentations, and other projects. Each individual subject calls upon particular approaches, and may involve laboratory experiments, role-playing exercises, shop work, and field trips.

Outside of the classroom, secondary school teachers prepare lectures, lesson plans, and exams. They evaluate student work and calculate grades. In the process of planning their class, secondary school teachers read textbooks, novels, and workbooks to determine reading assignments; photocopy notes, articles, and other handouts; and develop grading policies. They also continue to study alternative and traditional teaching methods to hone their skills. They prepare students for special events and conferences and submit student work to competitions. Many secondary school teachers also serve as sponsors to student organizations in their field. For example, a French teacher may sponsor the French club and a journalism teacher may advise the yearbook staff. Some secondary school teachers also have the opportunity for extracurricular work as athletic coaches or drama coaches. Teachers also monitor students during lunch or break times and sit in on study halls. They may also accompany student groups on field trips, competitions, and events. Some teachers also have the opportunity to escort students on educational vacations to foreign countries, to Washington, D.C., and to other major U.S. cities. Secondary school teachers attend faculty meetings, meetings with parents, and state and national teacher conferences.

Some teachers explore their subject area outside of the requirements of the job. *English* and *writing teachers* may publish in magazines and journals, *business* and *technology teachers* may have small businesses of their own, *music teachers* may perform and record their music, *art teachers* may show work in galleries, and *sign-language teachers* may do freelance interpreting.

REQUIREMENTS
High School
You should follow your guidance counselor's college preparatory program and take advanced classes in such subjects as English, science, math, and government. You should also explore an extracurricular activity, such as theater, sports, and debate, so that you can offer these additional skills to future employers. If you're already aware of which subject you'd like to teach, take all the available courses in that area. You should also take speech and composition courses to develop your communication skills.

Postsecondary Training
There are over 500 accredited teacher education programs in the United States. Most of these programs are designed to meet the certification requirements for the state in which they're located. Some states may require that you pass a test before being admitted to an

education program. You may choose to major in your subject area while taking required education courses, or you may major in secondary education with a concentration in your subject area. You'll probably have advisors (both in education and in your chosen specialty) to help you select courses.

In addition to a degree, a training period of student teaching in an actual classroom environment is usually required. Students are placed in schools to work with full-time teachers. During this period, undergraduate students observe the ways in which lessons are presented and the classroom is managed, learn how to keep records of such details as attendance and grades, and get actual experience in handling the class, both under supervision and alone.

Besides licensure and courses in education, prospective high school teachers usually need 24 to 36 hours of college work in the subject they wish to teach. Some states require a master's degree; teachers with master's degrees can earn higher salaries. Private schools generally do not require an education degree.

Certification or Licensing

Public school teachers must be licensed under regulations established by the department of education of the state in which they teach. Not all states require licensure for teachers in private or parochial schools. When you've received your teaching degree, you may request that a transcript of your college record be sent to the licensure section of the state department of education. If you have met licensure requirements, you will receive a certificate and thus be eligible to teach in the public schools of the state. In some states, you may have to take additional tests. If you move to another state, you will have to resubmit college transcripts, as well as comply with any other regulations in the new state to be able to teach there.

Other Requirements

Working as a secondary school teacher, you'll need to have respect for young people and a genuine interest in their success in life. You'll also need patience; adolescence can be a troubling time for children, and these troubles often affect behavior and classroom performance. Because you'll be working with students who are at very impressionable ages, you should serve as a good role model. You should also be well organized, as you'll have to keep track of the work and progress of many students.

EXPLORING

By going to high school, you've already gained a good sense of the daily work of a secondary school teacher. But the requirements of a teacher extend far beyond the classroom, so ask to spend some time with one of your teachers after school, and ask to look at lecture notes and record-keeping procedures. Interview your teachers about the amount of work that goes into preparing a class and directing an extracurricular activity. To get some firsthand teaching experience, volunteer for a peer tutoring program. Many other teaching opportunities may exist in your community. Look into coaching an athletic team at the YMCA, counseling at a summer camp, teaching an art course at a community center, or assisting with a community theater production.

EMPLOYERS

Secondary school teachers are needed at public and private schools, including parochial schools, juvenile detention centers, vocational schools, and schools of the arts. They work in middle schools, junior high schools, and high schools. Though some rural areas maintain schools, most secondary schools are in towns and cities of all sizes. Teachers are also finding opportunities in charter schools, which are smaller, deregulated schools that receive public funding.

STARTING OUT

After completing the teacher certification process, including your months of student teaching, you'll work with your college's placement office to find a full-time position. The departments of education of some states maintain listings of job openings. Many schools advertise teaching positions in the classifieds of the state's major newspapers. You may also directly contact the principals and superintendents of the schools in which you'd like to work. While waiting for full-time work, you can work as a substitute teacher. In urban areas with many schools, you may be able to substitute full time.

ADVANCEMENT

Most teachers advance simply by becoming more of an expert in the job that they have chosen. There is usually an increase in salary as teachers acquire experience. Additional training or study can also bring an increase in salary.

A few teachers with management ability and interest in administrative work may advance to the position of principal. Others may advance into supervisory positions, and some may become *helping teachers* who are charged with the responsibility of helping other teachers find appropriate instructional materials and develop certain phases of their courses of study. Others may go into teacher education at a college or university. For most of these positions, additional education is required. Some teachers also make lateral moves into other education-related positions such as guidance counselor or resource room teacher.

EARNINGS

Most teachers are contracted to work nine months out of the year, though some contracts are made for 10 or a full 12 months. (When regular school is not in session, teachers are expected to conduct summer teaching, planning, or other school-related work.) In most cases, teachers have the option of prorating their salary up to 52 weeks.

According to the Bureau of Labor Statistics, the median annual salary for secondary school teachers was $43,280 in 2001. The lowest 10 percent earned $27,980; the highest 10 percent earned $67,940 or more.

The American Federation of Teachers reports that the national average salary for all teachers was 43,250 during the 2000–01 school year. Beginning teachers earned approximately $28,986 a year.

Teachers can also supplement their earnings through teaching summer classes, coaching sports, sponsoring a club, or other extracurricular work.

On behalf of the teachers, unions bargain with schools over contract conditions such as wages, hours, and benefits. A majority of teachers join the American Federation of Teachers or the National Education Association. Depending on the state, teachers usually receive a retirement plan, sick leave, and health and life insurance. Some systems grant teachers sabbatical leave.

WORK ENVIRONMENT

Although the job of the secondary school teacher is not overly strenuous, it can be tiring and trying. Secondary school teachers must stand for many hours each day, do a lot of talking, show energy and enthusiasm, and handle discipline problems. But they also have the reward of guiding their students as they make decisions about their lives and futures.

Secondary school teachers work under generally pleasant conditions, though some older schools may have poor heating and electrical systems. Though violence in schools has decreased in recent years, media coverage of the violence has increased, along with student fears. In most schools, students are prepared to learn and to perform the work that's required of them. But in some schools, students may be dealing with gangs, drugs, poverty, and other problems, so the environment can be tense and emotional.

School hours are generally 8:00 A.M. to 3:00 P.M., but teachers work more than 40 hours a week teaching, preparing for classes, grading papers, and directing extracurricular activities. As a coach, or as a music or drama director, teachers may have to work some evenings and weekends. Many teachers enroll in master's or doctoral programs and take evening and summer courses to continue their education.

OUTLOOK

The U.S. Department of Education predicts that employment for secondary teachers will grow by 16.6 percent through 2010 to meet rising enrollments and to replace the large number of retiring teachers. The National Education Association believes this will be a challenge because of the low salaries that are paid to secondary school teachers. Higher salaries will be necessary to attract new teachers and retain experienced ones, along with other changes such as smaller classroom sizes and safer schools. Other challenges for the profession involve attracting more men into teaching. The percentage of male teachers at this level continues to decline.

In order to improve education for all children, changes are being considered by some districts. Some private companies are managing public schools. Though it is believed that a private company can afford to provide better facilities, faculty, and equipment, this hasn't been proven. Teacher organizations are concerned about taking school management away from communities and turning it over to remote corporate headquarters. Charter schools and voucher programs are two other controversial alternatives to traditional public education. Charter schools, which are small schools that are publicly funded but not guided by the rules and regulations of traditional public schools, are viewed by some as places of innovation and improved educational methods; others see charter schools as ill-equipped and unfairly funded with money that could better benefit local school districts. Vouchers, which exist only in a few cities, allow students to attend private schools courtesy of tuition vouchers; these vouchers are paid for with public tax dollars. In theory, the vouchers allow for more choices in education for poor and minority students, but private schools still have the option of being highly selective in their admissions. Teacher organizations see some danger in giving public funds to unregulated private schools.

Top Art Graduate Programs, by Specialty

U.S. News & World Report prepares annual ranking lists for graduate school programs. The following lists show the top ranked schools for various art degrees.

Ceramics

1. New York State College of Ceramics at Alfred University
http://nyscc.alfred.edu

2. Cranbrook Academy of Art (Mich.)
http://www.cranbrook.edu/art

3. University of Washington
http://net.art.washington.edu

4. California College of Arts and Crafts
http://www.ccarts.edu

5. Louisiana State University
http://www.art.lsu.edu

6. Ohio University
http://www.ohiou.edu/art

7. Rhode Island School of Design
http://www.risd.edu

8. Ohio State University
http://www.arts.ohio-state.edu

9. University of Colorado at Boulder
http://www.colorado.edu/finearts

10. California State University at Long Beach
http://www.art.csulb.edu

11. Pennsylvania State University at University Park
http://www.sva.psu.edu/svawebsite/sva.swf

12. University of California at Davis
http://art.ucdavis.edu

13. University of Minnesota at Twin Cities
http://artdept.umn.edu

Graphic Design

1. Rhode Island School of Design
http://www.risd.edu

(continues)

Top Art Graduate Programs, by Specialty

(continued)

2. Yale University (Conn.)
   http://www.yale.edu/art

3. Cranbrook Academy of Art (Mich.)
   http://www.cranbrook.edu/art

4. Art Center College of Design (CA)
   http://www.artcenter.edu

5. Virginia Commonwealth University
   http://www.vcu.edu/graduate

6. Carnegie Mellon University (Pa.)
   http://www.cmu.edu/cfa

7. North Carolina State University
   http://ncsudesign.org

8. University of Illinois at Urbana-Champaign
   http://www.art.uiuc.edu

9. Pratt Institute (N.Y.)
   http://www.pratt.edu

10. School of Visual Arts (N.Y.)
    http://www.schoolofvisualarts.edu

Industrial Design

1. Art Center College of Design (Calif.)
   http://www.artcenter.edu

2. Rhode Island School of Design
   http://www.risd.edu

3. Carnegie Mellon University (Pa.)
   http://www.cmu.edu/cfa

4. Cranbrook Academy of Art (Mich.)
   http://www.cranbrook.edu/art

5. Pratt Institute (N.Y.)
   http://www.pratt.edu

Multimedia and Visual Communications

1. California Institute of the Arts
   http://www.calarts.edu

(continues)

Top Art Graduate Programs, by Specialty

(continued)

2. Carnegie Mellon University (Pa.)
   http://www.cmu.edu/cfa

3. School of the Art Institute of Chicago
   http://www.artic.edu/saic

4. University of California at Los Angeles
   http://www.arts.ucla.edu

5. School of Visual Arts (N.Y.)
   http://www.schoolofvisualarts.edu

6. New York University
   http://www.nyu.edu/education/art

7. University of California at San Diego
   http://visarts.ucsd.edu

8. Art Center College of Design (Calif.)
   http://www.artcenter.edu

9. Rensselaer Polytechnic Institute (N.Y.)
   http://www.arts.rpi.edu

10. Rhode Island School of Design
    http://www.risd.edu

Painting/Drawing

1. Yale University (Conn.)
   http://www.yale.edu/art

2. School of the Art Institute of Chicago
   http://www.artic.edu/saic

3. University of California at Los Angeles
   http://www.arts.ucla.edu

4. Rhode Island School of Design
   http://www.risd.edu

5. Maryland Institute College of Art
   http://www.mica.edu

6. Tyler School of Art at Temple University (Pa.)
   http://www.temple.edu/tyler

7. San Francisco Art Institute
   http://www.sfai.edu

(continues)

Top Art Graduate Programs, by Specialty

(continued)

8. University of Texas at Austin
   http://www.utexas.edu/cofa/a_ah

9. Indiana University at Bloomington
   http://www.iub.edu

10. Cranbrook Academy of Art (Mich.)
    http://www.cranbrook.edu/art

11. Virginia Commonwealth University
    http://www.vcu.edu/graduate

Photography

1. School of the Art Institute of Chicago
   http://www.artic.edu/saic

2. Rhode Island School of Design
   http://www.risd.edu

3. University of New Mexico
   http://www.unm.edu/~finearts

4. Rochester University of Technology (N.Y.)
   http://www.rit.edu/~661www

5. Katherine K. Herberger College of Fine Arts at Arizona State University
   http://art.asu.edu

6. San Francisco Art Institute
   http://www.sfai.edu

7. Yale University (Conn.)
   http://www.yale.edu/art

8. California Institute of the Arts
   http://www.calarts.edu

9. University of Arizona
   http://web.cfa.arizona.edu

10. University of California at Los Angeles
    http://www.arts.ucla.edu

Printmaking

1. University of Wisconsin at Madison
   http://www.education.wisc.edu/art

(continues)

Top Art Graduate Programs, by Specialty

(continued)

2. University of Iowa
   http://www.uiowa.edu/~art

3. Arizona State University
   http://web.cfa.arizona.edu

4. University of Georgia
   http://www.gradsch.uga.edu

5. University of Tennessee at Knoxville
   http://web.utk.edu/~art

6. School of the Art Institute of Chicago
   http://www.artic.edu/saic

7. University of Texas at Austin
   http://www.utexas.edu/cofa/a_ah

8. Cranbook Academy of Art (Mich.)
   http://www.cranbrook.edu/art

9. Rutgers State University (N.J.)
   http://finearts.camden.rutgers.edu/art

10. Rhode Island School of Design
    http://www.risd.edu

Sculpture

1. Virginia Commonwealth University
   http://www.vcu.edu/graduate

2. Yale University (Conn.)
   http://www.yale.edu/art

3. School of the Art Institute of Chicago
   http://www.artic.edu/saic

4. University of California at Los Angeles
   http://www.arts.ucla.edu

5. Cranbrook Academy of Art (Mich.)
   http://www.cranbrook.edu/art

6. Rhode Island School of Design
   http://www.risd.edu

7. Maryland Institute College of Art
   http://www.mica.edu

(continues)

Top Art Graduate Programs, by Specialty

(continued)

8. Ohio State University
   http://www.arts.ohio-state.edu

9. Tyler School of Art at Temple University (Pa.)
   http://www.temple.edu/tyler

10. California Institute of the Arts
    http://www.calarts.edu

11. Syracuse University (N.Y.)
    http://vpa.syr.edu

Source: *U.S. News & World Report* (ranked in 2003)

FOR MORE INFORMATION

For information about careers and current issues affecting teachers, contact or visit the websites of the following organizations:

American Federation of Teachers
555 New Jersey Avenue, NW
Washington, DC 20001
Tel: 202-879-4400
Email: online@aft.org
http://www.aft.org

National Education Association
1201 16th Street, NW
Washington, DC 20036
Tel: 202-833-4000
http://www.nea.org

For information on accredited teacher education programs, contact
National Council for Accreditation of Teacher Education
2010 Massachusetts Avenue, NW, Suite 500
Washington, DC 20036-1023
Tel: 202-466-7496
Email: ncate@ncate.org
http://www.ncate.org

TELEVISION EDITORS

QUICK FACTS

School Subjects Art English **Personal Skills** Artistic Communication/ideas **Work Environment** Primarily indoors Primarily one location **Minimum Education Level** Some postsecondary training **Salary Range** $19,430 to $36,900 to $100,000+	**Certification or Licensing** None available **Outlook** Faster than the average **DOT** 132 **GOE** 11.08.01 **NOC** 5225 **O*NET-SOC** 27-4032.00

OVERVIEW

Television editors take an unedited draft of videotape and use specialized equipment to improve the draft until it is ready for viewing. It is the responsibility of the television editor to create the most effective product possible. Television editors may also be employed in the film industry. There are approximately 16,000 film, video, and television editors employed in the United States.

HISTORY

The television industry has experienced substantial growth in the last few years in the United States. The effect of this growth is a steady demand for the essential skills that television editors provide. With recent innovations in computer technology, much of the work that these editors perform is accomplished using sophisticated computer programs. All of these factors have enabled many television editors to find steady work as salaried employees of television production companies and as independent contractors who provide their services on a per-job basis.

In the early days of the industry, editing was sometimes done by directors, studio technicians, or others for whom this work was not their specialty. Now every videotape, including the most brief television advertisement, has an editor who is responsible for the continuity and clarity of the project.

THE JOB

Television editors work closely with producers and directors throughout an entire project. These editors assist in the earliest phase, called preproduction, and during the production phase, when actual filming occurs. Their skills are in the greatest demand during postproduction, the completion of primary filming. During preproduction, in meetings with producers, editors learn about the objectives of the film or video. If the project is a television commercial, for example, the editor must be familiar with the product the commercial will attempt to sell. If the project is a feature-length motion picture, the editor must understand the story line. The producer may explain the larger scope of the project so that the editor knows the best way to approach the work when it is time to edit the film. In consultation with the director, editors may discuss the best way to accurately present the screenplay or script. They may discuss different settings, scenes, or camera angles even before filming or taping begins. With this kind of preparation, film and television editors are ready to practice their craft as soon as the production phase is complete.

Editors are usually the final decision-makers when it comes to choosing which segments will stay in as they are, which segments will be cut, or which may need to be redone. Editors look at the quality of the segment, its dramatic value, and its relationship to other segments. They then arrange the segments in an order that creates the most effective finished product. They rely on the script and notes from the director, along with their natural sense of how a scene should progress, in putting together the film, commercial, or show. Editors looks for the best shots, camera angles, line deliveries, and continuity.

Some editors specialize in certain areas of television or film. *Sound editors* work on the soundtracks of television programs or motion pictures. They often keep libraries of sounds that they reuse for various projects. These include natural sounds such as thunder or raindrops, animal noises, motor sounds, or musical interludes. Some sound editors specialize in music and may have training in music theory or performance. Others work with sound effects. They may use unusual objects, machines, or computer-generated noisemakers to create a desired sound for a film or TV show.

REQUIREMENTS
High School
Broadcast journalism and other media and communications courses may provide you with practical experience in video editing. Because television editing requires a creative perspective along with technical skills, you should take English, speech, theater, and other courses that will allow you to develop writing skills. Art and photography classes will involve you with visual media. If you're lucky enough to attend a high school that offers film classes, either in film history or in production, be sure to take those courses. Finally, don't forget to take computer classes. Editing work constantly makes use of new technology, and you should become familiar and comfortable with computers as soon as possible.

Postsecondary Training
Some studios require a bachelor's degree for those seeking positions as television editors. However, actual on-the-job experience is the best guarantee of securing lasting employment. Degrees in communications or liberal arts fields are preferred, but courses in cinematography and audiovisual techniques help editors get started in their work. You may choose to pursue a degree in such subjects as English, journalism, theater, art, or film. Community and two-year colleges often offer courses in the study of film as literature. Some of these colleges also teach video and film editing. Universities with departments of broadcast journalism offer courses in video and film editing and also may have contacts at local television stations.

Training as a television editor takes from four to 10 years. Many editors learn much of their work on the job as an assistant or apprentice at larger studios that offer these positions. The apprentice has the opportunity to see the work of the editor up close. The editor may eventually assign some of his or her minor duties to the apprentice, while the editor makes the larger decisions. After a few years, the apprentice may be promoted to editor or may apply for a position as a television editor at other studios. Training in video and film editing is also available in the military, including the Air Force, Marine Corps, Coast Guard, and Navy.

Other Requirements

You should be able to work cooperatively with other creative people when editing a project. You should remain open to suggestions and guidance, while also maintaining your confidence in the presence of other professionals. A successful editor has an understanding of the history of television and a feel for the narrative form in general. Computer skills are also important and will help you to learn new technology in the field. You may be required to join a union to do this work, depending on the studio. "You should have a good visual understanding," Steve Swersky says. "You need to be able to tell a story, and be aware of everything that's going on in a frame."

EXPLORING

Many high schools have film clubs, and some have cable television stations affiliated with the school district. Often school-run television channels give students the opportunity to actually create and edit short programs. Check out what's available at your school.

Believe it or not, a good way to prepare for a career as a television editor is to read. Reading literature will help develop your understanding of the different ways in which stories can be presented.

You should be familiar with all different kinds of television and film projects, including documentaries, short films, feature films, TV shows, and commercials. See as many different projects as you can and study them, paying close attention to the decisions the editors made in piecing together the scenes.

Large television stations occasionally have volunteers or student interns. Most people in the industry start out doing minor tasks helping with production. These production assistants get the opportunity to see all of the professionals at work. By working closely with an editor, a production assistant can learn television operations as well as specific editing techniques.

EMPLOYERS

Some television editors work primarily with news programs, documentaries, or special features. They may develop ongoing working relationships with directors or producers who hire them from one project to another. Many editors who have worked for a studio or postproduction company for several years often become independent contractors. They offer their services on a per-job basis to producers of commercials and films, negotiating their own fees, and typically have purchased or leased their own editing equipment.

STARTING OUT

Because of the glamour associated with television work, this is a popular field that can be very difficult to break into. With a minimum of a high school diploma or a degree from a two-year college, you can apply for entry-level jobs in many television studios, but these jobs won't be editing positions. Most studios will not consider people for television editor positions without a bachelor's degree or several years of on-the-job experience.

One way to get on-the-job experience is to complete an apprenticeship in editing. However, in some cases, you won't be eligible for an apprenticeship unless you are a current employee of the studio. Therefore, start out by applying to as many television studios as possible and take an entry-level position, even if it's not in the editing department. Once you start work, let people know that you are interested in an editor apprenticeship so that you'll be considered the next time one becomes available.

Those who have completed bachelor's or master's degrees have typically gained hands-on experience through school projects. Another benefit of going to school is that contacts that you make while in school, both through your school's placement office and alumni, can be a valuable resource when you look for your first job. Your school's placement office may also have listings of job openings. Some studio work is union regulated. Therefore you may also want to contact union locals to find out about job requirements and openings.

ADVANCEMENT

Once television editors have secured employment in their field, their advancement comes with further experience and greater recognition. Some editors develop good working relationships with directors or producers. These editors may be willing to leave the security of a studio job for the possibility of working one-on-one with the director or producer on a project. These opportunities often provide editors with the autonomy they may not get in their regular jobs. Some are willing to take a pay cut to work on a project they feel is important.

Some editors choose to stay at their studios and advance through seniority to editing positions with higher salaries. They may be able to negotiate better benefits packages or to choose the projects they will work on. They may also choose which directors they wish to work with. In larger studios, they may train and supervise staffs of less experienced or apprentice editors.

Some sound or sound-effects editors may wish to broaden their skills by working as general editors. Some television editors may, on the other hand, choose to specialize in sound effects, music, or some other editorial area. Some editors who work in television may move to motion pictures or may move from working on commercials or television series to television movies.

EARNINGS

Television editors are not as highly paid as others working in their industry. They have less clout than directors or producers, but they have more authority in the production of a project than many other film technicians. According to the Bureau of Labor Statistics, the median annual wage for television, film, and video editors was $36,900 in 2001. A small percentage of editors earn less than $19,430 a year, while others earn over $72,480. The most experienced and sought after television and film editors can command much higher salaries, even more than $100,000 a year.

WORK ENVIRONMENT

Most of the work done by editors is done in television studios or at postproduction companies using editing equipment. The working environment is often a small, cramped studio office. Working hours vary widely depending on the project. During the filming of a commercial, for instance, editors may be required to work overtime, at night, or on weekends to finish the project by an assigned date. "As stressful as the work can be," Steve Swersky says, "we joke around that it's not like having a real job. Every day is a fun day."

During filming, editors may be asked to be on hand at the filming location. Locations may be outdoors or in other cities, and travel is occasionally required. More often, however, the television or film editor edits in the studio, and that is where the bulk of the editor's time is spent.

Disadvantages of the job involve the editor's low rank on the totem pole of television industry jobs. However, most editors feel that this is outweighed by the advantages. Television editors can view the projects on which they have worked and be proud of their role in creating them.

OUTLOOK

The outlook for television editors is very good. In fact, the U.S. Department of Labor predicts faster than average employment growth for television and film editors over the next decade. The growth of cable television and an increase in the number of independent film studios will translate into greater demand for editors. This will also force the largest studios to offer more competitive salaries in order to attract the best television and film editors.

The developments of companies such as Avid Technology, which engineered and introduced many of the digital editing tools used today, will continue to greatly affect the editing process. Editors will work much more closely with special effects houses in putting together projects. When using more effects, television and film editors will have to edit scenes with an eye towards special effects to be added later. Digital editing systems are also available for home computers. Users can feed their own digital video into their computers, then edit the material, and add their own special effects and titles. This technology may allow some prospective editors more direct routes into the industry, but the majority of editors will have to follow traditional routes, obtaining years of hands-on experience.

FOR MORE INFORMATION

The ACE features career and education information for film and television editors on its Web page, along with information about internship opportunities and sample articles from the magazine Cinemeditor.

American Cinema Editors (ACE)
100 Universal City Plaza
Building 2282, Room 234
Universal City, CA 91608
Tel: 818-777-2900
Email: amercinema@earthlink.net
http://www.ace-filmeditors.org

This union counts film and television production workers among its craft members. For education and training information as well as links to film commissions and production companies, check out the IATSE website.

International Alliance of Theatrical Stage Employees, Moving Picture Technicians, Artists and Allied Crafts of the United States and Canada (IATSE)
1430 Broadway, 20th Floor
New York, NY 10018
Tel: 212-730-1770
http://www.iatse-intl.org

For information on NATAS scholarships and to read articles from Television Quarterly, *the organization's official journal, visit the NATAS website.*

National Academy of Television Arts and Sciences (NATAS)
111 West 57th Street, Suite 600
New York, NY 10019
Tel: 212-586-8424
Email: hq@natasonline.com
http://www.emmyonline.org

TOY AND GAME DESIGNERS

QUICK FACTS

School Subjects Art English	**Certification or Licensing** None available
Personal Skills Artistic Communication/ideas	**Outlook** Faster than the average **DOT** 142
Work Environment Primarily indoors Primarily one location	**GOE** 01.02.03
Minimum Education Level Bachelor's degree	**NOC** 2252
Salary Range $28,800 to $49,830 to $200,000+	**O*NET-SOC** 27-1021.00

OVERVIEW

Toy and game designers develop and create a variety of entertainment products, from stuffed animals and action figures to video games and virtual pets. While these creative specialists often determine the general design to be used, they usually work with a team of developers (including editors, illustrators, production managers, and playtesters) to manufacture a product for an intended audience.

Classified as *industrial designers*, toy and game designers work primarily for publishers, development firms, and manufacturing companies. Most designers work as freelancers; there are probably no more than a few thousand full-time professionals employed in the United States.

HISTORY

While toy artisans and craftsworkers had been practicing their craft for centuries, they didn't receive any kind of formal recognition until the Renaissance. Although the toys and games of that period were relatively simple compared to those that we know today, the introduction of automatic and mechanical toys created a sense of wonder among the people of the time.

The toy-making industry formally emerged in Germany, with the town of Nuremburg serving as a distribution center for local toy makers. By the end of the 1700s, toy sellers and designers were able to reach large numbers of customers through the use of catalogs.

In the United States, colonial period toys were made from scraps of cloth, wood, and even corncobs. Many of the designs for these folk toys were passed from one generation to the next. Throughout the 1700s, Americans continued to create homemade toys and games. In the late 1830s, William Tower organized a guild of toy makers in Massachusetts. A decade later, the American toy and game industry was born.

Many early toys and games were produced on the side by designers and artists working in tool manufacturing or cabinetmaking. It was not until after World War II that the toy and game industry grew big enough to support full-time professional designers.

Today, toy and game designers create everything from interactive dolls to role-playing video games. Advanced technology combined with the growing use of computers and the Internet will give designers of the future unlimited opportunities to create unforgettable products for children and adults alike.

THE JOB

Whether they are self-employed or work on staff, most toy and game designers have similar duties and responsibilities. In general, designers are charged with creating the primary design of a new toy or game or for changing an existing product. In addition, designers must present ideas to management and/or clients, write up design documents describing every step required in creating a product, and work with either staff or outside sources to complete a project.

The first step in developing any design is to determine the needs of the client. In the toy and game industry, client needs focus not only on the physical product but also on safety issues (especially items intended for children under the age of three), the cost of the design, the age-appropriateness of the product, and marketplace competition.

Once designers have clearly defined their clients' needs, they usually conduct research on product use, materials, and production methods needed to create an appealing and competitive product. They also must make sure that the item, or a similar one, is not already in existence. According to the Toy Industry Association (TIA), approximately 7,000 new products are introduced every year. With so many new products flooding the market, a toy or game must be original to catch the customer's eye and drive sales.

Once all the research is completed, the designer creates a prototype (a mockup, sketch, computer-aided control drawing, or plan drawn to scale) to present for client or management approval. Prototypes often are quite detailed so that clients can easily understand how the finished toy or game will actually look and operate. Indeed, much of a designer's work involves the communication of ideas to clients, management, co-workers, and others.

After the general design has been approved, designers work with other team members or outside professionals to develop the actual product. In addition to graphic designers, illustrators, and production personnel, designers usually interact with or oversee the activities of developers, editors, playtesters, marketing specialists, and engineers as a toy or game goes through the various production stages.

Along with creative and artistic work, designers do a lot of writing. For example, they are usually responsible for writing the first draft of game rules or product instructions. Designers also have to write explanations of complex design concepts and the goals of a toy or game.

In addition to all of these responsibilities, *independent toy and game designers*, also known as *independent inventors*, face other challenges. They must determine from the start, for example, whether they will sell their ideas to toy manufacturers (or have a broker sell the ideas for them) or manufacture and distribute their products themselves.

Self-employed designers who opt to sell their products or ideas must find a publisher or manufacturer and a distributor once the toy or game has been designed. Most companies seeking new products from outside sources purchase them from design firms and from independent inventors and agents with whom they already have an established business relationship. Milton Bradley and Parker Brothers, for example, prefer to work only with designers they know.

For this reason, independent designers may have a hard time penetrating the industry at the start of their careers. However, some major companies, having been forced to reduce their research and development departments because of economic pressures, are now turning to outside professionals more than ever. Games, in particular, are increasingly being designed by freelancers and then developed in-house by large toy manufacturers. In addition, independent designers may find opportunities at small- and medium-sized firms, which often are more receptive to the ideas of freelancers than larger companies.

Designers who decide to publish their own games or manufacture their own toys are, in effect, starting their own businesses. They need to either contribute a considerable sum of their own money to their start-ups or find investors. In addition, these designers must to be able to contract for production services at reasonable prices, track orders from retailers, ensure the timely delivery of all ordered products, and create promotional materials that stir customer interest.

As is true for all start-up businesses, proper planning is vital. Independent designers need to create a business plan, develop product ideas, project sales, and determine the most cost-effective ways to manufacture, distribute, and market their products. They also must attend trade shows, make sure that accounts are billed, and keep accurate records. To protect their invention, these self-employed designers must obtain a patent or trademark, especially if they hope to sell their products to a manufacturer or publisher once they have met with success in the marketplace.

Ultimately, designers who think that they want to start their own toy or game companies must realize that most of their time will be spent running their businesses, not designing products. They should also be aware that about 90 percent of all new businesses fail in the first two years. On the other hand, many hugely successful toys and games, such as Monopoly, Uno, and Scrabble were designed and marketed by independent, inspired inventors.

REQUIREMENTS
High School

While in high school, you can take a variety of classes to prepare for more advanced courses offered at colleges and universities. In the creative arena, take various art and design classes. Other recommended courses are animation, creative writing, photography, filmmaking, music, and theater.

While art courses are important for aspiring toy and game designers, a solid liberal arts background is invaluable. Therefore, you should study a variety of subjects, including math, anthropology, computer science, public speaking, history, and literature. Classes that emphasize writing are especially vital, since designers must be able to communicate complicated design ideas to co-workers and clients alike.

Postsecondary Training

In general, most toy and game designers must have a bachelor's degree, even for entry-level positions. By earning a bachelor's degree in either industrial design or fine arts at a four-year college or university, you will be exposed to a variety of courses that will help you land an entry-level job and rise up through the ranks as a designer. Classes include art and art history, designing and sketching, principles of design, and other specialized studies. Liberal arts and business courses, such as merchandising, business administration, marketing, and psychology, will also prove to be invaluable. Taking specialized courses in areas of particular interest to you is recommended. For example, if you're thinking about becoming a video game designer, computer programming and computer-aided design classes will be helpful.

While many colleges and universities across the nation and abroad offer excellent programs in industrial design and fine arts, some institutions provide specialized curricula geared especially to toy and game designers. The Fashion Institute of Technology in New York, for example, allows students to earn a bachelor of fine arts degree in toy design. In addition, the International Game Developers Association provides a list of schools located around the world for students interested in video game design. (See the end of this article for contact information.)

Other Requirements

In addition to being creative and imaginative, you also need to be able to communicate ideas, both visually and verbally, and be able to work independently and as part of a development team. While motivation and perseverance are essential for success in the industry, it is equally important to be able to solve problems, be open to the ideas of others, and see beyond your own personal preferences in order to create what customers want.

Whether you work for yourself or for a company, self-discipline is vital. Both independent and staff designers must be able to initiate their own projects, budget their time wisely, and meet deadlines and production schedules. In addition to having business sense and sales ability, staff and freelance designers must stay on top of new products and developments in the field.

EXPLORING

If you're thinking about becoming a toy or game designer, there are many ways that you can investigate the field. Attend an industry show to keep abreast of the latest products and to meet toy and game developers, publishers, and manufacturers. The American

International Toy Fair, the biggest toy trade show in the United States, showcases toy and entertainment products from approximately 1,500 manufacturers, distributors, importers, and sales agents around the world.

Subscribing to industry-related publications can give you a sense of what is expected of toy and game designers, as well as where the market is heading. In addition to its regular monthly issues, *Playthings* magazine (http://www.playthings.com) publishes a special *Buyers Guide,* which contains material geared especially for designers and inventors.

To gain some hands-on experience, you may want to join a "virtual company" whose members design games at low or no cost in their spare time. Volunteer to help at a variety of websites that focus on toys and gaming. Although toy and game firms usually hire professionals as playtesters (individuals hired to test new products), contact manufacturers to see if they are looking for in-house or off-site volunteers.

Getting to know designers working in toys and games can serve as a handy resource and contact. As mentors, they can help you break into the field by introducing you to employers and manufacturers and provide guidance once you have landed your first job.

EMPLOYERS

Unlike workers in other industries, most toy and game designers are self-employed. Many create toys and games on a part-time basis in addition to working other jobs. Alternatively, some designers who opt to develop their own toys or publish their own games actually create their own businesses, handling all operational aspects required, from idea conception to marketing and production.

The small number of full-time toy and game designers is employed primarily by publishers, development firms, and manufacturing companies. While most industrial designers work for consulting firms or large corporations, toy and game designers can find job opportunities at every kind of toy company, from small start-ups to the industry giants, such as Parker Brothers, Milton Bradley, and Mattel.

STARTING OUT

Without experience, aspiring toy and game designers usually begin as *design assistants.* Assistants handle much of the background work needed for developing products. Through this work, assistants can learn more about the toy and game market so that, in time, they can become lead designers. Large firms are more likely than smaller companies to hire assistants, who usually have little or no experience.

If a design opportunity is not available, you may want to consider a related position as a production assistant or playtester. Many designers actually get their jobs only after working in other positions in the industry.

Employers looking to hire designers often contact local universities or industry associations. In addition, many place ads in local newspapers in search of qualified candidates. Regardless of how you make your initial move into the field, be sure to develop a portfolio of your design work and familiarize yourself with the products and future plans of potential employers.

Provided you have the necessary capital, it is relatively easy to enter the industry as a start-up; toy and game companies frequently purchase ideas after they have been made successful. On the other hand, larger firms usually do not accept new product ideas from independent inventors. These companies find it more cost effective to employ staff designers than to pay royalties to freelancers.

ADVANCEMENT
Although it is virtually impossible to find an entry-level job as a toy or game designer, people with ambition and potential can find many opportunities to get into the industry and then rise through the ranks. A variety of junior positions, such as those in playtesting or customer service, can springboard qualified people into assistant designing jobs. After several years of experience, capable assistants at large companies, guided and nurtured by senior or lead designers, can then become toy and game designers themselves.

Once a designer penetrates the toy and game industry, there are various advancement paths possible. A creative director at Parker Brothers, for example, began as a production assistant. From there she went on to become a graphic designer, a senior designer, the assistant art director, and, finally, the creative director.

While most people in the industry opt to work either for a company or for themselves, some staff designers decide to leave their salaried positions and start their own businesses. Others become department heads, industry executives, or agents who negotiate the sale of ideas to various toy and game companies.

EARNINGS

In general, toy and game designers earn approximately as much as industrial designers in other specialty fields.

The U.S. Department of Labor reports that the median salary of commercial and industrial designers was $49,830 in 2001. The lowest paid 10 percent earned $28,800 or less, while the highest paid 10 percent earned $79,690 or more.

According to the International Game Developers Association, a video game designer employed full time with one to two years of experience can earn an average of $50,000 a year. With more experience, designers may advance to the position of lead designer or creative director, with an earning potential of approximately $80,000. The most talented game designers can earn $200,000 or more.

However the earnings for independent designers can be rather bleak. In the game designing arena, independent designers earn only about $2,000 for a typical game, although top designers can make up to $5,000 per game.

Unlike independent designers, professionals on staff often receive a variety of benefits in addition to their salaries, depending on the organization for which they work. These benefits may include health and life insurance, paid vacation and sick days, and pension plans.

WORK ENVIRONMENT

The environment in which toy and game designers work varies, depending on the employer. Manufacturing firms and design companies usually provide designers with well-lit, comfortable offices or other spaces. These design professionals generally work a regular 40-hour workweek, although overtime is occasionally required in order to complete projects by designated deadlines. Self-employed designers often work longer hours, especially when they are establishing themselves in the industry.

Both staff and freelance designers frequently schedule their days in order to accommodate clients. It is not unusual for a design specialist to meet with a client in the evenings or on weekends, for example. Such meetings may take place in the designer's office, at the client's home or place of business, or at other locations, such as manufacturing plants or showrooms.

Toy and game designers work with other professionals, including editors, illustrators, graphic designers, playtesters, and production workers. The abilities to communicate and to get along with others are imperative. In addition, many designers must work under pressure in order to please clients and finish projects on time. Finally, while most designers feel a sense of satisfaction and pride from developing creative ideas and products, some occasionally feel frustrated when their designs are rejected or substantially changed.

OUTLOOK

According to the *Occupational Outlook Handbook*, employment opportunities for all designers are expected to grow faster than the average over the next decade. Demand for toy and game designing professionals in particular will result from continued emphasis on the quality and safety of products, as well as on toys and games that are easy to understand and appropriate for their intended audiences. Increasing global competition will also play a role in the demand for toy and game designers.

Emerging technologies will continue to positively impact the employment outlook for design professionals as well. Those designers who have knowledge of and experience with high-tech toys, CD-ROM versions of board games, and interactive video games will definitely have a competitive edge in the job market.

According to the TIA, the average American child lives in a home with three televisions, two VCRs, three radios, two CD players, a video game player, and a computer. Children today are often more tech-savvy than their parents; toy companies need to cater their designs to meet the younger generations' increasing demand for high-technology products.

Although employment growth is expected, the Department of Labor notes that all designers will face intense competition for available job openings. Since many talented designers are attracted to the toy and game industry, those without formal design education, creativity, and perseverance will have trouble establishing careers in the field. Independent designers will also continue to have difficulty penetrating the industry. On the upside, many job openings will be available for qualified designers as demand continues and as designers leave the field for a variety of reasons.

FOR MORE INFORMATION

For information on obtaining a bachelor's degree in toy design, contact
Fashion Institute of Technology
Seventh Avenue at 27th Street
New York, NY 10001-5992
Tel: 212-217-7999

Email: FITinfo@fitsuny.edu
http://www.fitnyc.suny.edu

For career information, contact
Industrial Designers Society of America
45195 Business Court, Suite 250
Dulles, VA 20166
Tel: 703-707-6000
Email: idsa@idsa.org
http://www.idsa.org

For information on industry issues, education options, and scholarship opportunities, contact the following organizations:
International Council of Toy Industries
80 Camberwell Road
London SE5 0EG United Kingdom
Email: info@toy-icti.org
http://www.toy-icti.org

International Game Developers Association
600 Harrison Street
San Francisco, CA 94107
Tel: 415-947-6235
Email: info@igda.org
http://www.igda.org

For industry information and other resources aimed at both kids and parents, contact
Toy Industry Association, Inc.
1115 Broadway, Suite 400
New York, NY 10010
Tel: 212-675-1141
Email: info@toy-tia.org
http://www.toy-tia.org

aesthetics: study of the nature and value of art objects

art: stemming from the word "artificial," a creative and skilled form of expression that conveys emotions through man-made creations

art deco: art movement embracing styles from the 1920s and 1930s; categorized by abstraction, distortion, and simplification of objects and people through the use of different shapes and bright colors

background: area of a painting or photograph that appears furthest away from the viewer (opposite of foreground)

balance: arrangement of elements of an artwork that gives the piece a feeling of stability

baroque: art movement in which artists sought to display emotion, movement, and variety in their works

cels: used in animation, these sheets of clear plastic contain the images of cartoon characters and are photographed in succession to give the illusion of movement

center of interest: area of an artwork intended to attract the most attention

ceramics: art form involving the making of clay sculptures, such as vases, bowls, and figures; pieces are sculpted by hand or using wheels and then fired in kilns at high temperatures to harden and set their color

composition: how elements of a piece of artwork are positioned in relation to each other

contrast: difference between two elements in an artwork, such as darkness and light

foreground: area of a painting or photograph that appears closest to the viewer

impressionism: art movement made popular by artists such as Claude Monet and Paul Cézanne that is categorized by the artists' use of light and shadow

kerning: adjusting the spacing between letters to give them the appearance of more even spacing

kiln: high-heat oven used to bake and set clay art

landscape: artwork that features nature, such as paintings of sunsets, waterfalls, or mountain ranges

middle ground: area of the artwork that appears between the foreground and the background

palette: flat piece of wood, plastic, or even paper that is used by painters to mix and hold paints while working

pop art: art movement of the 1950s and 1960s categorized by the use of popular cultural images such as advertisements and food labels within artwork; made popular by artists such as Andy Warhol and Roy Lichtenstein

portfolio: case for holding material, such as illustrations, photographs, or other artwork; term also used to describe the work within such a case

portrait: painting or photograph focusing on an individual's face

primary colors: colors (red, yellow, and blue) that can be used to mix all other colors in the art spectrum

printmaking: process of making prints by pressing paper or other thin materials between blocks or plates covered with ink

secondary colors: colors (orange, green, and violet) created by mixing equal amounts of two primary colors

still life: artistic depiction of an arrangement of inanimate objects, such as a bowl of fruit or a vase of flowers

texture: the way a piece of art literally or visually feels; artists can simulate uneven texture in a two-dimensional work by adding shadows or other methods

FURTHER READING

Cox, Mary. *2003 Artist's & Graphic Designer's Market.* Cincinnati, Ohio: Writers Digest Books, 2002.

Doyle, Michael E. *Color Drawing: Design Drawing Skills and Techniques for Architects, Landscape Architects, and Interior Designers,* 2d ed. Hoboken, N.J.: John Wiley and Sons, 1999.

Fleishman, Michael. *Starting Your Career as a Freelance Illustrator or Graphic Designer.* New York: Allworth Press, 2001.

Gair, Angela. *Artist's Manual: A Complete Guide to Painting and Drawing Materials and Techniques.* San Francisco: Chronicle Books, 1996.

Gershenfeld, Alan, Mark Loparco, and Cecilia Barajas. *Game Plan: The Insider's Guide to Breaking In and Succeeding in the Computer and Video Game Business.* Irvine, Calif.: Griffin Trade Paperback, 2003.

Glaser, Jane R., et al. *Museums: A Place to Work: Planning Museum Careers.* London: Routledge, 1996.

Jones, Sue Jenkyn. *Fashion Design.* New York: Watson-Guptill Publications, 2002.

Leland, Nita. *Exploring Color.* Cincinnati, Ohio: North Light Books, 1998.

Lumet, Sidney. *Making Movies.* New York: Vintage Books, 1996.

Olver, Elizabeth. *The Art of Jewelry Design: From Idea to Reality.* Cincinnati, Ohio: North Light Books, 2002.

Thompson, Jessica Cargill. *40 Under 40: Young Architects for the New Millennium.* Los Angeles: Taschen Books, 2000.